INTERDISCIPLINARY CONNECTIONS TO SPECIAL EDUCATION: IMPORTANT ASPECTS TO CONSIDER

ADVANCES IN SPECIAL EDUCATION

Series Editors: Festus E. Obiakor and Jeffrey P. Bakken

Recent Volumes:

ADVANCES IN SPECIAL EDUCATION   VOLUME 30A

INTERDISCIPLINARY CONNECTIONS TO SPECIAL EDUCATION: IMPORTANT ASPECTS TO CONSIDER

EDITED BY

JEFFREY P. BAKKEN
Bradley University, Peoria, IL, USA

FESTUS E. OBIAKOR
Valdosta State University, Valdosta, GA, USA

United Kingdom − North America − Japan
India − Malaysia − China

Emerald Group Publishing Limited
Howard House, Wagon Lane, Bingley BD16 1WA, UK

First edition 2015

British Library Cataloguing in Publication Data
A catalogue record for this book is available from the British Library

ISBN: 978-1-78441-660-7
ISSN: 0270-4013 (Series)

Printed and bound by CPI Group (UK) Ltd, Croydon, CR0 4YY

CONTENTS

v

LIST OF CONTRIBUTORS

Michael O. Afolayan	M&P Consulting, Springfield, IL, USA
Precious O. Afolayan	District Administrator, Springfield Illinois School District 186, Springfield, IL, USA
Jeffrey P. Bakken	Graduate School, Bradley University, Peoria, IL, USA
Tachelle Banks	Department of Teacher Education, Cleveland State University, Cleveland, OH, USA
Christy Borders	Department of Special Education, Illinois State University, Normal, IL, USA
D. Antonio Cantu	Department of Teacher Education, Bradley University, Peoria, IL, USA
Gary L. Cates	Department of Psychology, Illinois State University, Normal, IL, USA
Beto Davison Avilés	Department of Leadership in Education, Nonprofits, and Counseling, Bradley University, Peoria, IL, USA
Pauline Harris-Obiakor	Educational Opportunity Center, University of Wisconsin Milwaukee, Milwaukee, WI, USA
Karla Hull	Department of Curriculum, Leadership, and Technology, Valdosta State University, Valdosta, GA, USA
Stacey Jones Bock	Department of Special Education, Illinois State University, Normal, IL, USA
Lynda Kasky-Hernández	Department of Psychology, Illinois State University, Normal, IL, USA

Martha Laughlin   Department of Marriage and Family
                          Therapy, Valdosta State University,
                          Valdosta, GA, USA

Sunday Obi   School of Education, Kentucky State
                          University, Frankfort, KY, USA

Festus E. Obiakor   Department of Early Childhood and
                          Special Education, Valdosta State
                          University, Valdosta, GA, USA

Anne Risen   Director of Special Education, Pekin
                          Elementary District #108, Pekin, IL, USA

D. Michael Risen   Department of Leadership in Education,
                          Human Services and Counseling, Bradley
                          University, Peoria, IL, USA

Lori Russell-Chapin   Department of Leadership in Education,
                          Nonprofits, and Counseling, Bradley
                          University, Peoria, IL, USA

Christopher J. Rybak   Department of Leadership in Education,
                          Nonprofits, and Counseling, Bradley
                          University, Peoria, IL, USA

Julia B. Stoner   Department of Special Education, Illinois
                          State University, Normal, IL, USA

Jenny Tripses   Department of Leadership in Education,
                          Human Services and Counseling, Bradley
                          University, Peoria, IL, USA

Kate Warner   Department of Marriage and Family
                          Therapy, Valdosta State University,
                          Valdosta, GA, USA

PREFACE

Interdisciplinary Connections to Special Education is divided into two volumes: Volume 30A, *Important Aspects to Consider* and Volume 30B, *Key Related Professionals Involved.*

Individuals with disabilities have been supported in the school system since 1975. Since then, the field of special education has changed drastically and currently, many professionals involved in educating individuals with disabilities were not previously involved. For students to benefit to their fullest potential many key professionals need to be involved and key data needs to be collected to assure proper education and success for these individuals. What was done in the past has changed and current best practices involve many different professionals that were not even considered in the past. Through time, energy, growth, and research, practices have changed over time to now benefit students and their families at a level that was not previously considered.

This volume in *Advances in Special Education* focuses on *Interdisciplinary Connections to Special Education: Important Aspects to Consider*. The volume is a comprehensive examination into connections that need to be made and the data and considerations that need to take place when trying to meet the individual needs of a student with disabilities. The volume begins with a rationale of why interdisciplinary relations are important. Next, the volume addresses key stakeholders that should be involved in the process of developing individualized education programs (IEPs) like special educators, general educators, counselors, psychologists, school leaders, and related professionals. These chapters are followed by chapters that address families, communities, and the government. The book concludes with a chapter that addresses the comprehensive support model.

The volume is composed of 11 chapters written by university professors who are actively involved in teaching special education courses and engaged in research related to these topics. It should be used as a supplementary text for advanced undergraduate special education majors and graduate students who are looking for detailed and comprehensive information for their research papers or theses.

Festus E. Obiakor
Jeffrey P. Bakken
Volume Editors

CHAPTER 1

RATIONALE FOR INTERDISCIPLINARY/ MULTIDISCIPLINARY RELATIONS IN SPECIAL EDUCATION

Jeffrey P. Bakken

ABSTRACT

This chapter provides a brief history of the multidisciplinary process and how it has evolved over time. A rationale for why the process has changed is provided and how involving more professionals to obtain more specific assessment data and provide more direct input aids in the development of the student's individualized education program (IEP). In addition, a discussion on the incorporation of more reliable and accurate data directly from these individuals shows that a more educationally relevant IEP can be developed for students so that there is a better opportunity for academic success in the school. Incorporating more professionals, when possible, however, requires more planning, but ultimately this process will provide more accurate and reliable data to aid the process for the student, family, and teachers, and everyone will feel more a part of the process.

Keywords: Data; services; decision-making; multidisciplinary

Interdisciplinary Connections to Special Education: Important Aspects to Consider
Advances in Special Education, Volume 30A, 1–12
ISSN: 0270-4013/doi:10.1108/S0270-40132015000030A001

INTRODUCTION

Why is it important to incorporate a multidisciplinary team when making decisions and developing an individualized education program (IEP) for a student with a disability? What is the rationale for involving as many specialists as possible that relate to functions and abilities of the student? Will a better IEP be created with more input from a variety of individuals? What important data about the student can each specialist bring to the team? This chapter discusses answers to these questions and develops a rationale for why a multidisciplinary team is essential to planning and preparing an IEP for a student with a disability.

HISTORICAL PERSPECTIVES

After many parents/advocates voiced their opinions over time and individuals and organizations voiced their concerns regarding the education and treatment of individuals with disabilities, along with some very instrumental court cases, changes were made in our educational system. Two important cases were *Pennsylvania Association for Retarded Children (PARC) v. Commonwealth of Pennsylvania, 343 Fed. Supp. 279* (1972) and *Mills v. Board of Education of the District of Columbia, 348 F. Supp. 866* (1972). In both the PARC and Mills cases, the judges struck down local laws that excluded children with disabilities from schools. They established that children with a disability have a right to a public education and access to education. These among other factors contributed to Public Law 94-142 being established in 1975. Public Law 94-142 had been the basis for assuring that all children with disabilities have available free appropriate public education (FAPE), assuring that rights of parents and their children are protected, providing financial assistance to states, and assessing the effectiveness of those efforts. Before the enactment of this law, the education needs of millions of children with disabilities were not being fully met (especially those with cognitive disabilities and mental illnesses, who were excluded from schools). Children who played with other children in their local neighborhoods were unable to attend the neighborhood school because of their disability. Because of this law, all students are now entitled to FAPE; they cannot be excluded from school solely because of disability.

Students with disabilities must receive the special education and related services that they need, but for them to get FAPE, several provisions must be in place. "The following are basic principles that need to be met:

(a) their needs to be child find and zero reject procedures in place, (b) identification and assessment must be nondiscriminatory, (c) an individualized education program (IEP) must be developed for students identified with a disability, (d) students should be placed in their least restrictive environment, (e) procedural safeguards – such as parents' rights to participate in the educational decision-making process for their child, due process, and mediation when there are disagreements need to be in place, (f) the participation of parents throughout the entire process, and (g) transition after school needs to be considered. Subsequent reauthorizations of this Act through the years brought greater clarification and enhancements to these significant principles originally developed" (Ashbaker, 2011, p. 31).

According to Individuals with Disabilities Education Improvement Act (IDEA) reauthorization of P.L. 94-142, each student suspected of having a disability will be evaluated in all areas of the suspected disability with assessments that are nondiscriminatory. This assessment should be conducted by a team of evaluators who are knowledgeable and trained in the use of assessments and capable of gathering relevant and specific information from a variety of sources. In addition, the evaluation materials and procedures selected must be administered in ways that are not racially or culturally discriminatory. The child cannot be subjected to unnecessary tests and assessments that are not needed in order to obtain proper assessment data on the student (Ashbaker, 2011). Nondiscriminatory identification and assessment are requirements that are necessary when evaluating children suspected of having a disability. Thanks to numerous court cases over the years, knowledge and procedures have improved. The *Larry P. v. Riles* (1984) case highlighted unfair placement based on identification, assessment, and evaluation methods. A federal district court in California banned the use of standardized intelligence quotient (IQ) instruments to evaluate African-American students for placement in classes for students with educable mental retardation known today as intellectual or cognitive disabilities. The court ruled that such tests contained racial and cultural bias and discriminated against students from culturally and racially different backgrounds. Local education agencies now must conduct a full individual evaluation before beginning to provide special education and related services to a child with a disability (IDEA, 20 U.S.C. 1414(a) (1)).

IDEA and its reauthorizations require "that assessment materials be administered in the child's native language or mode of communication (such as sign language) and that the tests are validated for the specific purpose for which they are used. Tests must be administered and interpreted by trained personnel, and more than one test must be used to make a determination.

Nondiscriminatory evaluation means that students must be evaluated in ways that do not discriminate based on language, culture, or race. This evaluation provides information to be used to determine the child's eligibility for special education and related services, and the team must identify information that is instructionally useful in planning for the child's educational needs. This program is documented in the child's written individualized education program" (Ashbaker, 2011, p. 33). This information then helps to plan the appropriate placement for the child. For example, the first step in deciding placement options is always deciding what needs to be done. Only after deciding what we wish to do for and with an individual with learning disabilities (FAPE), can we judge the placement and amount of service that needs to be provided to attain the goals (Brigham & Bakken, 2013).

THE MULTIDISCIPLINARY TEAM

A multidisciplinary team, by its name, is made up of a multitude of professionals that can bring their knowledge and expertise to the table in regards to a student with a disability. By involving many professionals with a multitude of perspectives, better outcomes can be formulated and achieved. In addition, more data, regarding the student, are considered in the decision-making process. Not only are more data available, but the accuracy of the data is improved as direct professionals in designated areas are the ones that are collecting, analyzing, and reporting the results. For example, if the student was having issues with mobility, a physical therapist would be invited to collect data (assess the student) and present their results at the IEP meeting. This multiple perspective process enables the team to make more educated decisions regarding the development of an IEP for the student with a disability. Thus, this IEP will be more comprehensive and address the areas that could be missed if the team was not a comprehensive unit.

Why did teams expand and become more multidisciplinary? What was the reasoning for this shift in philosophy? Most of it had to do with the student with a disability. It was apparent after careful analysis that the individuals involved were not able to thoroughly investigate the entire child. It was very clear that a few individuals could not collect the most appropriate data nor could they interpret and make educational decisions on it if it was not their area of expertise. Many times, areas were just not assessed as there was no one with the expertise needed to evaluate the student or the team never thought of that as an option. More data were needed by other professionals that could aid in the decision-making process. Although finding a common time for many different professionals to meet can be cumbersome, ultimately, it is important to develop the most appropriate and functioning IEP for the student, parents, and teachers. Involving more professionals is more effective and efficient in providing more accurate information about the student and thus allows these individuals to develop a better plan for him/her to progress in the curriculum and/or prepare for independence in society.

Dealing with Assessment

Years ago, only a few individuals seemed to be responsible for conducting assessments and making educational decisions for students with disabilities. The norm was that the school psychologists conducted all of the assessments (IQ and achievement), and in most cases, they were implementing standardized tests to get their results. They would then share their results with the parents, special education teacher, and other related professionals. Parental involvement on IEP team ensures that parents have the right to participate in making decisions regarding the education of their child, including placement decisions and development of the IEP. Over the past several decades since the passage of P.L. 94-142, the emphasis on family involvement in school decision making has increased in response to federal mandates, and also because research supports that home—school collaboration yields positive results for children (Elizalde-Utnick, 2002; Hubbard & Adams, 2002). In a discussion of techniques to increase home—school collaboration, Esler, Godber, and Christenson (2002) observed that such positive partnerships are correlated with higher school achievement. Furthermore, parents must be provided with a copy of the evaluation report and the documentation of eligibility determination, provisions which imply that assessment personnel are obligated to provide understandable results in written reports (Plotts, 2012). In complying with federal mandates, school districts recognize the value of parental input into educational planning and programming for exceptional children. Parents have the right and responsibility to be actively involved in their child's educational programming, and professionals must be prepared to accept parents as coequal members of the team. According to Ashbaker (2011), there are advantages of parental participation, namely:

1. Parents are the most knowledgeable resource concerning their child.
2. Parent's participation in the conference increases their awareness of their child's disability.

3. Parent participation improves the likelihood that they will implement recommendations of the team.
4. Parent participation increases the likelihood that recommendations from the team will meet the needs of the individual parents and children.
5. Participation of the parent increases the development of parent–professional relationships.
6. Including parents in this process potentially increases their role as co-instructors.
7. Parent participation increases communication in the future.

Traditionally, psychological tests were supposed to uncover uneven development, and they were typically given by a psychologist. When students performed erratically, failed easier questions requiring recall on recently or remotely presented information, or on tasks which require manipulation of objects, it was noted on the assessment. In addition, if students were unable to reproduce a visual perception in graphic form or confused aspects on the intellective and manipulative aspects of the tests, these discrepancies often revealed that there might be a problem. Given that psychologists were the only ones with assessment data, they were then responsible for deciding if students were eligible for special education services and where in the educational environment they would receive these services. "Too often the assessment process just involves giving a student norm-referenced tests that are used to determine eligibility, an action that Reschly (2000) noted was inappropriate because it would not result in the type of information necessary to plan a student's IEP. Although norm-referenced tests can give the team clues to help identify students' needs to accurately plan instruction more fine-grained assessments using procedures such as curriculum-based assessment, curriculum-based measurement, direct observation, and functional behavioral assessment are needed (Yell, Thomas, & Katsiyannis, 2012). Such tests and procedures will be much more useful to the team in determining the students' present levels of performance and skill deficits in areas in which they need individualized instruction or programming" (Yell & Gatti, 2012, p. 6). Standardized assessments, however, did not typically find current classroom-based knowledge of students; they only found out a more general and global view of what the child knew. In addition, these data did not help the classroom teacher in regards to what the student actually knew versus what they did not know and where they should be placed in their respective curriculum. Once decisions were made, teachers still needed to assess students within the curriculum to find out what the student actually knew and did not know and where classroom instruction would begin. This reliance on the use of standardized testing soon shifted to curriculum-based assessments that could actually tell what the student knew and what they did not know within the school's curriculum. Combined with an IQ test, the student's potential versus actual knowledge could be calculated.

Over time, as the field changed, individuals became more educated, a shift from only using standardized assessments was made, and data and opinions from other professionals were incorporated to best meet the needs of the individual student with disabilities. When curriculum-based assessments are implemented to assess where in the curriculum the student should be placed (what the student knows vs. what he/she is having trouble with), continuous assessments must continue in order to evaluate progress that the student is making. New terminology in the field calls this *progress monitoring*. It is crucial that all students participate in progress monitoring to investigate student and teacher progress (Cuenca, Douglas, & Bakken, 2012). The initial formation of true multidisciplinary teams was beginning to be developed. As indicated, the multidisciplinary team which includes the teacher, school psychologist, parent, and other specialists who have knowledge or can assess the strengths and weaknesses of the individual child in question serves as the most functional method of collaboration towards achieving an IEP that will be accurate and comprehensive and benefit the child. Many times, however, other professionals besides the teacher and school psychologist are not included in the evaluation of the student. To derive the best results possible and to develop the most informational and accurate IEP, every professional who can be available to assess and provide input should be included in this process. Through this team approach, many aspects of the whole child are available for observation and management.

Clearly the 2004 reauthorization of IDEA (2004) indicated that the multidisciplinary team must include the parents, not less than one general education teacher of the child (if the child is or may be participating in the general education environment), not less than one special education teacher, the person responsible for assessment who can interpret the instructional implications of evaluation results, an administrator (or other representative who has knowledge of instruction in special and regular education and the availability of resources of the school), any other persons with knowledge or special expertise as appropriate, and, whenever appropriate, the student (Plotts, 2012). An effective team approach does not need to have all of the members in attendance to implement or modify its approach to the pupil's education. There does, however, need to be constant communication between the parties for progress to be made. For example, if the deaf educator was a part of the process, but could not attend the meeting in person, they could print out a summary of what they did with the student, the results, and recommendations and provide this document to all members of the committee prior to the meeting. The relationship of the professional team members with the administration of the school cannot be too highly stressed. See Table 1 for evaluation requirements according to IDEA.

The Individualized Education Program

Every child who receives special education services must have an IEP. The IEP is a written document that details the student's strengths and needs in any area affected by the disability and identifies the goals and objectives for improvement in those areas. The emphasis of the IEP is on progress in the general curriculum, addressing special factors that may influence a student's ability to learn (e.g., behavior or communication needs, or limited English proficiency). The IEP is the documentation that shows that a student is receiving free and appropriate education (Ashbaker, 2011).

The IEP is developed by a collaborative team including the regular and special educators, a parent of the student, a representative of the school administration (representative of the local education agency), and any related service providers who may contribute to the process by knowing about the student or about educational services for the student. It should be noted that the special education teacher or administrator should ensure that parents attend the initial IEP meeting. It is important to keep good documentation of all attempts to get parents to come to the meeting (e.g., phone calls, emails, or notes) in case they cannot be contacted or choose not to come. Another option to consider is to change the day, time, or place of the meeting to allow the parent(s) to attend. Sometimes, parent work schedules prevent them from attending an IEP meeting held during the typical school day. Scheduling a meeting outside the normal school day to fit a parent's schedule benefits everyone and shows parents that you are vested in their input. In addition, because the classroom teacher knows the curriculum and ways to help a student access it, the teacher should participate in developing the IEP. This team considers the student's present levels of educational

Table 1. IDEA's Evaluation Requirements.

Evaluation Requirements	Description
The team must use a variety of assessment tools and strategies to gather relevant functional, developmental, and academic information, including information provided by the parent, that may assist in determining (a) whether the student has a disability and (b) the content of the student's IEP.	Assessments should not only involve formal tests, but curriculum-based measurements, functional-based assessments, interviews, observations, and other procedures that will assist the team to determine eligibility and instructional needs.
The team cannot use a single measure or assessment as the sole criterion for determining whether a student has a disability or determining an appropriate educational program for a student.	No single measure (e.g., an IQ test) can be the basis for determining eligibility of instructional programming.
The team must use technically sound instruments to assess the contribution of cognitive, behavioral, physical, and developmental factors.	Assessment procedures that are used should have good technical characteristics and be appropriate to assess different factors that may be involved with a student's disability.
Assessment and other evaluation materials (a) must not be discriminatory on a racial or cultural basis; (b) must be provided and administered so as to yield accurate information on what a student knows and can do academically, developmentally, and functionally; (c) must be used for purposes for which the assessments are reliable and valid; (d) must be administered by trained and knowledgeable personnel; and (e) are administered in accordance with the instructions provided by the producer of the assessments.	The persons who conduct the assessments must have been trained in administering tests and other assessment procedures. Moreover, all assessments must be reliable, valid, and accurate assessments of academic and functional factors.
A student must be assessed in all areas of suspected disability.	When a student is assessed, the team must ensure that all areas of concern are addressed.
Assessment tools and strategies must provide information and directly assist the team in determining the educational needs of a student.	It is important that assessments not only be used for determining eligibility but that they are useful for instructional planning.

Source: Yell and Gatti (2012, p. 5).

performance and makes plans for improvement during the year. The IEP team then decides what special education and related services are required to help the student achieve the goals and objectives that were developed. In addition, the IEP team must determine how to measure progress, how often this should occur, and how to inform parents about the student's progress toward accomplishing the IEP goals. Finally, the team must meet at least annually to update the IEP (Ashbaker, 2011), but if problems arise or changes are needed, the team can reconvene whenever it is appropriate.

Full individual evaluation by the IEP team means that eligibility must be determined by a multidisciplinary team based on information from an individualized evaluation in a number of areas such as language, cognitive–intellectual, adaptive behavior, academic, emotional, medical–physical, and behavioral, with specific areas of formal and informal assessment determined by the IEP team. Multidisciplinary teams are mandated to ensure that different perspectives from diverse groups are considered, to limit the decision-making authority of any one individual, and to involve parents (Plotts, 2012). Although mandated by law, it is not very common to include as many different individuals as these volumes suggest. All of these individuals, however, can contribute very valuable information to the process.

Developing students' IEPs refers to the process of creating a student's individualized program of special education and related services. Thus, the IEP is the blueprint of a student's FAPE. IDEA mandates the process and procedures for developing the IEP. Because of problems in the past of getting appropriate individuals to attend the IEP meeting, IDEA mandates the persons who must be on IEP team. Clearly, other school-based personnel are permitted, but not required, to attend the IEP meeting. Table 2 lists and describes the required members of students' IEP teams.

It is important to note that other professionals who have a specific expertise are not required to come, but it is suggested they be included and participate. Although not mandated to come, the belief of including any key professional who can provide input and assessment data that will lead to a more comprehensive view of the student as well as a more directed IEP is suggested. Including members on the IEP team who have specialized expertise in areas that may be needed to meet the unique educational needs of a student (e.g., community aspects, auditory or visual needs, or health-related professionals) should always be considered. Of course, this will depend on the needs of the particular student. It is important that everyone involved come to the IEP meeting with an open mind and seriously consider suggestions made by everyone in attendance. An IEP should never be developed prior to the meeting. Individuals may come with a draft of their section of the IEP but write "draft" at the top of the IEP to ensure that everyone understands that it is not a final IEP. The actual IEP should be

Table 2. IEP Team Members.

IEP Team Members	Description
The parents of the student[a]	Either one or both of a student's parents.
General education teacher of the student[a]	At least one general education teacher who has had or does have the student.
Special education teacher of the student[a]	At least one special education teacher who has had or does have the student.
Local education agency representative[a]	A representative of the school district. This person is often a principal or assistant principal of the student's school.
Individual who can interpret the instructional implications of the assessment/evaluation[a]	A person who understands and can interpret the instructional implications of the assessment. This person is often a school psychologist although it may be another person already on the IEP team (e.g., special education teacher).
Other persons who have knowledge of special expertise regarding the student, including related services personnel	The student's parents or the school personnel may appoint other members who have knowledge of the student or the student's disability.
The student, when appropriate	The student must be invited to the IEP team if transition services are considered.

Source: Yell and Gatti (2012, p. 7).
[a]Required members.

formulated and developed at the meeting including all relevant data and participants involved.

CONCLUSION

This chapter provided a rationale for involving more professionals who can obtain more specific assessment data to aid in the development of the student's IEP. Multiple professionals providing multiple perspectives working together and analyzing many different types of data can help develop and build relationships. These relationships can then give the involved individuals ownership in the IEP process. This ownership and being a part of a team will allow them to better plan for the student's success and allow the team to collaborate and incorporate best practices for him/her. Thus, incorporating more professionals, when possible, will allow those involved to share and explain specific relevant data to each other that will allow discussions and formulations of academically more relevant IEPs for the student and family.

REFERENCES

Ashbaker, B. (2011). History of legal and legislative acts concerned with special education. In A. F. Rotatori, F. E. Obiakor, & J. P. Bakken (Eds.), *The history of special education* (Vol. 21, pp. 21–45). Advances in Special Education. Bingley, UK: Emerald Group Publishing Limited.

Brigham, F. J., & Bakken, J. P. (2013). Identification and assessment of students with learning disabilities. In J. P. Bakken, F. E. Obiakor, & A. F. Rotatori (Eds.), *Learning disabilities: Current perspectives and issues* (Vol. 24, pp. 55–74). Advances in Special Education. Bingley, UK: Emerald Group Publishing Limited.

Cuenca, Y., Douglas, K. H., & Bakken, J. P. (2012). Making data-based decisions. In. J. P. Bakken (Ed.), *Response to intervention in the core content areas: A practical approach for educators* (pp. 91–112). Waco, TX: Prufrock Press.

Elizalde-Utnick, G. (2002). Best practices in building partnership with families. In A. Thomas & J. Grimes (Eds.), *Best practices in school psychology IV* (pp. 413–429). Bethesda, MD: National Association of School Psychologists.

Esler, E. N., Godber, Y., & Christenson, S. L. (2002). Best practices in supporting home-school collaboration. In A. Thomas & J. Grimes (Eds.), *Best practices in school psychology IV* (pp. 389–411). Bethesda, MD: National Association of School Psychologists.

Hubbard, D. D., & Adams, J. (2002). Best practices in facilitating meaningful family involvement in educational decision making. In A. Thomas & J. Grimes (Eds.), *Best practices in school psychology IV* (pp. 377–387). Bethesda, MD: National Association of School Psychologists.

Individuals with Disabilities Education Improvement Act or 2004, 20 U.S.C. § 1400 et seq. (2004). Reauthorization of the Individuals with Disabilities Education Act of 1990.

Larry P. v. Riles. (1984). United States Court of Appeals, 1984. 793 F.2d 969 (9th Cir.).

Mills v. Board of Education of the District of Columbia. 348 F. Supp. 866. (D.D.C.1972).

Pennsylvania Association for Retarded Children v. Commonwealth 334 F. Supp. 1257 (E.D. Pa 1971) and 343 F. Supp. 279 (E.D. Pa. 1972).

Plotts, C. A. (2012). Assessment of students with emotional and behavioral disorders. In J. P. Bakken, F. E. Obiakor, & A. F. Rotatori (Eds.), *Behavioral disorders: Identification, assessment, and instruction of students with EBD* (Vol. 22, pp. 51–85). Advances in Special Education. Bingley, UK: Emerald Group Publishing Limited.

Reschly, D. (2000). Assessment and eligibility determination in the Individuals with Disabilities Education Act of 1997. In C. Telzrow & M. Tankersley (Eds.), *IDEA Amendments of 1997: Practice guidelines for school-based teams* (pp. 65–104). Bethesda, MD: National Association of School Psychologists.

Yell, M. L., & Gatti, S. L. N. (2012). Legal issues and teachers of students with emotional and behavioral disorders. In J. P. Bakken, F. E. Obiakor, & A. F. Rotatori (Eds.), *Behavioral disorders: Identification, assessment, and instruction of students with EBD* (Vol. 22, pp. 1–29). Advances in Special Education. Bingley, UK: Emerald Group Publishing Limited.

Yell, M. L., Thomas, S. S., & Katsiyannis, A. (2012). Special education law for leaders and administrators of special education. In J. B. Crockett, B. S. Billingsley, & M. L. Boscardin (Eds.), *Handbook of leadership and administration for special education* (pp. 69–96). New York, NY: Taylor & Francis.

CHAPTER 2

THE ROLE OF SPECIAL EDUCATORS IN INTERDISCIPLINARY CONNECTIONS

Tachelle Banks

ABSTRACT

This chapter presents a synopsis of teaching students with disabilities and the qualities of schools that can enable effective teaching of all students, including those who have disabilities. A review of legal mandates that teachers must understand are outlined and serve as a framework encouraging interdisciplinary collaboration. This chapter seeks to inform the reader of the role of special educators and related professionals, including families, to improve school outcomes for students with disabilities.

Keywords: Special education; related service providers; collaboration; families

Interdisciplinary Connections to Special Education: Important Aspects to Consider
Advances in Special Education, Volume 30A, 13–34
ISSN: 0270-4013/doi:10.1108/S0270-40132015000030A002

INTRODUCTION

Since 1975, there have been two major developments for students with mild/moderate disabilities in special education programs in U.S. schools. First, the number of students served steadily increased from approximately 3.7 million to over 6 million, reflecting an extraordinary achievement in terms of access (National Center for Education Statistics, 2011; U.S. Department of Education, 1995, 2005). Second, the placement patterns for these students served under the *Individuals with Disabilities Education Improvement Act* (IDEA) of 2004 reflected high enrollment in general education classes. For example, the national average for the percentage of students aged 6–21 who spent at least 80% of their time in general education classrooms grew from 31.6% in 1989 to 51.9% in 2004 (U.S. Department of Education, 2005) some states (i.e., Vermont, North Dakota, Oregon, and Colorado) significantly exceeded this national average by supporting more than 70% of their students with disabilities in general education settings (U.S. Department of Education, Office of Special Education Programs, 2005), and more than 90% of students aged 6–21 were educated in regular classrooms for at least some portion of the school day (National Center for Education Statistics, 2011).

In addition to advancing the inclusion of students with disabilities in general education classrooms, the academic performance of students with high-incidence disabilities has been increasingly evaluated. Federal laws have mandated that students with disabilities participate on state tests and that states report these test results to the public (IDEA, 1997). Unfortunately, IDEA imposed no consequences on states that did not comply with these mandates, and many were slow to meet the law's mandates. It was not until the passage of the No Child Left Behind (NCLB) Act (2001) that states enacted significant, large-scale changes to their testing and accountability systems to increase participation of students with disabilities in the core curriculum and ensure that the progress of these students was monitored and reported. The 2004 reauthorization of IDEA expanded testing requirements at the state level for students with high-incidence disabilities, as local school districts were required to develop and implement alternate assessments aligned with the state's academic content standards. In addition, states reported (a) the number and performance of students with disabilities taking regular state assessments and how many of them received accommodations to participate in those assessments, (b) how many students with disabilities participated in alternate assessments aligned with the state standards, and (c) the number of students with disabilities taking alternate assessments aligned with alternate achievement standards. Finally, the performance of students with high-incidence disabilities must be compared with the achievement of all children, including children without disabilities, on those assessments.

It is important to note that placement in inclusive classroom settings and access to the general education curriculum are important issues for all students with disabilities (Skiba, Michael, Nardo, & Peterson, 2002; Skiba, Peterson, & Williams, 1997). The 2004 reauthorization of IDEA stipulated that states allow districts to use multitiered systems of support (MTSS) strategies such as response-to-intervention (RtI) and positive behavior support (PBS) for determining if a child has a specific learning disability or behavioral disability.

Based on the aforementioned points, it has become clear that special educators play divergent roles in interdisciplinary connections in education. It is clear that special educators by law have to work with students, parents/ family members, other professionals as needed, and community agencies. Outside the law, special educators will be unsuccessful in their jobs if they fail to collaborate, consult, and cooperate with internal and external stakeholders of their job. This is the focus of this chapter.

WORKING WITH STUDENTS

To meet the varied and diverse educational needs of students with disabilities in inclusive classrooms, the reauthorization of IDEA (2004) required states to allow districts to use MTSS strategies such as RtI and PBS for determining if a child has a specific learning disability or behavioral disability. RtI involves early identification of students' learning problems and the use of increasingly intensive lessons, or interventions, to address those problems before they become entrenched (Samuels, 2011). The RtI three-tiered conceptual model is designed to shift the focus of educators from finding a disability or within-child deficits to focusing on providing the best instruction for all students in the general education classroom. The RtI model emphasizes early intervention, with a focus on making sure children receive appropriate instruction at the "first tier" or general education classroom level, and the push to match instruction to a student's needs based on ongoing classroom assessment

(Utley, Obiakor, & Bakken, 2011; Vaughn, & Fuchs, 2003; Vaughn, Linan-Thompson, & Hickman, 2003; Vaughn, Mathes, Linan-Thompson, & Francis, 2005; Vellutino, Scanlon, Small, & Fanuele, 2003).

PBS has specific characteristics associated with it and these include (a) the development of positive behavioral expectations, (b) specific methods to teach these expectations to staff and students, (c) proactive supervision or monitoring of behaviors, (d) contingency management systems to reinforce and correct behavior, and (e) methods to measure outcomes and to evaluate progress across three tiers with specific core elements at different levels. These levels are:

(1) Primary prevention/school-wide level, including universal school-wide management strategies to reduce disruptive behavior and teach prosocial skills to all students;
(2) Secondary prevention level, including targeted or group-based intervention strategies for students at-risk of developing more serious antisocial behaviors (about 5–10%); and
(3) Tertiary prevention level, including functionally derived treatment strategies for the small number of students (about 1–3%) who engage in more chronic patterns of antisocial behavior (Horner, Crone, & Stiller, 2001; Horner, Sugai, Todd, & Lewis-Palmer, 2005).

The previously described evidence-based approaches to instruction and behavior support have served to pave the way for marching toward successful inclusion of students with disabilities in general education classrooms. No longer are students with high incidence disabilities separated from mainstreamed students (Praisner, 2003); instead, efforts are made to provide effective education for students with disabilities in inclusive general education classrooms. The professional literature has now focused on the preparedness of educators and administrators to develop and implement effective inclusive programs and support within their general education classrooms (Obiakor, Harris, Mutua, Rotatori, & Algozzine, 2012).

INCLUSION OF STUDENTS WITH DISABILITIES

In order for the inclusion to be effective, there must be collaboration between general and special education teachers. However, these two teacher groups have not always been effective in teaming together. Research has shown that teacher expectations influence student behavior, self-esteem, and achievement; therefore, if a teacher has a negative attitude toward students with disabilities, then those students most likely will not be successful in the teacher's classroom (Obiakor, 1999). Research has also shown that administrators' attitudes toward students with disabilities are important for successful inclusion, since they are most influential in developing and operating educational programs in their schools. Research also has shown that many school districts implement inclusion without adequate professional development or preparation for using interventions beforehand (Obiakor et al., 2012).

Successful models for effective inclusive schools and classrooms need to be analyzed and described in ways that are useful by practitioners in their classrooms. Researchers of peer-reviewed literature often write of the positive impact of inclusive education, focusing on the social skills learned by students, the sharpening of pedagogical skills by teachers, and the role of inclusive education in the promotion of Civil Rights (Broderick, Mehta-Parekh, & Reid, 2005; Polat, 2010; Soodak, 2003). Most importantly, research has shown how students with disabilities benefit academically from inclusive education. This practitioner literature has also focused on the necessity of teachers receiving preparation in inclusive education as part of their teacher education programs (Florian & Linklater, 2010; Jordan, Schwartz, & McGhie-Richmond, 2009). Scholarly articles have made suggestions on implementing inclusive education, but descriptions of such approaches are typically minimally discussed and do not provide sufficient direction for teachers and other school professionals.

Several studies have provided information that is useful for practitioners in understanding the complex range of issues they must address in schools as they develop and implement inclusive practices. For example, Daane, Beirne-Smith, and Latham (2000) examined administrators' and teachers' perceptions of the collaborative efforts of inclusion in the elementary grades by conducting a survey of 324 elementary general education teachers, 42 special education teachers, and 15 building administrators. The results showed that teachers and administrators agreed that while collaboration is essential to support inclusive education, it was often not a comfortable experience for many professionals due to (a) conflict of personalities, (b) lack of planning time, and (c) limited time in the classroom by the special education teacher.

Survey responses further revealed that both general and special education teachers believed that the inclusive classroom was not the most effective environment for students with disabilities, although administrators believed that it was. Respondents also felt that general education teachers were not prepared to teach students with disabilities, and these teachers lacked the confidence and support needed in addressing the needs of these students (Daane et al., 2000). This investigation provides critical information for practitioners that must be addressed as they work to develop and implement effective inclusive programs.

In another investigation that provided a rich description of inclusive education, Idol (2006) described how special education services were provided in four elementary schools and four secondary schools in a large metropolitan school district. The schools were purposefully selected as settings with well-developed special education programs in which the staff believed they provided strong and supportive programs for educating students with disabilities. The schools were also selected so that one half were from the top and the other from the bottom of a continuum from no inclusion to full inclusion. Idol thus provides a description of a range of perspectives on providing high-quality educational services for students with disabilities in a cross-section of schools that are similar to those in many local education agencies. The results of this investigation revealed that only one of the elementary schools had placed an emphasis on special education and inclusion in their school improvement plan, and included students with disabilities within the general education classroom for all of the school day. Many students with disabilities in the other three elementary schools were educated for some or most of the school day in separate special education classrooms. Administrators in these schools were asked how students with disabilities were best educated. Three of the building administrators were in favor of inclusion only if an instructional assistant or a special educator were provided to support the general education teacher. Teachers and instructional assistants in all four elementary schools stated that they were applying the skills necessary for effective inclusion, which included (a) adaptation of instruction, (b) modification of curriculum, and (c) classroom management and student discipline.

Many teachers in the four elementary schools had additional comments that were generally positive about students with disabilities and inclusion. For example, these teachers indicated that they liked having instructional assistants and valued special education teachers in their classrooms, felt that statewide test scores were not affected by inclusive programs, did not like pull out programs, liked inclusive programs, and felt that mainstreaming be used rather than inclusion for students with more serious emotional problems. These teachers also stated that there was a need for more professional development related to inclusion, more opportunities were needed to visit schools with successful inclusive programs, better training for instructional assistants was needed, and more use of mainstreaming rather than inclusion for students with serious emotional problems should occur. Finally, elementary teachers addressed the need to respect "the special challenges (inclusion) presented to the classroom teacher and providing support" (Idol, 2006, p. 85) to these teachers.

For secondary settings, in the schools that were more inclusive (one middle school and one high school), referral rates to special education were much lower than at the other two schools. Possible reasons for this were providing more support by special educators and other support personnel for students with disabilities in the general education classrooms; providing support programs for tutoring, counseling, and career development; and the use of consulting teachers to support instruction. In addition, support services in these schools were typically provided for all students who needed assistance, and not just students with disabilities. In contrast, the schools that were less inclusive had higher referral rates. Possible reasons for this included provision of more separate class and resource programs for students with disabilities, providing fewer classes with support in the general education classroom, and providing classroom resources only for students with disabilities.

All secondary administrators reported that they were supportive of inclusion, but only if support services were provided in the general education classroom. Interestingly, while four administrators reported that they were good collaborators and worked well with teachers, the administrator in the most inclusive secondary school said that he was a good collaborator who worked well with most teachers, but not all of them. Secondary teachers perceived that they were skilled at adapting instruction and modifying the curriculum for student needs, addressing student discipline and classroom management issues, and collaborating with other professionals. In three of the secondary schools, the majority of teachers favored educating students with disabilities in general education classes with assistance from a special educator. However, in one high school, equal proportions of teachers supported inclusion and part-time special education classroom support. Across all schools, a majority of teachers felt that support provided in the general education classrooms should be for all students, and not just those with disabilities.

Most secondary educators felt that students with disabilities did not adversely affect the education of typical students. Additional comments from these educators indicated that they made distinctions between including students with academic versus behavioral problems and felt that they could better manage and support students with academic problems. Many of the teachers also noted that more personnel were needed to provide adequate support in general education classrooms for students with disabilities. Finally, many of these teachers indicated the need for additional professional development related to inclusion.

Idol (2006) noted that this investigation provided strong "support for including students with special education challenges in general education programs" (p. 94). However, she also provided several recommendations from educators in these settings to support inclusive practices, including more professional development for teachers in areas that support effective classroom practice, visits to successful inclusive schools, use of heterogeneous learning groups, and more professional development of instructional assistants. Finally, teachers across the schools made recommendations for policy and practice, including:

- Reconsider the viability of self-contained classes for students with disabilities;
- Consider mainstreaming rather than inclusion for some students with emotional/behavior disorders;
- Consider redistributing all students with disabilities to their neighborhood schools for more equitable distribution of students with different types of disabilities;
- Provide open and clear communication regarding why some students are provided more assistance in the general education classroom, including those who are provided instructional or curricular modifications;
- Ensure that the entire school staff is well prepared related to the use of consulting teachers, instructional assistants, and cooperative teaching;
- Make sure that special education teachers work with the principal and other professionals to determine how to best use their professional time working with students.

The studies by Daane et al. (2000) and Idol (2006) provide rich, descriptive information that is useful for practitioners as they develop and implement effective inclusive programs in their schools and classrooms. These investigations serve to provide practitioners with a realistic picture of what should be expected as they work in inclusive settings, and some of the complexity that is associated with these activities. More investigations are needed that provide this type of information that is usable by teachers and principals as they work to provide more effective inclusive schools and classrooms for all students with disabilities. Ecological models, which address educational phenomena, assert that students are involved in multiple environments where they play different roles. In each environment, they are expected to show certain behaviors; sometimes this can create conflicts, perhaps due to a discrepancy between the individual's skills in meeting the requirements of that environment or because the environment does not meet the individual's needs. As a result, comprehensive service provision includes meeting the educational social emotional needs of students with disabilities in home and community environments.

WORKING WITH FAMILIES

Research supports that teachers themselves are influenced by parental involvement. A teacher plays a major role in the grades and ratings a student receives in class, and a high degree of parental involvement likely influences how the teacher perceives and even grades the child (Jeynes, 2005). Research has shown that parental involvement has a significant influence on student achievement (Barnard, 2004; Fan & Chen, 2001). Becher's (1986) literature review on parental involvement found that there was "substantial evidence" which shows that students whose parents are involved in their schooling have increased academic performance and overall cognitive development. Data from the National Assessment of Educational Progress (NAEP) have found that parental levels of education and parental involvement in schools have a significant influence on student performance. The NAEP data report a 30-scale point differential on standardized achievement tests between students with involved parents compared to those students whose parents were not involved (Dietel, 2006). Researchers have also found that parental involvement is associated with a greater likelihood of aspiring to attend college and actually enrolling (Cabrera & Steven, 2000; Horn, 1998), as well as with higher grades (Lee, 1993; Muller & Kerbow, 1993), higher eighth grade mathematics and reading achievement (Lee, 1993; Sui-Chu & Willms, 1996), lower rates of behavioral problems (Lee, 1993), and a lower likelihood of high school dropout and truancy (McNeal, 1999). Sanders and Harvey (2002) conducted a case study of school—community partnerships and found that when schools were willing to structure authentic two-way communication with parents, levels of parental involvement increased considerably.

Using Bourdieu's cultural capital framework, Lareau and Horvat's (1999) study explores how some low-income black parents had great difficulty in communicating with their child's teachers as a result of the distrust they had of the educational system stemming from the historical legacy of racism. School teachers expecting parents to be positive, supportive, and trustful of their judgments were disappointed when black parents criticized and expressed anger at them for the differential treatment of black students. The criticism of teachers by black parents turned into negative cultural capital when their class-specific behaviors clashed with the expected norms of conformity and being positive of the middle-class white teachers, leading to the social exclusion of low-income black parents. Despite the worries that some middle-class black parents had concerning the possible differential treatment of their children, they were able to more effectively activate their cultural capital by closely monitoring their child's progress without letting school officials know of their distrust for the system. The attempts by a low-income black family to activate cultural capital for their daughter were rebuffed by school officials as a result of an informal implicit standard of what parental involvement should be like that delegitimized the concerns of those who did not conform to it (i.e., low-income black parents experiencing social exclusion).

Fine (1993) examined three major urban parent involvement projects in Baltimore, Philadelphia, and Chicago. All were undergoing specific efforts aimed at "involving" parents and giving them a greater voice. In Baltimore, the "With and for Parents" program sought to collaborate with its middle school and empower parents individually; however, it eventually ended up becoming a crisis intervention program, resulting from a failure to redistribute power and resources at the family–school level. Philadelphia pursued shared decision making and school-based management, which placed parents on decision-making bodies with educators and administrators. Fine notes that in those structures, teachers and parents were placed in adversarial positions as a result of larger bureaucratic action, noting specifically that both of their interests would be better served in a democratic coalition against those structures. In the late 1980s, Chicago passed legislation calling for their schools to be governed by local school councils comprising mainly of parents, along with community representatives, teachers, and principals. However, as a result of a fiscal crisis, some of the power that parents were to have in these positions was undermined as restrictive decisions that had to be made to accommodate the monetary shortfall, as well as low-income parents being taken less seriously as a result of their limited cultural capital. Fine argues that real parent involvement will result when parents become organized as political bodies working to transform public life, rather than to just help particular families in a crisis intervention mode.

Henderson and Mapp (2002) conducted an examination and synthesis of 51 recently conducted (all but two are from 1995 to 2002) studies on family involvement and student achievement. The three overarching themes in the studies center around the impact of family on student achievement; effective strategies for connecting schools, families, and community; and the development of community organizing as a tool for mobilizing parents as a means of holding schools accountable. This study reinforces the "positive and convincing relationship between family involvement and benefits for students, including improved academic achievement" (p. 24). More importantly, new literature concerning the effects of parent and community organizing in urban areas was explored, demonstrating the impact that comes from establishing a power base (leading to changes in policy, resources, school culture, etc.) in an effort to hold schools accountable. Henderson and Mapp provide a set of recommendations aimed at educators, parents, and community members, as well as researchers ranging from the acknowledgment that all parents are involved in some form in the education of their children, to conducting research that is more rigorous and focused using "more culturally sensitive and empowering definitions of parent involvement" (p. 69). In light of this research, legislation has been passed to create more meaningful ways for parents to play a concerted, more active role in their children's education (Henderson, 1987). Parents and teachers need specific information to maximize the efficacy of parental involvement (Jeynes, 2005). The next section discusses the role of special educators in interdisciplinary connections in collaborating with families with disabilities to foster greater parental involvement. Parents have the power to intimidate teachers and some do. Teachers have varied talents in their personal interaction skills. Some interact better with students than with parents. Some teachers feel poorly prepared to establish relationships with parents whose lives are very different from their own.

Park, Alber-Morgan, and Fleming (2011) remarked about additional roadblocks to actively involving parents. Though particular interventions such as functional behavioral assessment and positive behavior supports have been successful for decreasing negative behaviors (Heward, 2009), it is critical to take into account the individual family when selecting strategies for home and school implementation. Particular factors such as culture, family structure, work schedules, and socioeconomic status may impact the success or failure of various programs (Moes & Frea, 2000). Accounting for individual family difference is an important consideration for the success of intervention programs.

COLLABORATIVE TEAM-CENTERED RELATIONSHIPS BETWEEN SCHOOL PERSONNEL AND FAMILY MEMBERS

Turnbull et al. (2007) noted the importance of school personnel articulating not only *how* teachers and families should interact but also focusing on *what* specific services are essential. It is difficult for families to make informed decisions about their choices if they do not have a comprehensive awareness of the array of services available. In line with the previous discussion on working with the family instead of only the child with a disability, many researchers highlight the notion of "family support" that encompasses a wide range of components (Lucyshyn, Dunlap, & Albin, 2002; Park et al., 2011; Turnbull, Turnbull, Erwin, Soodak, & Shogren, 2010). Simpson, Peterson, and Smith (2011) propose a comprehensive framework of support components. Table 1 lists the components of the comprehensive framework of support.

Table 1.   Comprehensive Framework of Support Components.

a. Qualified and committed professionals	Well-trained teachers and support personnel understand the challenges faced by families of children with emotional disabilities. These personnel are vital in providing jargon-free information about the recommended interventions for the child. Unfortunately, regular classroom teachers feel ill equipped to handle the multiple challenges of meeting the needs of the child and the family.
b. Proven academic support systems	Academic and curricular issues often are placed on a backburner for children with emotional disabilities; however, it is important to engage the child in meaningful learning experiences at school and at home.
c. Environmental supports	Children with emotional disabilities tend to be more successful when their school and home environments include clear rules, consistent routines, and organized physical space.
d. Social skill and social interaction support	Opportunities for social interaction in a variety of settings provide useful practice for children. Providing families with information on and resources for developing the child's social interactions skills is beneficial for the harmony of the classroom environment as well as the home environment.
e. Coordinated community support	Due to the stress placed on the family, awareness of and enrollment in a network of services provides much needed assistance to families. Parents and families of children with disabilities often have complex needs, typically considered beyond the purview of schools, such as health, legal, housing, recreation, employment, and financial.

Families have complex needs and rarely in the categorical system of service provision is attention paid to the overall plan of assistance. When a vehicle for arranging this interagency collaboration and coordination of services does not formally exist in a community, schools may be the focal point for developing this (Cohen, Linker, & Stutts, 2006). Schools may help by establishing a framework for such services to exist.

Van Hove et al. (2009) discuss the relationship between the extent to which families can participate in the educational process of their child and the specific characteristics of the families' capabilities and problems. Families can participate more or less depending on such variables as their interests, the severity of the child's problems, the impact of the child's problems on the family members, work availability and hours, and availability of respite care (Dyson, 2010). If services are to be provided that meet the expressed needs of the family in a team format, the burden of training rests on all members of the team – the school, the family, and the service agencies.

Probably the best method of reporting pupil progress is through properly structured parent–teacher conferences. Such meetings allow for exchanging information about the student and clearing up misconceptions about the student's program. Parents may ask questions about areas that might otherwise be unclear or misunderstood. The key to conducting meaningful conferences is planning. The following are some general considerations to bear in mind when setting up conferences:

1. Allow enough time to adequately discuss each student.
2. Be aware that some parents may have conflicts with the allotted times; they should be allowed to make appointments at other times.
3. Develop some structure or format for keeping the conference on-task and flowing.
4. Communicate in clear, understandable language, avoiding educational jargon.
5. Make the setting comfortable, but businesslike.
6. Allow for questions during the course of the conference, not only at the end.
7. Make provisions for parents who may have to bring young children.
8. Make provisions for parents who arrive early and have to wait for their appointment.
9. Be on time.
10. Have folders available containing representative samples of the student's schoolwork (parents who arrive early may examine these while waiting).

11. Be flexible, but make every attempt to follow the schedule.
12. If problem areas are identified, inform parents how they may help in resolving the problems.

The National Peer Technical Assistance Network's Partnership for Children's Mental Health (1997) evaluated a variety of approaches to parent—teacher collaboration in their report *Family-Professional Partnerships: Moving Forward Together*. The report articulates five "Continuum of Service" configurations of collaborative team supports. These include:

(a) Professional-Centered: In the Professional-Centered approach, the relationship between the family and the teachers is adversarial and at times hostile. The parent is viewed (consciously or unconsciously) as part of the child's problem. The professional has the answers and the parent needs to listen to the expert advice.
(b) Family-Focused: The school professionals are still the experts, and the family is seen as a "helper" who is to follow the directions provided by the experts.
(c) Family-Allied: The school professionals and the family members have something to offer in this view. There is more sharing of information and less telling of what to do.
(d) Family-Centered: The family is seen as the "customer," and the job of the professional is to support the parent as the primary agent in helping the child. The school personnel believe the parents are responsible for and capable of determining what is best for their child.
(e) Team-Centered: Decisions about supports are made in what is referred to as a "wraparound model" (1997, p. 34). Family members and school personnel investigate assets, resources, and various interventions and match those with the child as part of a collective agreement.

In summary, communication involves sending, receiving, and perceiving information. This is reasonably straightforward and seemingly simple; however, effective communication is complex. In order for it to occur, there must be careful structuring by the facilitator who, in this case, is the teacher. Effective communication can lead to mutually beneficial collaborative team-centered relationships between school personnel and family members, thus resulting in potential growth for the child.

WORKING WITH OTHER EDUCATIONAL PROFESSIONALS

Multidisciplinary teams (MDTs) were originally conceptualized and mandated by P.L. 94-142 as a procedural safeguard for identification and placement of students in special education (Pryzwansky & Rzepski, 1983). The function of these teams was to assist general educators in their efforts to support students in the least restrictive settings. The team decision-making requirement was based on the premise that group decision making was superior to individual decision making (Abelson & Woodman, 1983).

Since the early 1980s, the role of teams in schools has expanded. Today MDTs may also function as a problem-solving unit to assist teachers in maintaining students in general classrooms (Pryzwansky & Rzepski, 1983; Truscott, Cohen, Sams, Sanborn, & Frank, 2005). Specifically, school team roles have taken two general forms: teacher assistance teams (TATs) and pre-assessment teams. The TAT model engages within-building personnel in collaborative and problem-solving processes. TATs are intended to provide problem-solving *assistance* to general education teachers in regard to students who are at risk for referral to special education. The TAT can be used to clarify classroom problems, collect and review student assessment data, develop interventions, set instructional or management goals, modify curriculum, generate strategies for whole classes, and/or prepare for parent conferences (Chalfant & Van Dusen Pysh, 1989). Since TATs were established, investigations of team effectiveness have reported success in intervening in classroom difficulties (Gilmer, 1985; Talley, 1988). High levels of teacher and team satisfaction with the process have been reported (Chalfant & Van Dusen Pysh, 1989).

TATs and MDTs often provide assistance and problem solving through development and implementation of strategies, adaptations, and interventions to be used to support struggling students. A teacher may seek the assistance of one of these teams to effectively meet the needs of a student. As a teacher begins work with the TAT or MDT, the professional group tends to look to categories of interventions that may provide the supports students and teachers require for success. While those interventions vary across teachers, students, and settings, most initial interventions fall within one of three categories: (a) curricular, (b) environmental, and/or (c) management. Table 2 provides examples of curricular, environmental, and management adaptations that may be suggested in informal collaborative situations.

Table 2.   Chart of Curricular, Environmental, and Management
                  Adaptations Examples.

Curricular Modifications	Environmental Modifications	Management Modifications
Tape lessons or instructions	Change the student's seat assignment	Establish home–school communication system
Simplify vocabulary of test items, practice sheets	Assign preferential seating	Post rules and consequences for behavior
Provide tests in segments	Post class routine	Put student on daily or weekly progress report
Provide visual or memory aids such as number lines, formulas, pictures, and charts	Move location of classroom supplies to minimize distractions	Keep graphs, charts, or calendars of student progress
Highlight main ideas and supporting details in text	Assign student study partner	Establish contingency contract
Provide study outlines and guides	Provide one-on-one tutoring	Ignore inappropriate behavior
Reduce quantity of material to be read	Use small group instruction	Give verbal or nonverbal signals (winks, hand signals, etc.) to monitor behavior
Have student keep an assignment notebook	Provide a monitoring buddy	Move closer to student to monitor behavior
Provide a sample or practice test	Establish time expectations for assignment completion	Establish list of reinforcers for student
Provide opportunities for extra drill	Provide verbal cues to indicate beginning and ending instructional time	Offer social reinforcers for student
Use special supplementary material	Provide visual, tactile, or auditory prompts to indicate appropriate behavior	Offer tangible reinforcers (points, tokens, stickers)
Provide text written at student's reading level		Provide immediate reinforcement for correct responses
Provide self-checking materials		Implement a token or point system
Provide immediate correction of errors		Implement self-recording of behavior
Teach learning strategies		
Ask student to repeat directions		

Curricular adaptations target the academic tasks required for classroom success. Ideally, the classroom teacher analyzes student data and adapts learning objectives, materials, and teaching methods to ensure a better academic match between each teacher's instructional objectives and individual students' demonstrated academic or social behaviors. Taping lessons or texts, using parallel instructional materials, or giving a test in segments are examples of curricular modifications that teachers may use to provide support to a student experiencing academic difficulties. *Environmental adaptations* focus on analyzing and adapting the classroom ecology to accommodate individual learners. For example, general educator may provide preferential seating, establish time expectations for assignment completion, or move instructional supplies to reduce distractions to help a student experience classroom success. *Management adaptations* are designed to provide behavioral support to a student. These adaptations offer reinforcement for appropriate behavior as well as environmental–behavioral support for students. Providing daily or weekly progress reports, using nonverbal signals to monitor behavior, or using tangible reinforcers are only a few examples of early interventions that may be implemented for students experiencing behavioral difficulties.

FUTURE DIRECTIONS

Teaching is a profession of ever-changing demands, and the need to develop new skills and approaches to use with students is considered essential. Teachers prepared in isolation fail to produce significant transformations in the school culture (Blanco, 1999). Considerable evidence has indicated that both general and special educators believe they are inadequately prepared to serve students with disabilities in general education classrooms. Many general education teachers are not prepared to provide differentiated and diversified instructional methods that are needed in inclusive classrooms. To facilitate confidence and competence, "teachers need systematic and intensive training that includes research-based best practices in inclusive schools" (Burstein, Sears, Wilcoxen, Cabello, & Spagna, 2004, p. 105). Teachers must also engage in professional development as an ongoing part of their professional role (Fisher, Frey, & Thousand, 2003). A number of areas of professional development are important, but research done by Fisher et al. (2003) suggests five high priority focus areas: (1) collaborative teaming and teaching, (2) curricular and instructional modifications, (3) accommodations and personal supports, (4) assistive technology, and (5) positive behavioral supports.

If implemented properly, collaborative and inclusive education services can (a) be less expensive to implement and operate than special education services, (b) have a broader reach than traditional special education in terms of positive educational and social impacts on children and youth, (c) contribute significantly to the ongoing professional development and job satisfaction of educators, and (d) produce better morale and team effort in the school environment. Legislative and policy provisions are also important for the development of inclusive schools and supportive communities. These general principles must be backed up by operational strategies that can get the key officials and leaders to fully commit to implementing inclusion (Obiakor et al., 2012). If any area demands accountability, it is the education system that shapes our future and the future of our children and youth. Below are quality indicators that inform what inclusion must look like in the future:

1. Leadership
2. School climate
3. Curriculum, instruction, and assessment
4. Program planning and implementation
5. Individual student supports
6. Family—school partnerships
7. Collaborative planning
8. Professional development
9. Planning for continued best practice improvement

SUMMARY AND CONCLUSIONS

This chapter addressed many facets of school-related issues that impact student performance and teacher productivity. Teachers and students are part of a larger, complex system of education that must accept guidance from their district, legislators, researchers, parents, and state departments of education. Understanding the larger picture of how student behavior fits within our present laws, expectations, and research allows teachers to consider factors that extend beyond the daily work they accomplish with students with and without disabilities. The influences of NCLB and IDEA are felt from the state levels to the local education agencies, to the campus, to the teacher and child. Issues that impact the equivocal educational experiences of high-risk learners, such as students who have disabilities, must be understood within the efforts being undertaken to address and correct the problems.

One way of better meeting the needs of children with disabilities is establishing good communication with the family, related, and other educational professionals. Parents have to be recognized as special educators, the true experts on their children; professional people — teachers, pediatricians, psychologists, and others — have to learn to be consultants to parents (Muscott, 2002). The complexity of teaching students with disabilities and encouraging collaborative participation from diverse groups of professionals and that involvement often extends outside the classroom to the community and home. It is important that teachers understand where the parents are, their strengths, and what they can contribute to the educational process of their child at any given stage. Seeing the child with disabilities as an element of an interactive family system requires the coordination of services to meet the complex needs of children and youth. Schools may need to be the central coordinating agent for these services.

REFERENCES

Abelson, M. A., & Woodman, R. W. (1983). Review of research on team effectiveness: Implications for teams in schools. *School Psychology Review*, *12*, 125–136.

Barnard, W. M. (2004). Parent involvement in elementary school and educational attainment. *Children and Youth Services Review*, *26*(1), 39–62.

Becher, R. (1986). *Parents and schools*. (ERIC Document Reproduction Service No. ED269137).

Blanco, R. (1999). Towards schools for all with the involvement of all. In BULLETIN 48, April 1999. *The Major Project of Education* (pp. 55–71). Paris: UNESCO.

Broderick, A., Mehta-Parekh, H., & Reid, D. K. (2005). Differentiating instruction for disabled students in inclusive classrooms. *Theory Into Practice*, *44*(3), 194–202.

Burstein, N., Sears, S., Wilcoxen, A., Cabello, B., & Spagna, M. (2004). Moving towards inclusive practices. *Remedial and Special Education*, *25*(2), 104–115.

Cabrera, A. F., & Steven, M. (2000). Overcoming the tasks on the path to college for America's disadvantaged. *New Directions for Institutional Research*, *27*(3), 31–43.

Chalfant, J. C., & Van Dusen Pysh, M. (1989). Teacher assistance teams: Five descriptive studies on 96 teams. *Remedial and Special Education*, *10*(6), 49–58.

Cohen, R., Linker, J. A., & Stutts, L. (2006). Working together: Lessons learned from school, family, and community collaborations. *Psychology in the Schools*, *43*(4), 419–428.

Daane, C. J., Beirne-Smith, M., & Latham, D. (2000). Administrators and teachers perceptions of the collaborative efforts of inclusion in the elementary grades. *Education*, *121*, 331–339.

Dietel, R. (2006). *Get smart: Nine ways to help your child succeed in school*. San Francisco, CA: Jossey Bass.

Dyson, L. (2010). Unanticipated effects of children with learning disabilities on their families. *Learning Disability Quarterly, 33*(1), 43–55.

Fan, X., & Chen, M. (2001). Parental involvement and students' academic achievement: A meta-analysis. *Educational Psychology Review, 13*(1), 1–22.

Fine, M. (1993). (Ap)parent involvement. *Equity and Choice, 9*(3), 4–8.

Fisher, D., Frey, N., & Thousand, J. (2003). What do special educators need to know and be prepared to do for inclusive schooling to work? *Teacher Education and Special Education, 26*, 42–50.

Florian, L., & Linklater, H. (2010). Preparing teachers for inclusive education: Using inclusive pedagogy to enhance teaching and learning for all. *Cambridge Journal of Education, 40*(4), 369–386. doi:10.1080/0305764X.2010.526588

Gilmer, J. F. (1985). *Factors related to the success and failure of teacher assistance teams in elementary schools*. Unpublished doctoral dissertation, University of Arizona, Tucson.

Henderson, A. (1987). *The evidence continues to grow*. Columbia, MD: National Committee for Citizens in Education.

Henderson, A., & Mapp, K. (2002). *A new wave of evidence: The impact of school, family, and community connections on student achievement*. Austin, TX: Southwest Educational Development Laboratory.

Heward, W. (2009). *Exceptional children* (9th ed.), Upper Saddle, NJ: Pearson.

Horn, J. G. (1998). Stakeholders' evaluation of rural/small schools. *Rural Educator, 20*(1), 5–11.

Horner, R., Crone, D., & Stiller, B. (2001). The role of school psychologists in establishing positive behavior support: Collaborating in systems change at the schoolwide level. *Communiqué, 29*(6), 10–12.

Horner, R. H., Sugai, G., Todd, A. W., & Lewis-Palmer, T. (2005). School-wide positive behavior support. In L. Bambara & L. Kern (Eds.), *Individualized supports for students with problem behaviors: Designing positive behavior plans* (pp. 359–390). New York, NY: Guilford.

IDEA. (1997). *Individuals with Disabilities Education Act (IDEA) 1997/Services to parentally placed private school students with disabilities*. Retrieved from http://www2.ed.gov/about/offices/list/oii/nonpublic/idea1.html

Idol, L. (2006). Toward inclusion of special education students in general education: A program evaluation and study of eight schools. *Remedial and Special Education, 27*(2), 77–94.

Individuals with Disabilities Education Act of 2004. Pub.L. No. 108–446, § 101, 118 Stat. 2647.

Jeynes, W. (2005). A meta-analysis of the relation of parental involvement to urban elementary school student academic achievement. *Urban Education, 40*(3), 237–269.

Jordan, A., Schwartz, E., & McGhie-Richmond, D. (2009). Preparing teachers for inclusive classrooms. *Teaching and Teacher Education, 25*, 535–542.

Lareau, A., & Horvat, E. M. (1999). Moments of social inclusion and exclusion: Race, class, and cultural capital in family-school relationships. *Sociology of Education, 72*(1), 37–53.

Lee, S. (1993). Family structure effects on student outcomes. In B. Schneider & J. S. Coleman (Eds.), *Parents, their children, and school* (pp. 43–75). Boulder, CO: Westview Press.

Lucyshyn, J. M., Dunlap, G., & Albin, R. W. (2002). *Families and positive behavior support: Addressing problem behavior in family contexts.* Baltimore, MD: P. H. Brookes.

McNeal, R. B., Jr. (1999). Parental involvement as social capital: Differential effectiveness on science achievement, truancy, and dropping out. *Social Forces, 78*(1), 117−144.

Moes, D., & Frea, W. (2000). Using an assessment of family context to inform intervention planning for the treatment of challenging behavior in a child with autism. *Journal of Positive Behavior Interventions, 2*(1), 40−46.

Muller, C., & Kerbow, D. (1993). Parent involvement in the home, school, and community. In B. Schneider & J. S. Coleman (Eds.), *Parents, their children, and schools* (pp. 13−42). Boulder, CO: Westview Press.

Muscott, H. S. (2002). Exceptional partnerships: Listening to the voices of families. *Preventing School Failure, 46*(2), 66−69.

National Center for Education Statistics. (2011). *The condition of education 2011 (NCES 2011-033).* Washington, DC: U.S. Department of Education, U.S. Government Printing Office.

National Peer Technical Assistance Network's Partnership for Children's Mental Health. (1997). *Family-professional relationships: Moving forward together.* Alexandria, VA: Federation of Families for Children's Mental Health.

No Child Left Behind Act of 2001. Pub.L.107−110, 115 stat. 1425.

Obiakor, F. E. (1999). Teacher expectations of minority exceptional learners: Impact of "accuracy" of self-concepts. *Exceptional Children, 66*, 39−53.

Obiakor, F. E., Harris, M., Mutua, K., Rotatori, A., & Algozzine, B. (2012). Making inclusion work in general education classrooms. *Education & Treatment of Children, 35*(3), 477−490.

Park, J. H., Alber-Morgan, S. R., & Fleming, C. (2011). Collaborating with parents to implement behavioral interventions for children with challenging behaviors. *Teaching Exceptional Children, 43*(3), 22−30.

Polat, N. (2010). A comparative analysis of pre- and in-service teacher beliefs about readiness and self-competency: Revisiting teacher education for ELLs. *System, 38*, 228−244.

Praisner, C. (2003). Attitudes of elementary school principals toward inclusion of students with disabilities. *Exceptional Children, 69*(2), 135−145.

Pryzwansky., W., & Rzepski, B. (1983). School-based teams: An untapped resource for consultation and technical assistance. *School Psychology Review, 23*(2), 174−179.

Samuels, C. A. (2011). CA district uses RTI to boost achievement for all. *Education Digest: Essential Readings Condensed for Quick Review, 77*(1), 53−56.

Sanders, M. G., & Harvey, A. (2002). Beyond the school walls: A case study of principal leadership for school-community collaboration. *Teachers College Record, 104*(7), 1345−1368.

Simpson, R., Peterson, R., & Smith, C. (2011). Critical educational program components for students with emotional and behavioral disorders: Science, policy, and practice. *Remedial and Special Education, 32*(3), 230−242.

Skiba, R. J., Michael, R. S., Nardo, A. C., & Peterson, R. (2002). The color of discipline: Sources of racial and gender disproportionality in school punishment. *The Urban Review, 34*(4), 317−342.

Skiba, R. J., Peterson, R., & Williams, T. (1997). Office referrals and suspension: Disciplinary intervention in middle schools. *Education and Treatment of Children, 20*(3), 295−315.

Soodak, L. C. (2003). Classroom management in inclusive settings. *Theory Into Practice*, *42*(4), 327–333.

Sui-Chu, E. H., & Willms, J. D. (1996). Effects of parental involvement on eighth-grade achievement. *Sociology of Education*, *69*(2), 126–141.

Talley, R. (1988). *End of year school psychological services report. School year 1987–1988*. Jefferson, KY: Jefferson County Public Schools.

Truscott, S. D., Cohen, C. E., Sams, D. P., Sanborn, K. J., & Frank, A. J. (2005). The current state(s) of prereferral intervention teams: A report from two national surveys. *Remedial and Special Education*, *26*(3), 130–140.

Turnbull, A., Summers, J., Turnbull, R., Brotherson, M., Winton, P., Roberts, R., ... Stroup-Rentier, V. (2007). Family supports and services in early intervention: A bold vision. *Journal of Early Intervention*, *29*(3), 187–206.

Turnbull, A., Turnbull, H., Erwin, E., Soodak, L., & Shogren, K. (2010). *Families, professionals, and exceptionality: Positive outcomes through partnerships and trust* (6th ed.), Upper Saddle River, NJ: Prentice Hall.

U.S. Department of Education. (1995). *OCR empowers others to prevent illegal discrimination*. Retrieved from https://www2.ed.gove/about/offices/list/ocr/AnnRpt95/edlite-ocr95rp4.html

U.S. Department of Education, Office of Special Education Programs. (2005). *Annual report to Congress on the implementation of the Individuals' with Disabilities Education Act*. Washington, DC: Author.

Utley, C. A., Obiakor, F. E., & Bakken, J. P. (2011). Culturally responsive practices for culturally and linguistically diverse students with learning disabilities. *Learning Disabilities: A Contemporary Journal*, *9*(1), 5–18.

Van Hove, G., De Schauwer, E., Mortier, K., Bosteels, S., Desnerck, G., & Van Loon, J. (2009). Working with mothers and fathers of children with disabilities: Metaphors used by parents in a continuing dialogue. *European Early Childhood Education Research Journal*, *17*(2), 187–201.

Vaughn, S., & Fuchs, D. (2003). Redefining learning disabilities as inadequate response to instruction: The promise and potential problems. *Learning Disabilities Research & Practice*, *18*(3), 137–146.

Vaughn, S., Linan-Thompson, S., & Hickman, P. (2003). Response to instruction as a means of identifying students with reading/learning disabilities. *Exceptional Children*, *69*(4), 391–409.

Vaughn, S., Mathes, P., Linan-Thompson, S., & Francis, D. J. (2005). Teaching English language learners at risk for reading disabilities to read: Putting research into practice. *Learning Disabilities Research & Practice*, *20*(1), 58–67.

Vellutino, F. R., Scanlon, D. M., Small, S. G., & Fanuele, D. (December, 2003). Response to intervention as a vehicle for distinguishing between reading disabled and non-reading disabled children: Evidence for the role of kindergarten and first grade intervention. Paper presented at the National Research Center on Learning Disabilities Responsiveness-to-Intervention Symposium, Kansas City, MO.

CHAPTER 3

ROLE OF GENERAL EDUCATORS IN A MULTIDISCIPLINARY TEAM FOR LEARNERS WITH SPECIAL NEEDS

D. Antonio Cantu

ABSTRACT

We have witnessed, over the past century, an evolution in the manner in which students with disabilities are educated. Indeed, the quality of education students with special needs receive, in many ways, may be more aptly termed a revolution — from a legal and pedagogical perspective. The tremendous strides special education has made during this period of time has resulted in the current situation in which students with special needs are placed in the least restrictive environment, which often is an inclusive classroom in which general education and special education teachers work together in a collaborative, co-teaching environment. This chapter traces the events, legislation, and court cases that provide the historical context for this situation. In addition, models and essential components of co-teaching are examined, as well as the roles and requisite skills of general education and special education co-teachers. Of critical importance, in the success of co-teaching, is the need for special

Interdisciplinary Connections to Special Education: Important Aspects to Consider
Advances in Special Education, Volume 30A, 35−57
ISSN: 0270-4013/doi:10.1108/S0270-40132015000030A003

education and general education teachers to approach the curriculum planning and instructional processes in a collaborative and cooperative manner in order to achieve optimum results from the resulting co-teaching partnership. Finally, the assessment of special education and general education co-teaching efficacy is discussed, specifically through the use of three assessment rubrics used to evaluate co-teaching, co-planning, and co-assessment.

Keywords: Alternative teaching; collaboration; co-teaching; IDEA; IEP; inclusion; mainstreaming; team teaching

Today, the institution of public education is dedicated to the teaching of all students, which includes those with physical, mental, or emotional disabilities. The history of teaching students with special needs – including whether, where, and how to teach them – however, serves to illustrate this has not always been the case. To be certain, only after decades of lobbying and advocacy, which resulted in a myriad of state and federal laws, court decisions, and civil rights initiatives, have students with disabilities been afforded access to the same educational opportunities as those students that do not have special needs. A thorough understanding of this historical timeline or journey is requisite to fully appreciating the essential role that both special education and general education teachers play in the success of students with special needs, and the critical importance of their collaborative efforts in yielding these education gains/results. Prior to examining the need for special education and general education teachers to develop co-teaching partnerships, however, it is important to review the events of the twentieth century, which have served to inform and shape how we approach special education in the classroom of the twenty-first century.

EARLY HISTORY OF SPECIAL EDUCATION

For far too long, individuals with disabilities have been excluded or segregated on account of their differences (Osgood, 2008). This situation was further compounded by the fact that the concept of public education for all students in America has been anything but guaranteed, resulting in an educational landscape best characterized by Katz (1976) as, "a patchwork of arrangements for schooling that included dame schools, academies, evening schools, Latin grammar schools, English grammar schools, pauper schools, and colleges" (p. 14). With only a select number of individuals, for several generations, having the opportunity to attend school, potential students with disabilities were often among those who were excluded.

The movement to provide education for all students gained momentum with urbanization. Increased immigration, overcrowding, crime, and other factors included with the rise of cities served as a catalyst for many groups to support public schools as a remedy or cure for societal ills, that is, as a prevention for crime, as well as a vehicle for assimilation of immigration, promotion of Christian values, and propagation of patriotism (Katz, 1976).

The first school established to assist students with a disability, that is, hearing impairments, was founded at Hartford, Connecticut, in 1817 by Thomas Hopkins Gallaudet (Albrecht, 2006). This was followed shortly thereafter, in the 1830s, by Samuel Gridley Howe's founding of a school for those students who were blind or deaf (Gargiulo & Kilgo, 2011). Howe went on to found another school for students with disabilities, although the moniker of the school served to illustrate the insensitivity of the period, that is, "The Massachusetts School for the Idiotic and Feebleminded Youth" (Gargiulo & Kilgo, 2011, p. 17). Nonetheless, Howe became the leading expert on educating the disabled. Another American education reformer, Dorothea Dix, was also an advocate for the disabled. She was able to help establish 32 state-operated mental institutions (Gargiulo & Kilgo, 2011). Despite some advances, institutions for students with disabilities or exceptionalities were not part of the American educational landscape until near the end of the nineteenth century (Gargiulo & Kilgo, 2011).

LEGAL GENESIS OF SPECIAL EDUCATION

The legal genesis for educational opportunities being afforded to students with disabilities can be traced to the Fourteenth Amendment of the U.S. Constitution. While supporters of the Fourteenth Amendment intended to provide civil rights to African-Americans, a legal byproduct was that students with disabilities were granted the same rights as the rest of the citizenry (Yell, 2006).

Originally, compulsory school attendance laws did not include students with disabilities. Even though there were fines if children between 8 and 18 years of age did not attend school at least 12 weeks per year, parents with children who had disabilities were exempt from these laws (Katz, 1976). As recent in U.S. history as the Progressive Era, students with disabilities were being institutionalized rather than enrolled in public schools (Osgood, 2008). This led to isolation and a lack of awareness, relative to disabilities, on the part of the general public.

This awareness, however, would soon be brought to the forefront in American society in the form of returning veterans who were disabled during World War I and World War II. As the number of disabled Americans increased, the public perception of individuals with disabilities improved significantly (Colarusso & O'Rourke, 2004). Simultaneous with this, the Civil Rights Movement also brought about significant advances, including the historic *Brown v. Board of Education* Supreme Court decision of 1954 (Antosh & Imparato, 2014). In their decision, the Supreme Court ruled that "separate educational facilities are inherently unequal" (Yell, 2006). Although the focus of the *Brown* decision was on racial segregation, it would later serve as a legal basis for calls to end segregation based on disabilities.

SPECIAL EDUCATION LEGISLATIVE INITIATIVES

The Cold War, in particular the race to the moon, also served to benefit students with disabilities in the United States, as a result of increased funding for public education in response to the Soviet Union launching Sputnik in 1957. The resulting *National Defense Education Act* (NDEA) of 1958 provided funding in the form of grants to promote science and math in public schools (Martin, Martin, & Terman, 1996). A lesser-known legislative companion to this act was Public Law 85-926 − signed four days after the NDEA − which allocated federal funding to colleges for training teachers to work with children who had mental disabilities (Martin et al., 1996). This was followed a few years later, in 1966, by the establishment of the Bureau for the Education of the Handicapped (BEH), as part of Title VI of the *Elementary and Secondary Education Act* (ESEA) (Martin et al., 1996).

On the state level, students with disabilities were either turned away or placed in inadequate school settings. For example, many of those with physical disabilities were placed in settings alongside students with mental disabilities, with only partial funding being allocated to local school districts. To address this inappropriate treatment, Congressional hearings were held in 1975, revealing that 4.5 million children were receiving insufficient educational services or no services whatsoever (Martin et al., 1996). It became apparent that states needed funding from the federal government to subsidize special education.

Indeed, federal intervention was required to bring about change, given school districts were allowed to refuse services to students that were "uneducable," with the definition of "uneducable" being determined by the local administration (Martin et al., 1996). Significant change was needed, and it finally occurred as a result of the *Education for All Handicapped Children Act* (Public Law 94-142) in 1975, which ensured that students with disabilities would have equal access to free and appropriate public education (Martin et al., 1996).

Parents soon began serving as advocates for children with disabilities. Their primary goal was to acquire the same access to appropriate education, delivered in the same classroom as their child's academic peers. From these efforts, inclusion was born. Inclusion served to enhance students' self-esteem and confidence, as well as to gain exposure to the same curriculum, and similar experiences relative to socialization (Walther-Thomas, 1997). Some of the benefits of inclusion include age-appropriateness and an increase in the ability to function with less difficulty in the outside world (Hunt, Farron-Davis, Beckstead, Curtis, & Goetz, 1994).

SPECIAL EDUCATION JUDICIAL MILESTONES

Failure to provide proper placements resulted in litigation during the early 1970s, as parents began to use the Fourteenth Amendment's section about due process to secure prior notice, changes in their child's placement, and a right to appeal a change (Martin et al., 1996). *Pennsylvania Association for Retarded Children (PARC) v. Commonwealth of Pennsylvania* established the right of a least restrictive placement for students, and in *Mills v. Board of Education*, the court ruled that school districts could not invoke inadequate resources as a reason to deny services to students with disabilities (Martin et al., 1996).

SEMINAL SPECIAL EDUCATION LEGISLATION

Another seminal piece of legislation that afforded students access to services was the *Rehabilitation Act* of 1973. This act prohibits agencies from receiving federal funds if they discriminate against people with disabilities (Yell, 2006). A major provision of the *Rehabilitation Act* was Section 504. This section calls for a "free appropriate public education to each student with disabilities, regardless of the nature or severity of the disability; [which] ... means providing regular or special education and related aids and services designed to meet the individual educational needs of disabled persons as adequately as the needs of nondisabled persons are met ... [so] that each student with disabilities is educated with nondisabled students to the maximum extent appropriate" (Smith, 2001).

By 1975, Public Law 94-142 was passed, requiring annual meetings, and an individualized education program (IEP) for each student with a disability and the right to education in a least restrictive environment. This federal law, also referred to as the *Education for All Handicapped Children Act*, became the prevailing special education mandate until 1990 (Martin et al., 1996). In that year, the *Elementary for All Handicapped Children Act*, otherwise known as the *Individuals with Disabilities Education Act*, became law. The year 1990 also witnessed passage of the *Americans with Disabilities Act* (ADA), which afforded people with disabilities protection of civil rights in all segments of society, including employment, access to buildings, and tele-communications (Hunt & Marshall, 2002).

TWENTY-FIRST CENTURY SPECIAL EDUCATION LEGISLATIVE LANDSCAPE

The most recent legislation to affect students with disabilities is *No Child Left Behind* (NCLB), passed in 2001, although this act was designed to assist students both with and without disabilities (Slavin, 2006). Perhaps, the most important aspect of NCLB is the requirement that all students receive high-quality teaching and achieve success in the classroom.

To this end, NCLB required accountability in the form of report cards issued for each school measuring how different subgroups in the school performed, relative to meeting what became known as Adequate Yearly Progress (AYP). AYP included measures for reading/language arts and math, and applied to the following: "... not only to students on average, but also to students in subgroups, including economically disadvantaged students, students with disabilities, English-language learners, African-American students, Asian-American students, Caucasian students, Hispanic students, and Native American students" (Editorial Projects in Education Research Center, 2011). The AYP findings are public knowledge, being printed in the newspapers, reported in the media, and found on each state and school district website. Parents are able to look at how a prospective school is performing in a particular region prior to making the decision to move. As a result, schools were made more transparent. The goal of NCLB perhaps is best summarized in a recent issue of *Education Week* as follows:

> Under NCLB, AYP is used to determine if schools are successfully educating their students. The law requires states to use a single accountability system for public schools to determine whether all students, as well as individual subgroups of students, are making progress toward meeting state academic content standards. The goal is to have all students reaching proficient levels in reading and math by 2014 as measured by performance on state tests. Progress on those standards must be tested yearly in grades 3 through 8 and in one grade in high school. The results are then compared to prior years, and, based on state-determined AYP standards, used to determine if the school has made adequate progress towards the proficiency goal. (Editorial Projects in Education Research Center, 2011, July 18)

THE CONCEPT OF CO-TEACHING

To facilitate all students being given an opportunity to learn, the concept of co-teaching received increased attention and emphasis. Co-teaching is often implemented in an effort to increase the performance of students with disabilities on state-mandated tests (Cramer & Nevin, 2006). Co-teaching involves a highly qualified content teacher engaging with students of all abilities, while working cooperatively with a special education teacher (Bauwens, Hourcade, & Friend, 1989). This allows students to receive services in the least restrictive environment with their peers, providing their educational needs can still be met.

Conceptually, co-teaching is different from team teaching. While two teachers working together in a classroom provide an obvious benefit of a lower student-to-teacher ratio, team teaching would often entail a content teacher delivering a lecture one time to a large group of students rather than the same lecture four times to smaller groups. Then, once the lecture was delivered, groups were divided up and assigned to the co-teachers for more individualized discussion, engagement, and assessment (Friend, Cook, Hurley-Chamberlain, & Shamberger, 2010).

The pedagogical pendulum, however, would swing from the team teaching approach to co-teaching as a result of the growing emphasis on inclusion rather than pull-out programs, to provide students with special needs services without the social stigma attached to having class away from one's peers. This directly addressed one major shortcoming of pull-out programs, which relied solely on special education teachers who were qualified in pedagogical approaches but may not have the same level of content knowledge as a core teacher (Warger & Aldinger, 1986). Team teaching and co-teaching differ in that the former reduces student-to-teacher ratio, while the latter is a different pedagogical approach and educational philosophy where the skill set of both the general education and special education teachers are maximized to provide all students with the best possible teaching and learning environment (Friend et al., 2010).

THE ROLE OF CO-TEACHING IN A LEAST RESTRICTIVE ENVIRONMENT

Indeed, special education legislation and court decisions serve to show that students with special needs must be placed in the least restrictive learning environment, which oftentimes is a general education classroom, unless a student's needs are not met by placement in an inclusive setting. Inclusion, according to Idol (2006), is achieved when "students with disabilities receive their entire academic curriculum in the general education program" (p. 78). The problem, however, is that far too many general education teachers, and a certain number of special education teachers, are not familiar with the models of co-teaching that are required to teach students with special needs in an inclusive general education classroom (Monahan & Marino, 1996). However, the U.S. Department of Education's (2014) *Annual Report to Congress on the Implementation of the Individuals with Disabilities Education Act* documents the increasing importance of collaboration between general education and special education teachers to effectively teach the growing number of students with special needs who are being taught in regular classrooms:

> From 2003 through 2012, the percentage of students ages 6 through 21 served under IDEA, Part B, educated inside the regular class 80% or more of the day increased from 49.9 percent to 61.5 percent. The percentage of students ages 6 through 21 served under IDEA, Part B, educated inside the regular class no more than 79% of the day and no less than 40% of the day decreased from 27.7 percent in 2003 to 19.5 percent in 2012. Similarly, the percentage of students educated inside the regular class less than 40% of the day decreased from 18.5 percent to 13.8 percent between these years. The percentage of students ages 6 through 21 served under IDEA, Part B, educated in "other environments" increased from 3.9 percent in 2003 to 5.2 percent in 2012. (U.S. Department of Education, 2014, p. xxvi)

Therefore, collaboration between the general education and the special education teacher remains the key to achieving this end (DeSimone & Parmar, 2006). There is no one formula, however, for how to develop this type of collaborative partnership; as Eccleston (2010) reminds us, "different educational institutions will achieve collaboration between their general educators and special educators in as many ways as there are people to collaborate" (p. 40). When operationalized in an effective manner, co-teaching teams can play an essential role in meeting the needs of students with special needs (Colarusso & O'Rourke, 2004). Such efforts, however, have still not achieved the level of success originally hoped for, even two decades after Fuchs and Fuchs (1994), in their seminal work on this topic, alerted us that "special education has big problems, not least of which is that it must redefine its relationship with general education"(p. 305). Hunt and Marshall (2002) remind us this is not only a more efficacious pedagogical approach but is also a legal mandate, that is, "… educational programs for exceptional children require that parents and professionals work together, or collaborate, to meet the best interest of the child" (p. 99). This is why the role of co-teaching, which Nichols, Dowdy, and Nichols (2010) define as "a collaboration effort between a general education teacher and special education teacher" (p. 647), in inclusive K-12 classrooms, is more important today than ever before.

MODELS OF CO-TEACHING AND ESSENTIAL COMPONENTS

There are a variety of collaborative models, that is, approaches and strategies, available to special education and general education teachers to use in developing co-teaching partnerships (Friend, Reising, & Cook, 1993; McCulley, Solis, Swanson, & Vaughn, 2012; Sileo, 2011). To facilitate that process, Friend et al. (2010) have identified six models of co-teaching, which are designed to meet the needs of students and to guide the curriculum planning and instructional process. The essential components of the six co-teaching models identified by Friend et al. (2010) are outlined in Fig. 1.

These six models provide a scaffolding that special education and general education teachers may use in creating co-teaching partnerships, which, otherwise, do not develop naturally in a school environment (Mastropieri et al., 2005; Scruggs, Mastropieri, & McDuffie, 2007; Weiss & Lloyd, 2003).

1. *One teach one observe* requires one teacher to engage in whole-class instruction, while the other teacher engages in collecting data on individual students or specific groups within the class.
2. *Station teaching* requires the creation of three teaching and learning stations, two of which are staffed/facilitated by the teachers and one in which the students must work independently. Students then rotate from station to station at designated times within the class period.
3. *Parallel teaching* requires both teachers to engage in instruction, which is differentiated, with two respective class groups in an effort to facilitate learning and increase student participation.
4. *Alternative teaching* requires that one of the teachers work with a smaller group of students to provide either remediation or enrichment, while the other teacher provides instruction to the larger group of students in the class.
5. *Teaming* requires both teachers to be actively engaged in whole-class instruction, taking advantage of the opportunity to engage in a variety of instructional strategies, both teacher-centered and student-centered.
6. *One teach one assist* requires that one teacher assume an instructional leadership role, while the other teacher make herself/himself available to provide more individual or small group assistance.

Fig. 1. Six Co-Teaching Models: Essential Components.

Table 1. Six Co-Teaching Models: Implementation Strategies.

1. *One teach, one observe* is ideally implemented to identify students who need support relative to engaging in class discussion or to collect information regarding student behavior for possible use in preparing or evaluating IEPs.
2. *Station teaching* is implemented in nearly any instructional situation, particularly when the teachers want the students to engage in small group (collaborative and cooperative) learning.
3. *Parallel teaching* is ideally implemented in teaching activities, such as science experiments, when students are engaged in small group or individualized hands-on authentic learning activities.
4. *Alternative teaching* is ideally implemented to provide differentiated instruction that can be delivered both in large-group and small-group or individualized classroom settings.
5. *Team teaching* is implemented in nearly any instructional situation, particularly when introducing a topic or when collaborative teaching is required to facilitate or enhance student understanding of a concept or issue, such as in a debate situation.
6. *One teach, one assist* is ideally implemented in teaching situations in which it is necessary to gauge student understanding — and possibly provide individual assistance — concurrent with the delivery of whole-group instruction.

The first step in the integration of these co-teaching strategies is for special education and general education teachers to identify when and how to use the six aforementioned co-teaching models. To that end, Sileo and van Garderen (2010) have identified the ideal teaching situations/contexts for integrating each of the six respective co-teaching strategies, as outlined in Table 1 (Sileo, 2011).

ROLES AND REQUISITE SKILLS OF CO-TEACHERS

Regardless of the co-teaching model being operationalized, special education and general education teachers must familiarize themselves with the strategy and the role each must play in the classroom arrangement in order to maintain parity, relative to their shared pedagogical responsibilities, and ensure the needs of each student in the classroom are being met (Dieker & Little, 2005). To assist in that effort, Solis, Vaughn, Swanson, and McCulley (2012) provide special and general educators with an overview of the role each one plays in some of the more popular co-teaching approaches (see Table 2).

Regardless of the model adopted by special education and general education teachers, they must develop skills that serve to strengthen their

Table 2.   Collaborative Models: Teaching Roles.

Type of Co-Teaching	Role of General Education Teacher	Role of Special Education Teacher
Whole class, teacher led	Lead teacher	Support
Two heterogeneous groups	Lead teacher	Lead teacher
Two homogeneous groups	Lead teacher (enrichment or extension)	Lead teacher (remediation or re-teaching)
Station teaching	Lead teacher	Lead teacher
Whole class + small group	Lead teacher (whole class)	Lead teacher (small group)
Whole class team teaching	Lead teacher	Lead teacher

Table 3.   Co-Teaching Partnership: Essential Skills.

1. Communication

Co-teachers must engage in honest and open communication, on a continuous basis, both during the planning and instructional processes.

2. Preparation

Co-teachers must engage in a thoughtful planning process that includes setting aside time for regular meetings, with well-defined protocol, using timelines with well-articulated goals, and by designing lesson plans that integrate co-teaching models of instruction.

3. Instruction

Co-teachers must engage in the simultaneous tasks of instruction and student monitoring, informed or guided by student performance data, that is constantly subject to reflection and evaluation of student performance and instructional efficacy.

4. Conflict resolution

Co-teachers must respect each other's pedagogical, personal, and cultural differences, in an attempt to address any potential problems in an embryonic stage of development before any disagreements escalate − with a goal of attaining a better understanding of each other's position.

collaborative teaching relationship (Gately & Gately, 2001; Piechura-Couture, Tichenor, Touchton, Macisaac, & Heins, 2006; Ploessl, Rock, Schoenfeld, & Blanks, 2010; Rice, Drame, Owens, & Frattura, 2007). Ploessl et al. (2010) have identified four skill sets that prove essential in the development of a co-teaching partnership. These skill sets, that is, communication, preparation, instruction, and conflict resolution, when fully developed, not only create a more satisfying and rewarding partnership but also allow for these professional collaborations to reach their full potential. Table 3 provides an overview of these essential skill sets (Ploessl et al., 2010).

These essential skills are requisite to the development of a successful co-teaching partnership. In addition, it is critical for special education and general education teachers to work collaboratively in the curriculum planning process, in an effort to meet the needs of both students with special needs and those without (Kloo & Zigmond, 2008; Scruggs et al., 2007). During the curriculum planning process, according to Lindeman and Magiera (2014), the general education teacher serves as the "content specialist," and the special education teacher serves as the "learning specialist" (pp. 41–42).

CO-TEACHING CURRICULUM PLANNING AND INSTRUCTIONAL PROCESSES

To facilitate the curriculum planning process, many special education and general education teachers have adopted the Magiera–Simmons Quality Indicator Model of Co-Teaching (Magiera, Simmons, & Hance, 2008), which identifies six steps or stages (outlined in Fig. 2) that must be followed in order to achieve optimum results from the formation of a co-teaching partnership designed for the inclusive classroom.

When implemented effectively, the curriculum planning process in the Magiera–Simmons Quality Indicator Model of Co-Teaching yields well-developed lesson plans that ensure that "classroom interactions between the partners are as satisfying as they are successful" (Ploessl et al., 2010, p. 162). To further define the curriculum planning process in a co-teaching model, Keefe, Moore, and Duff (2004) designed a template that special education and general education partners can use to facilitate the lesson planning process, which Ploessl et al. (2010) have modified by adding the visual images in the planning form included in Fig. 3 (p. 163).

ASSESSMENT OF CO-TEACHING EFFICACY

Given the special education and general education co-teaching model is not as common as other collaborative approaches, Murawski and Lochner

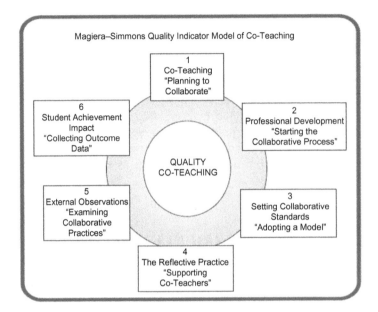

Stage 1: Planning – Deciding on District-Wide Collaboration
Co-teachers agree to collaborate and gain a better perspective on what co-teaching entails.

Stage 2: Professional Development – Receiving Training on Co-Teaching Delivery
Co-teachers must define key terms and concepts that are germane to co-teaching, including the following:

> Mainstreaming – the education of a student with special needs in a general education classroom when this is deemed to be the best learning environment, and least restrictive, for the student.

> Inclusion – teaching and learning environment in which all students (i.e., those with and without special needs) are taught in the same classroom, often facilitated by the integration of differentiated instruction and remediation.

> Collaboration – a reflective and deliberate process in which co-teachers jointly plan and implement instruction.

> Co-Teaching – approach or model in which co-teachers engage in a collaborative and cooperative delivery of instruction, ideally optimizing their respective pedagogical talents.

Fig. 2.   Magiera–Simmons Quality Indicator Model of Co-Teaching: Six Stages of Implementation. *Source*: Cook and Tankersley (2012) and Lindeman and Magiera (2014).

Stage 3: Setting Standards – Deciding What Is Important
Co-teachers must articulate expectations for all students, i.e., both those with
and without special needs, in an inclusive classroom.

Stage 4: Reflection – Clarifying Roles, Reinforcing Learning
Co-teachers engage in a process whereby they clarify their respective roles and
compare their instructional strategies.

Stage 5: External Observation – Procuring an Outside Partner
When warranted, co-teachers may seek input from outside partners in an attempt
to assess strengths and shortcomings relative to the manner in which they
approach co-teaching.

Stage 6: Student Achievement – Assessing the Students' Performance
Co-teachers must assess student performance in an attempt to evaluate their
instructional efficacy.

Fig. 2. (Continued)

(2010) created a checklist (see Fig. 4) that serves to guide administrators in
their efforts to evaluate co-teachers, relative to the following three aspects of
effective co-teaching: co-planning, co-instruction, and co-assessment (p. 4).

The checklist developed by Murawski and Lochner (2010) for school
administrators also includes a list of teaching behaviors, strategies, and
activities (in Fig. 5) that should be the focus of a classroom observation or
evaluation of co-teachers in a special education and general education co-
teaching model (p. 8).

Designed with a similar intent, Murawski and Lochner (2010) provide
administrators with a checklist (in Fig. 6) of what to listen for during a
classroom observation of co-teachers, to evaluate the efficacy of their
teaching performance (p. 9).

It is critical for special education and general education co-teachers to
develop a genuine understanding of each other as classroom teachers and
as professionals. Ploessl et al. (2010) summarized this desired professional
relationship between special education and general education teachers in a
collaborative co-teaching model as follows:

Co-teaching provides practitioners with an opportunity to better meet the academic
and behavioral needs of an increasingly diverse school-age population. However, for
such professional collaboration to reach its full potential, a genuine commitment is
needed. Casting aside preconceived, separate notions about teaching and learning in
order to work toward constructing shared beliefs, assumptions, and styles requires
ample time and strategic effort (p. 167).

Collaborative Planning Form Subject: _____ Period(s): _____ Prepared by: _____

	Teach/Observe	Stations	Parallel	Alternative	Team	Teach/Assist

Lesson Overview: Reading Comprehension; Skills With Problem Solving; Steps to Story Problem Solving
Standards Addressed: Reading Addendum 2.4; Math 2.2

Tasks to be Completed	Co-Teaching Model	Special Educator's Role/Responsibilities	General Educator's Role & Responsibilities
1. Anticipatory Set a) Class *Whip Around* b) Beginning *Ticket Check-in*	1. Teach / Observe	1a) Lead class *Whip Around discussion* 1b) Present *Ticket In*	1a) Observe *Whip Around* 1b) Observe *Ticket In*
2. Direct Instruction a) 3 digit subtraction b) Story problem	2. Parallel Teaching	2a) Review subtraction with 3 digits (remind to start in one's place) 2b) Model working story problem	2a) Review subtraction with 3 digits (remind to start in one's place) 2b) Model working story problem
3. Guided Practice a) Story problem	3. Parallel Teaching	3a) Guide students through a problem as a group	3a) Guide students through a problem as a group
4. Independent Practice a) Story problem	4. Parallel Teaching	4a) Assign independent problem (provide assistance as needed)	4a) Assign independent problem (provide assistance as needed)
5. Closure a) Review story problem steps b) *Free-flow writing*: What have they learned? How has it helped?	5. Teach/Observe	5a) Observe review of steps 5b) Observe *Free-flow writing*	5a) Teach new word problem to whole group while reviewing steps 5b) Lead *Free-flow writing*
Criteria for student success	Co-Teaching Model	Special Educator's Role & Responsibilities	General Educator's Role & Responsibilities
1) All students participate in classroom anticipatory set activities	1) Teach Observe	1) Assign students check, check plus, or check minus for *Ticket In*	1) Monitor and record students' behavior during *Whip Around* discussion
2) All students participate in story problem discussions and problem solving	2) Parallel Teaching	2) Grade independent story problem using story problem rubric	2) Grade independent story problem using story problem rubric
3) All students engage in *Free-flow writing*	3) Teach/Observe	3) Monitor and record student behavior and engagement during *Free-flow writing*	3) Grade *Free-flow writing* with check, check plus, or check minus Monitor and record student behavior and engagement during *Free-flow writing*
Learning Strategies (Evidence based): HighAccess	Co-Teaching Model	Special Educator's Role & Responsibilities	General Educator's Role & Responsibilities
1) Instructional Strategies	1) Teach/Observe	1a) *Ticket In* 1b) *Whip Around*	1a) Observe *Whip Around* 1b) Observe *Ticket In*
2) High Access instructional strategies	2) Parallel Teaching	2a) Open ended Discussion-Group 2b) *Thumbs up* 2c) Reciprocal Teaching	2a) Open ended Discussion-Group 2b) *Thumbs up* 2c) Reciprocal Teaching
3) High Access instructional strategies	3) Teach/Observe	3a) Observe *Free-flow writing* 3b) Observe *Thumbs up*	3a) Lead *Free-flow writing* 3b) Lead *Thumbs up*
Strategies to implement positive behavior support (Evidence based classroom behavior management):	Co-Teaching Model	Special Educator's Role & Responsibilities	General Educator's Role & Responsibilities
1) SRR Dollars	Parallel Teaching Teach/Observe Assist	1a) Observe *Safety, Respect, Responsibility* b) Provide clearly stated expectations c) Assist with stating expectations	1a) Observe *Safety, Respect, Responsibility* b) Provide clearly stated expectations c) Assist with stating expectations
2) 4:1 Ratio	Parallel Teaching Teach/Observe Assist	2) Deliver 4:1 Ratio	2) Deliver 4:1 Ratio
3) Participation Folder	Teach/Observe	3) Assist in implementation participation folder	3) Assist in implementation participation folder

Fig. 3. Co-Teaching Planning Form. *Source*: Ploessl et al. (2010, pp. 158−168) and Keefe et al. (2004, pp. 36−42).

To demonstrate the following aspects of Co-Teaching:	ASK FOR ITEMS	0 – Didn't See It 1 – Saw an Attempt 2 – Saw It Done Well		
CO-PLANNING	Example	0	1	2
Lesson Plans	Lesson plans should demonstrate that both teachers have had input in instructional planning and will actively engage all students at the appropriate levels. The CTSS© Teachers' Toolbox (www.coteachsolutions.com) and the Co-Teaching Lesson Plan book (www.nprinc.com) are excellent resources for co-planning.			
Modified Materials/ Syllabi	Co-teachers who have planned together proactively will have materials ready prior to the lesson. These may include books on tape, modified assignments, close-captioned video, manipulatives, etc.			
Letters Home/Syllabi	All materials that are sent home to parents/guardians can help demonstrate that co-teachers are engaged in co-planning. They should be co-signed and express parity between teachers.			
SHARE Worksheets	Co-teachers should have completed the SHARE worksheets recommended by Murawski (2003) and Murawski and Dieker (2004).			
Problem-Solving Worksheet	Co-teachers should be able to provide evidence of problem-solving. They can use a variety of formats (notes from planning) to work through major problems together.			
CO-INSTRUCTING	What Items Should Include	0	1	2
Behavior Documentation	Co-teachers should be able to produce documentation of data they collect while co-teaching. This documentation could include behaviors, homework, tardiness, social skills, classwork and/or participation in data collection.			
Tiered Lessons	Co-teachers should be able to demonstrate how lessons are tiered to provide differentiated instruction to a variety of individual learners. Lessons should address the high, average, and low achievers.			
Class Notes	Class notes (indicate what was taught during the class & specifically what was emphasized). They also include mnemonics taught, and in some cases, modifications made.			
CO-INSTRUCTING	What Items Should Include	0	1	2
Grade Book	Administrators can ask co-teachers to provide a copy of their grade books. Even if one teacher does the actual recording of the grades, it should be evident that both teachers had a hand in grading and communicating about assessments through notes or assignments.			
Accommodated Assignments	Assignments and assessments need to be tailored to individual needs. Co-teachers should be able to provide copies of modified tests, examples of accommodations given to student with special needs, and lists of IEP requirements.			
Description of How Students Are Individually Graded	Co-teachers should have proactively discussed grading and how they will accommodate different learners. They may even have documentation of when they called or wrote parents to inform them of how the student with special needs would be graded in the class.			

Fig. 4.   Co-Teaching Checklist: Ask for Items.

CO-TEACHING CHECKLIST

General Educator: _____   Special Educator: _____

Observer: _____   Date/Time: _____

LOOK FOR ITEMS	0 – Didn't See It 1 – Saw an Attempt 2 – Saw It Done Well		
	0	1	2
Two or more professionals working together in the same physical space. 0 = only one adult; two adults not communicating at all; class always divided into two rooms 1 = two adults in same room but very little communication or collaborative work 2 = two adults in same room; both engaged in class & each other (even if not perfectly)			
Class environment demonstrates parity and collaboration (both names on board, sharing materials, and space). 0 = no demonstration of parity/collaboration; room appears to belong to one teacher only 1 = some attempt at parity; both adults share materials and space 2 = clear parity; both names on board/report card; two desks or shared space; obvious feeling from teachers that it is "our room"			
Both teachers begin and end class together and remain in the room the entire time. 0 = one adult is absent or late; adults may leave room for time w/o reason related to this class 1 = one adult may be late but for remaining time, they work together 2 = both adults begin and end together, and are with students the entire time *note – if adults have planned to use a regrouping approach (e.g.,"parallel") and one adult takes a group of students out of the room (e.g., to the library), that is perfectly acceptable			
During instruction, both teachers assist students with and without disabilities. 0 = adults are not helping students or are only helping "their own" students 1 = there is some helping of various students but adults primarily stay with a few of "their own" 2 = it is clear that both adults are willing to help all students & that students are used to this			
The class moves smoothly with evidence of co-planning and communication between co-teachers. 0 = all planning appears to have been done by one adult and/or no planning is evident 1 = minimal planning and communication is evident; most appears to be done by one adult 2 = it is clear that both adults had input in lesson and communicate regularly as class progresses			
Differentiated strategies, to include technology, are used to meet the range of learning needs. 0 = there is no evidence of differentiation of instruction or use of technology in the classroom 1 = there is minimal differentiation and use of technology; most differentiation appears to be focused on groups rather than individuals 2 = it is clear that adults considered individual student needs; differentiation and use of technology is used when needed to meet individual student needs, as well as that of the group			
A variety of instructional approaches (5 co-teaching approaches) are used, include regrouping students. 0 = Students remain in large class setting; Adults rely solely on One Teach/One Support or Team 1 = Adults regroup students (using Alternative, Parallel, or Station) at least once 2 = Adults use more than one of the 5 approaches (Friend & Cook's One Teach/One Support, Team, Parallel, Station & Alternative); at least one of the approaches involves regrouping students *note – if teachers have been observed using other approaches in the past and only one approach is observed today (e.g., Stations), it is acceptable to recall previous observations and give a 2 for using a variety of approaches as adults have demonstrated competency			
Both teachers engage in appropriate behavior management strategies as needed and are consistent in their approach to behavior management. 0 = there is no obvious plan for behavior management, nor do adults appear to communicate about how they are approaching class management; possibly inappropriate class management 1 = behavior management strategies are utilized but there is very little clear evidence of how adults have communicated about their use 2 = it is evident that adults have discussed how they will approach classroom/behavior management and adults are consistent in their approach; clear communication between adults			
It is difficult to tell the special educator from the general educator. 0 = Observer could easily determine who was the general/special educator by their language/roles/ lack of parity. 1 = Observer could tell who was the general/special educator but there was a clear attempt at parity between the teachers. 2 = Observer would not be able to tell who was the general/special educator as parity was evident and adults shared the roles and responsibilities in the classroom.			
It is difficult to tell the special education students from the general education students. 0 = Observer could easily determine who were the general/special education students by their lack of integration (e.g., students at back or separated from class). 1 = Observer could tell who were the general/special education students but there was a clear attempt at inclusion of students for most activities. 2 = Observer would not be able to tell who were the general/special education students as parity was evident and adults shared the responsibilities for working with all students.			

Fig. 5. Co-Teaching Checklist: Look for Items.

CO-TEACHING CHECKLIST				
General Educator: _____		Special Educator: _____		
Observer: _____		Date/Time: _____		
	LISTEN FOR ITEMS	0 – Didn't See It 1 – Saw an Attempt 2 – Saw It Done Well		
		0	1	2
Co-teachers use language ("we";"our") that demonstrates true collaboration and shared responsibility.	*0 = Adults use "I" language frequently (e.g., "I want you to ..." Or "In my class ..."), lacking parity.* *1 = Adults attempt to use "we" language and include each other, but it is clear that one adult is more used to "ruling" the class.* *2 = Adults clearly use "we" language (e.g., "We would like you to..."), showing that they both share the responsibility and students know they are equally in charge.*			
Co-teachers phrase questions and statements so that it is obvious that all students in the class are included.	*0 = Class is very teacher-directed and little involvement by students; questions/statements are general and not inclusive of all students.* *1 = A few statements/questions are phrased to encourage participation from a variety of students.* *2 = A clear attempt is made by both adults to engage all students through the use of a variety of types of questions and statements.*			
Students' conversations evidence a sense of community (including peers with and without disabilities).	*0 = Students do not talk to one another ever during class or specific students are clearly excluded from the student interactions.* *1 = Most students appear to be included in the majority of student interactions.* *2 = It is evident from the students' actions and words that all students are considered an equal part of the class and are included in all student interactions.*			
Co-teachers ask questions at a variety of levels to meet all students' needs (basic recall to higher order thinking).	*0 = Adults do not use questions or ask questions geared just to one level (to the middle or "watered down").* *1 = Adults use closed and open questions at a variety of levels in a general manner.* *2 = Adults used closed and open questions at a variety of levels in a way that demonstrates they are able to differentiate for specific students in order to ensure maximum (appropriate) levels of challenge.*			

Fig. 6. Co-Teaching Checklist: Listen for Items.

CONCLUSION

It is apparent that the relationship between co-teachers is "a major crucial component influencing the success or failure of the inclusion of students with disabilities" (Mastropieri et al., 2005, p. 268). A successful co-teaching partnership, however, is always a work in progress and requires cooperation on the part of both the special education and the general education teacher. Gurgur and Uzuner (2011) remind us of what is needed to achieve this end:

> The strength in co-teaching emerges from the partnership itself, not from one of the co-teachers acting as an expert who holds all the right answers. Appreciate differences of opinion as opportunities to further develop the partnership by focusing on the new insights that will be gained through many conversations, rather than fixating on the outcome of one specific interaction. Effective co-teachers work hard to maintain one another's self-confidence and self-esteem and follow through with actions that match their words: They listen first and then speak and act with integrity. Moreover, co-teaching partners who acknowledge, deal with, and learn from conflict when it arises between them are more likely to positively affect pupil performance. (p. 591)

While co-teaching holds tremendous promise, there is perhaps more to be learned about the various collaborative special education and general education models than is known. In this regard, Friend et al. (2010) have noted that co-teaching "… demonstrates the potential as well as the complexities of collaboration that joins the fields of general education and special education" (p. 18). Indeed, more research is needed to determine the efficacy of different special education and general education co-teaching models, particularly focused on the larger context of school reform (Friend et al. 2010, p. 10). What is not questioned, however, is that classrooms of the twenty-first century truly have become "epicenters for collaboration between special educators [and] general educators …" (Hamilton-Jones & Vail, 2013, p. 57).

This is why it is critical for all classroom teachers to become familiar with collaborative models that provide the pedagogical blueprints for the construction of effective partnerships between special education teachers and general education teachers. If co-teaching partners "are willing to invest time and effort in enhancing communications skills, finding regular planning time, improving instructional approaches, and resolving conflicts," according to Ploessl et al. (2010), "they not only can reverse unproductive interactions but can even prevent them entirely" (p. 167).

To be certain, we have learned from our examination of events, legislation, and court cases that all students benefit from − and the classroom of the twenty-first century demands − creating a teaching and learning environment that meets the needs of all learners, with and without special needs. To achieve this goal, it is essential to invest the time and intellectual capital in creating effective co-teaching partnerships between special education and general education teachers. To that end, the co-teaching models discussed here serve to guide the formation of co-teaching partnerships and inform the co-planning and co-instruction processes. Indeed, when designed and implemented in a thoughtful, deliberate, and reflective manner, co-teaching benefits both general education and special education teachers, as well as their respective students.

REFERENCES

Albrecht, G. L. (2006). *Encyclopedia of disability: A history in primary source documents.* Thousand Oaks, CA: Sage.

Antosh, A., & Imparato, A. (2014, May 16). *The meaning of Brown for children with disabilities.* Retrieved from https://www.acslaw.org/acsblog/the-meaning-of-brown-for-children-with-disabilities. Accessed on April 11, 2015.

Bauwens, J., Hourcade, J. J., & Friend, M. (1989). Cooperative teaching: A model for general and special education integration. *Remedial and Special Education, 10*(2), 17–22.

Colarusso, R., & O'Rourke, C. (2004). *Special education for all teachers* (3rd ed.), Dubuque, IA: Kendall/Hunt Publishing.

Cook, B. G., & Tankersley, M. G. (2012). *Research-based practices in special education.* Upper Saddle River, NJ: Pearson Education.

Cramer, E., & Nevin, A. (2006). A mixed methodology analysis of co-teacher assessments. *Teacher Education and Special Education, 29*(4), 261–274.

DeSimone, J. R., & Parmar, R. S. (2006). Issues and challenges for middle school mathematics teachers in inclusion classrooms. *School Science and Mathematics, 106*(8), 338–348.

Dieker, L., & Little, M. (2005). Secondary reading: Not just for reading teachers anymore. *Intervention in School and Clinic, 40*(5), 276–283.

Eccleston, S. T. (2010). Successful collaboration: Four essential traits of effective special education specialists. *Journal of the International Association of Special Education, 11*(1), 40–47.

Editorial Projects in Education Research Center. (2011, July 18). Issues A-Z: Adequate Yearly Progress. *Education Week.* Retrieved from http://www.edweek.org/ew/issues/adequate-yearly-progress/

Friend, M., Cook, L., Hurley-Chamberlain, D., & Shamberger, C. (2010). Co-teaching: An illustration of the complexity of collaboration in special education. *Journal of Educational and Psychological Consultation, 20*(1), 9–27.

Friend, M., Reising, M., & Cook, L. (1993). Co-teaching: An overview of the past, a glimpse at the present, and considerations for the future. *Preventing School Failure, 37*(4), 6–10.

Fuchs, D., & Fuchs, L. S. (1994). Inclusive schools movement and the radicalization of special education reform. *Exceptional Children, 60*(4), 294–309.

Gargiulo, R., & Kilgo, J. (2011). *An introduction to young children with special needs: Birth through age eight.* Belmont, CA: Wadsworth.

Gately, S., & Gately, F. (2001). Understanding co-teaching components. *TEACHING Exceptional Children, 33*, 40–47.

Gurgur, H., & Uzuner, Y. (2011). Examining the implementation of two co-teaching models: Team teaching and station teaching. *International Journal of Inclusive Education, 15*(6), 589–610.

Hamilton-Jones, B., & Vail, C. O. (2013). Preparing special educators for collaboration in the classroom: Pre-service teachers' beliefs and perspectives. *International Journal of Special Education, 28*(1), 56–68.

Hunt, N., & Marshall, K. (2002). *Exceptional children and youth* (3rd ed.), Boston, MA: Houghton Mifflin Company.

Hunt, P., Farron-Davis, F., Beckstead, S., Curtis, D., & Goetz, L. (1994). Evaluating the effects of placement of students with severe disabilities in general education versus special education. *Journal of the Association for Persons with Severe Handicaps, 19*(3), 200–214.

Idol, L. (2006). Toward inclusion of special education students in general education. *Remedial and Special Education, 27*(2), 77–94.

Katz, M. S. (1976). *A history of compulsory education laws* [Fastback Series, No. 75]. Bloomington, IN: Phi Delta Kappa.

Keefe, E., Moore, V., & Duff, R. (2004). The four "knows" of collaborative teaching. *TEACHING Exceptional Children, 36*, 36–42.

Kloo, A., & Zigmond, N. (2008). Co-teaching revisited: Redrawing the blueprint. *Preventing School Failure, 52*, 12–20.

Lindeman, K. W., & Magiera, K. (2014). A co-teaching model: Committed professionals, high expectations, and the inclusive classroom. *Odyssey: New Directions in Deaf Education, 15*, 40–45.

Magiera, K., Simmons, R., & Hance, S. (2008). Secondary co-teaching: A quality process. *Impact on Instructional Improvement, 34*(1), 18–25.

Martin, E. W., Martin, R., & Terman, D. L. (1996). The legislative and litigation history of special education. *The Future of Children, 6*(1), 25–39.

Mastropieri, M. A., Scruggs, T. E., Graetz, J., Norland, J., Gardizi, W., & McDuffie, K. (2005). Case studies in co-teaching in the content areas: Successes, failures and challenges. *Intervention in School and Clinic, 40*(5), 260–270.

McCulley, L., Solis, M., Swanson, E., & Vaughn, S. (2012). Collaborative models of instruction: The empirical foundations of inclusion and co-teaching. *Psychology in the Schools, 49*(5), 498–510.

Monahan, R., & Marino, S. (1996). Teachers' attitudes toward inclusion: Implications for teacher education in schools 2000. *Education, 117*(2), 316–320.

Murawski, W. W., & Lochner, W. W. (2010). Observing co-teaching: What to ask for, look for, and listen for. *Intervention in School and Clinic, 20*(10), 1–10.

Nichols, J., Dowdy, A., & Nichols, C. (2010). Co-teaching: An educational promise for children with disabilities or a quick fix to meet the mandates of no child left behind? *Education, 130*(4), 647–651.

Osgood, R. L. (2008). *The history of special education: A struggle for equality in American public schools.* Westport, CT: Greenwood Publishing Group.

Piechura-Couture, K., Tichenor, M., Touchton, D., Macisaac, D., & Heins, E. D. (2006). Coteaching: A model for education reform. *Principal Leadership, 6*, 39–43.

Ploessl, D. M., Rock, M. L., Schoenfeld, N., & Blanks, B. (2010). On the same page: Practical techniques to enhance co-teaching interactions. *Intervention in School and Clinic, 45*(3), 158–168.

Rice, N., Drame, E., Owens, L., & Frattura, E. M. (2007). Co-instructing at the secondary level: Strategies for success. *TEACHING Exceptional Children, 39*, 12–18.

Scruggs, T. E., Mastropieri, M. A., & McDuffie, K. A. (2007). Co-teaching in inclusive classrooms: A metasynthesis of qualitative research. *Exceptional Children, 73*, 392–416.

Sileo, J. M. (2011). Co-teaching: Getting to know your partner. *TEACHING Exceptional Children, 45*(5), 32–38.

Sileo, J. M., & van Garderen, D. (2010). Creating optimal opportunities to learn mathematics: Blending co-teaching structures with research-based practices. *TEACHING Exceptional Children, 42*(3), 14–21.

Slavin, R. E. (2006). *Educational psychology: Theory and practice* (8th ed.). Boston, MA: Pearson.

Smith, T. E. C. (2001). Section 504, the ADA, and Public Schools. *LD Online.* Retrieved from http://www.ldonline.org/article/6108/. Accessed on April 10, 2015.

Solis, M., Vaughn, S., Swanson, E., & McCulley, L. (2012). Collaborative models of instruction: The empirical foundations of inclusion and co-teaching. *Psychology in the Schools, 49*(5), 498–510.

U.S. Department of Education. (2014). Office of Special Education Programs, 36th Annual Report to Congress on the Implementation of the Individuals with Disabilities Education Act. Retrieved from http://www2.ed.gov/about/reports/annual/osep/2014/parts-b-c/36th-idea-arc.pdf

Walther-Thomas, C. (1997). Co-teaching experiences: The benefits and problems that teachers and principals report over time. *Journal of Learning Disabilities, 30*(4), 395–407.

Warger, C. L., & Aldinger, L. E. (Eds.). (1986). *Preparing special educators for teacher consultation.* Toledo, OH: College of Education and Allied Professions, University of Toledo.

Weiss, M. P., & Lloyd, J. (2003). Conditions for co-teaching: Lessons from a case study. *Teacher Education and Special Education, 26,* 27–41.

Yell, M. L. (2006). *The law and special education* (3rd ed.), Upper Saddle River, NJ: Prentice Hall.

CHAPTER 4

ROLE OF COUNSELORS IN MULTIDISCIPLINARY INTERACTIONS IN SPECIAL EDUCATION

Beto Davison Avilés, Lori Russell-Chapin and Christopher J. Rybak

ABSTRACT

Professional school counselors have been in the public schools since the early 1900s. Fueled by the industrial revolution, the vocational guidance movement spawned the creation of high school guidance counseling programs. In 1907, Jesse B. Davis created one of the first vocational guidance programs at Central High School in Detroit, Michigan (Schmidt, 2014). In 1908, Frank Parsons, the father of vocational guidance, founded the Vocations Bureau that eventually became part of the Division of Education at Harvard University. These early efforts helped students develop vocationally, morally, and intellectually, and it would take nearly 70 years for children with exceptionalities to be similarly served in the public schools.

Interdisciplinary Connections to Special Education: Important Aspects to Consider
Advances in Special Education, Volume 30A, 59–79
Copyright © 2015 by Emerald Group Publishing Limited
All rights of reproduction in any form reserved
ISSN: 0270-4013/doi:10.1108/S0270-40132015000030A004

The purpose of this chapter is to explain the role of counselors in assisting students with exceptionalities. This will be examined by better understanding the counseling history, defining the terms of exceptionalities and transdisciplinary collaboration, and showcasing the many benefits of individual, group, and brain-based interventions.

Keywords: Counselors; multidisciplinary; neurofeedback; mindfulness

BACKGROUND

In 1975, the U.S. Congress passed the *Education for All Handicapped Children Act*. Since that time, students with disabilities have been receiving free and appropriate education and their educational future has been secured in special education law through the *Individuals with Disabilities Education Act* of 1990. Additional amendments passed in 1997 and 2004 expanding educational opportunities for school-age students and babies and toddlers (DO-IT, University of Washington, 2013). Finally, the *No Child Left Behind Act* of 2001 (NCLB) was signed into law in January 2002. Its purpose was to increase school accountability and academic achievement for all students, but most especially poor and minority students (Federal Education Budget Project, 2014).

Educational outcomes for students with disabilities since the passage of NCLB have been mixed. A report on NCLB by the National Council on Disability (NCD, 2008) indicated that since its adoption in 2002, students with disabilities have dropped out of school in higher numbers and the number of students who are using special education services has decreased. However, graduation rates have gone up. More recently, the NCD (2014) reported that National Assessment of Education Progress (NAEP) math and reading scores for students with disabilities are significantly lower than their nondisabled peers. This achievement gap increases for poor and minority students with disabilities. Moreover, students with disabilities drop out at rates more than twice that of students without disabilities and their college completion rates are lower (2014).

Additional challenges for students with disabilities appear in the form of bullying and behavioral/discipline referrals. The NCD (2014) reported that students with disabilities are more likely to be restrained or suspended out of school than students who are not identified by IDEA. Bullying is a significant concern for students with disabilities. Young, Ne'eman, and Gleser (2011) indicated that students with disabilities are more likely to be bullied than nondisabled students, including increased incidences of victimization. Most bullying takes place in educational settings; however, parents of students with disabilities report a lack of school response, with many finding out about bullying from their children (2011).

Mental health concerns also continue to significantly impact students with disabilities. Students receiving special education services who have mental health conditions have a dropout rate of over 50 percent, more than any other disability group (NCD, 2014). The stigma and discrimination associated with mental illness disproportionately affect students with disabilities and their families. The mental health needs of students with serious disturbances are often not addressed or met in public schools (NCD, 1996). Professional school and clinical mental health counselors are in unique positions to promote the academic, personal/social, and career development of all students, including students with disabilities (Schmidt, 2014).

TERMS AND DEFINITIONS

Students with disabilities are served under the *Individual with Disabilities Education Improvement Act* (IDEA). The U.S. Department of Education's IDEA website offers the following definition of a child with a disability: "Child with a disability means a child evaluated in accordance with Sec. Sec. 300.304 through 300.311 as having mental retardation, a hearing impairment (including deafness), a speech or language impairment, a visual impairment (including blindness), a serious emotional disturbance (referred to in this part as 'emotional disturbance'), an orthopedic impairment, autism, traumatic brain injury, an other health impairment, a specific learning disability, deaf-blindness, or multiple disabilities, and who, by reason thereof, needs special education and related services (U.S. Department of Education, n.d.). Services authorized under IDEA include appropriate specialized education and other related supports. Examples are counseling, advocacy, positive behavioral supports, physical/occupational/speech, and language therapies" (Rock & Leff, 2015).

PROFESSIONAL SCHOOL COUNSELORS

Professional school counselors serve and advocate for the needs of all students. The American School Counseling Association (ASCA) indicates that professional school counselors "Advocate for equitable school counseling policies and practices for every student and all stakeholders including use of translators and bilingual/multilingual school counseling program materials that represent all languages used by families in the school community, and advocate for appropriate accommodations and accessibility for students with disabilities" (ASCA, 2010, pp. 5–6). In order to carry out this mandate, professional school counselors are members of multidisciplinary teams (MDTs) that create and oversee special education programs and services. The school counselor's role in the MDT may include assessment, assistance in developing an Individualized Education Program (IEP), or consultation with other team members such as administrators, teachers, families, and other education professionals (e.g., psychologists and social workers) (Schmidt, 2014; Trolley, Haas, & Patti, 2009).

Professional school counselors also work directly with children through individual and group counseling, classroom guidance, and as a resource for information related to academic, personal/social, and career development. Parents and families also receive counseling and education services (Schmidt, 2014).

Services and Interventions

Schmidt (2014) described the services of a comprehensive school counseling program as containing the following major elements: counseling, consulting, coordinating, and appraising. Services dedicated to special education programs begin in preschool and continue through college (Trolley et al., 2009). Counseling services may be individual or group. Typically, individual counseling is problem-centered; however, it can also be developmental, focusing on building academic or personal/social skills (Schmidt, 2014).

While general goals for counseling address building on academic or social skills, counselors also realize that children with certain exceptionalities may benefit from specific interventions. Counseling techniques for children with developmental delays or significant cognitive impairments may focus on self-reliance and appropriate behaviors. In addition, counseling interventions involving peer-modeling and behavior modification techniques may be useful for children with developmental delays (Davison Avilés & Skaggs, 2000). School counselors can also help parents teach similar skills to their children (e.g., independent living and personal/social skills).

Children with emotional disturbances require consistency, stability, and trust (Davison Avilés & Skaggs, 2000). Key counseling skills here are the ability to identify children's feelings and frustrations and reflect them. Counseling interventions that teach self-management skills and relaxation training help these children manage challenging behavioral and emotional aspects of their disabling conditions. School counselors can provide psychoeducational counseling to parents to help them establish consistent schedules and rules, logical consequences, and encouragement. For both parent and child, managing stress, frustration, myths, and fears are important in effectively dealing with emotional disturbances (Davison Avilés & Skaggs, 2000; Schmidt, 2010).

Children with learning disabilities also benefit from counseling techniques supporting self-regulatory skills and managing frustration. Academic and personal self-concept is particularly important for children with learning disabilities involving intellectual ability, academic achievement, athletic competence, social acceptance, physical appearance, and behavior (Davison Avilés & Skaggs, 2000). Counseling children with learning disabilities should take into account any or all of these areas. Counseling may be (1) person-centered: active listening, clarifying, summarizing; (2) behavioral: structured problem solving, time management, academic/behavioral strategies; or (3) cognitive: focusing on accurate beliefs, reducing irrational beliefs, and positive self-reinforcement. School counselors should be mindful that counseling interventions often focus on verbal and reasoning skills, which may be weak in children with learning disabilities. Helping children understand their learning style and teaching reasoning and problem solving can help ameliorate reasoning and communication difficulties faced by children with learning disabilities (Davison Avilés & Skaggs, 2000; Stone & Dahir, 2006).

Attention deficit hyperactivity disorder (ADHD) is "the most frequently occurring disability associated with earning problems in the public schools of the United States" (Wright, 2012, p. 250). Professional school counselors are often among the first to be consulted when teachers or parents suspect a child has ADHD. Primarily a neurological disorder affecting executive functioning, ADHD is exemplified by impaired ability to focus on instructions in the home or classroom and difficulty carrying out learning tasks (2011). Children with this disorder vary in behavioral and cognitive symptoms, sometimes exhibiting impulsivity and hyperactivity, other times experiencing impaired attending and task completion.

It is important for counselors to keep in mind that for children with ADHD what appear to be behavior disorders may be the child's attempt to regulate a complex mix of behaviors, thoughts, and feelings. Coping behaviors may influence the learning environment, such as talking out loud while completing a task (Davison Avilés & Skaggs, 2000). Diagnosis is multidisciplinary, including physician, psychologist, parent, child, counselor, and teachers.

> Counseling interventions include knowing drug therapies (e.g., stimulants, antidepressants) and their effects, providing structured environments with limited stimuli and maintaining consistent schedules. Effective school counselors will respect the child's efforts at self-regulation and work within the child's ability to regulate. Both teachers and counselors will find using colors to communicate useful. For example, pairing colors with feelings can help children manage their affective states more successfully. Similarly, manipulatives and visuals, and pictures or written clues can help children become more capable in managing their environment. (Hall, Kaduson, and Schaefer, 2002)

Alternatively, cognitive–behavioral strategies may not be useful and may even be a drain on finite resources of regulation and attention. Finally, teaching children to delay behaviors will help them regulate interactions with teachers and peers (Cherkes-Julkowski, Sharp, & Stolzenberg, 1997; Davison Avilés & Skaggs, 2000; Wright, 2012).

Consulting, coordinating, and appraising services involve a school counselor working collaboratively with teachers, administrators, families, and other community professionals to support children's academic and personal/social development (Schmidt, 2014; Wright, 2012). In addition, Trolley et al. (2009) described school counselor participation in processes and services for special education in preschool and school-age populations. A detailed examination of these activities is beyond the scope of this chapter; however, in the following sections, we present a summary of common types of consulting, coordinating, and appraising provided by school counselors in special education services.

Consulting often involves school counselors providing information, instructional, and other school services such as integrating the guidance curriculum across the academic curriculum (Schmidt, 2014). Information services include providing access to community and school resources available to help special education educators, and children and families eligible for special education services. Instructional services involve classroom guidance and parent education. The former supports inclusion and group psychoeducational and developmental interventions for children with disabilities, while parent education is a means to disseminate information about special education disability categories and offer support for families facing challenges associated with meeting the needs of a child with disabilities (Trolley et al., 2009; Wright, 2012).

Preschool and School-Aged Children

Coordinating and appraisal services are linked in that they involve collecting and sharing data and the evaluation of those data (Schmidt, 2014). Coordinating in the context of special education, school counselor coordinating, and appraisal services begin at the preschool level with involvement in the Committee on Preschool Special Education (CPSE) (Trolley et al., 2009). The CPSE provides services to preschool children 3 years old to school age. School counselors are often unaware of the role of CPSEs in their county; however, Trolley et al. (2009) suggested that school counselors as "related services personnel" (p. 51) can assist the CPSE understand the history, strengths, and performance of preschool children thought to have functional delays or disorders. These data may include academic achievement, learning characteristics, and social development.

School counselors often coordinate services to school-age children who struggle academically. Before a child enters or is referred to special education services, she or he will have been continually involved in developmental and preventative assessments and interventions for academic or behavioral concerns through Response to Intervention (RtI) and Positive Behavior Intervention Supports (PBIS) (Schmidt, 2014; Wright, 2012). RtI is a multitiered model that uses "data to drive instruction … assess [a] student's academic performance and evaluate the effectiveness of instruction" (Trolley et al., 2009, p. 29). The intent of RtI is to put academic supports in place early in a child's academic career with the goals of remediating deficiencies or delays and reducing special education referrals. However, if special education services are deemed appropriate, the RtI process provides necessary academic and social data for identification and assessment of disabilities and subsequent educational interventions (Wright, 2012).

The school counselor roles in RtI are to assist in analyzing academic and behavioral data, collaborate with other school professionals in designing and monitoring instructional interventions, and refer to appropriate school and community agencies (Rock & Leff, 2015). For students at high risk, school counselors may engage in individual or small group counseling and continue those interventions through IEPs once students have been identified as eligible for special education services.

Similar to RtI, PBIS is a multilevel school-wide program that focuses on effective teaching and environmental supports to reinforce positive academic and behavioral skills (Rock & Leff, 2015). The school counselor participates in PBIS by helping develop "general school-wide policies and procedures that promote positive behavior among all students" (p. 366). School counselors provide instructional support through classroom guidance by teaching well-defined, expected behaviors. Coordinating and appraising efforts include developing procedures for gathering and assessing data on outcomes of the behavioral system.

School counselor special education coordinating and appraisal services may begin with preschool age children by participating in a specific MDT called the Committee on Special Education (CSE) (Trolley et al., 2009). CSEs are established in accordance with education laws specific to each state. Many elementary school counselors may not know about CPSEs (Trolley et al., 2009). Moreover, since fewer than 30% of 4 year olds in the United States were enrolled in state-funded preschool programs in 2012−2013, school counselors have fewer opportunities to interact with preschool populations (National Institute for Early Education Research, 2013). Nevertheless, counselors who are appropriately trained can provide direct services through play therapy and consulting services by providing parent education and access to resources for families with young children.

School counselor involvement in special education processes and services for school-age children include participating in MDT processes and decisions (Rock & Leff, 2015; Trolley et al., 2009). Sometimes called the CSE but more commonly known as the MDT, this group comprises a parent, teacher, special education teacher, school psychologist, other school district representative qualified to provide special education services, and other persons appropriate to providing services to the student (e.g., school counselor) (Trolley et al., 2009). This team establishes special education "classification, placement, programming, appropriate services (including counseling), testing modifications, and most importantly [writes] the IEP" (Trolley et al., 2009, p. 60).

Professional school counselors provide a comprehensive program that includes all students. Although not mandated, school counselors often participate in MDT meetings and provide expertise in student academic, personal/social, and career development. A non-exhaustive list of counselor responsibilities includes individual and small group counseling, referrals, appraisals such as functional behavioral assessments, and consultation on educational, career, and community resources. Some schools may designate the school counselor as the educational professional responsible for scheduling MDT meetings and notifying relevant parties (Schmidt, 2014; Wright, 2012).

TRANSDISCIPLINARY COLLABORATION: SCHOOL AND CLINICAL MENTAL HEALTH COUNSELORS

Transdisciplinary collaboration is an emerging concept borrowed from the education profession. "Where multidisciplinary or interdisciplinary inquiry may focus on the contribution of disciplines to an inquiry, transdisciplinary inquiry tends to focus on the inquiry or issue itself" (Antola Crowe, Brandes, Davison Aviles, Erickson, & Hall, 2013, p. 195). Community mental health services serve as an important yet often underutilized support for students with disabilities and their families. Clinical mental health professionals working in community and hospital settings can interact with professional school counselors in a transdisciplinary fashion where professional disciplines coalesce and focus on the needs of children with disabilities and their families and schools.

Community mental health agencies, social service agencies, and hospitals often interact with schools in providing mental health services to schools (Rock & Leff, 2015). As noted earlier, children with disabilities often have unmet mental health needs (NCD, 2014). Schools and school counselors seek out community mental health services and social services to help students with disabilities build on school-based academic success skills and develop interpersonal and social skills (Schmidt, 2014). Often schools seek to have these services provided within their buildings, eliminating the need for transportation to outside agencies.

School and clinical mental health counselors work best when their efforts are intentionally coordinated to meet the need of students with disabilities. Students in special education often have multiple services during their school day, making each educational minute precious. This requires school and clinical mental health counselors to adopt a transdisciplinary model focusing on the needs of students to efficiently and effectively provide necessary mental health support. Once necessary HIPPA and FERPA release forms have been signed, this can be accomplished through regular communication via phone and secure email and internet video conferencing. Careful scheduling and planning by all parties involved in students' education and care avoids scheduling distractions, provides structure and consistency, and keeps everyone focused on supporting the mental health needs of children in special education.

TRANSITION AND CAREER PLANNING IN THE SCHOOLS AND COMMUNITY

Processes and services supporting students with disabilities in their post-secondary development are multidisciplinary, involving both school and community professionals (Trolley et al., 2009). On the education side are administrators, teachers (general education and special education), transition coordinators, professional school counselors, school psychologists, and occupational/physical therapists. Community resources include mental health counselors, vocational rehabilitation services, social workers, business—education partnerships, adult education programs, and employment agencies/specialists (Trolley et al., 2009).

Students in special education have three major destinations after high school: college (community and four-year institutions) or career-technical training, employment, and supported settings (Trolley et al., 2009). In each of these circumstances, transition plans are required to help students and their families link with educational and community agencies to assure successful post-secondary outcomes.

Counselors occupy a central place in post-secondary services for students in special education. Council for the Accreditation of Counseling and Related Educational Programs (CACREP)-accredited counseling programs mandate training in career theory and interventions and diversity issues in student development (Holcomb-McCoy & Chen-Hayes, 2015; Niles & Harris-Bowlsbey, 2013). School counselors participate in career and educational planning and transitions as mandated in IEPs. School counselors engage in career interventions with students in special education transitioning to post-secondary environments, through individual or group career counseling, administering and interpreting career interest inventories and other career assessments, and helping students develop goals and find career-related resources. These resources may range from scholarships and other financial resources to training and apprenticeships in competitive employment (at least minimum wage and mostly nondisabled employees) (Trolley et al., 2009). Counselors in community settings also provide individual and group counseling. In addition, counselors can act as job coaches, employment and placement professionals, and advocates for adults with disabilities (Trolley et al., 2009).

GROUP AND INDIVIDUAL BRAIN-BASED COUNSELING IN SPECIAL EDUCATION

Research findings have shown that small group work is generally an effective approach to working with responsive services in schools (Whiston, Tai, Rahardja, & Eder, 2011). Group counseling can be an efficient way to bring services to larger numbers of individuals in schools and be equally as effective as individual treatment (Baskin et al., 2010). This has been true of groups designed to meet the special education needs of students in schools as well as groups offered in community and other settings. Examples of the use of group counseling approaches with various special educational needs are described as follows.

Social skills training groups have shown promise with respect to helping youth identified with high-functioning autism spectrum disorders (ASD) as demonstrated through improvement on the parent-rated social communication and social motivation (White, Koenig, & Scahill, 2010). Improvement in relationships skills are considered essential in assisting those adapting to ASD in having a greater quality of life and in reducing tendencies toward depression and anxiety (Duncan & Klinger, 2010). Groups can offer a strong opportunity for participants to learn and develop social relationship skills. Groups designed to help individuals with ASD are offered in community clinical settings as well as conducted in schools (2010). Such groups may include instruction on using specific social skills, practicing the social skill, and then role-playing to simulate differing settings to help cement the skill to a greater extent. An important aspect of the learning also includes learning means of self-monitoring in order to learn effective means of managing emotional reactions. Additionally, learning to apply the learning outside the group within community and other settings can further extend the learning and utility of the skills to more complex situations (2010).

A phenomenological research study of a social skills group for members diagnosed with ASD identified the specific power of group as a modality to provide a setting in which members could both learn new forms of interaction while having a safe place to practice initially and to report back after testing new social skills outside the group (Ware, Ort, & Swank, 2012). The group further provided a setting in which members could learn to experience and manage their emotions while also learning about the experiences of others.

Another approach for helping individuals with exceptionalities is the use of brain-based interventions. Brain-based intervention is defined as any skill and/or treatment having a focus on the brain using some type of neuromodulation, the alteration of some aspect of neuronal functioning (Chapin & Russell-Chapin, 2014). For example, with ASD-related symptoms, the use of mindfulness-based therapy delivered in a group setting would be beneficial (Kiep, Spek, & Hoeben, 2014). These researchers found this approach to be effective in both the short term of the nine-week group and longer term past the completion of the group. Improvements were found with respect to a number of emotional concerns including anxiety, depression, and rumination.

While developing effective coping skills in dealing with emotional regulation are important for any aged individual, some research suggests that earlier intervention may produce an even more potent beneficial impact for children. Bidgood, Wilkie, and Katchaluba (2010) developed a group-based emotion management program for younger and older cohorts where they found that the program proved especially effective with children in grades 1−3 showing greater improvement across the five areas rated by the Behavioral and Emotions Rating Scale as compared to older students in grades 4−6 and 7−8. They used the program acronym of STEAM that focused on Supporting Tempers, Emotions and Anger Management (Bidgood et al., 2010). Such findings support the view described by Zelazo and Lyons (2012) that suggested mindfulness training in early childhood may offer an especially potent boost to the social cognitive development that occurs.

A meta-analytic review was conducted with respect to 75 research studies in schools that involved programs designed to foster increased social and emotional skills of their students (Sklad, Diekstra, De Ritter, & Ben, 2012). These researchers found an overall documented improvement across seven areas of functioning including "social skills, antisocial behavior, substance abuse, positive self-image, academic achievement, mental health, and prosocial behavior" (p. 892). The strongest positive impact noted occurred with respect to academic achievement.

A growing area of research and treatment for youth including those with special education needs involves the use of mindfulness-based interventions (Burke, 2014). Mindfulness-based programs offer systematic methods of helping participants change their way of relating to their own thoughts and feelings in ways that remain under the control of the participating person (Myers, Winton, Lancioni, & Singh, 2014). As Burke (2014) pointed out, the effectiveness of treatments are more likely enhanced by school and family environments that help support positive behavioral changes. Some mindfulness training approaches have included parents to utilize this aspect in supporting the changes for the children while also giving tools to the parents to help them better manage their family interactions. Singh et al. (2010) conducted a research project offering mindfulness training for both parents and children with ADHD. Findings from that study suggested that important personal transformation occurred for both parent and child that contributed to an increased level of satisfaction with their interactions with the child for the parents (Singh et al., 2010). Another study focusing on ADHD treatment found that mindfulness training for children along with mindful parenting training for their parents resulted in a significant reduction in symptoms by both children and parents along with a reduction in parental stress levels (Van der Oord, Bogels, & Peijnenburg, 2012). In this study, teachers noted a significant reduction in inattention by the students but no other ADHD symptoms for the children.

Other researchers have introduced teaching children mindful awareness practices and incorporating ratings from teachers and parents in analyzing the results (Flook et al., 2010). These researchers found that the children taught these skills as a group in their classrooms over an eight-week period exhibited an increase in executive control, higher levels of metacognition, and improved behavioral regulation with the largest gains noted for those children who began with the greatest difficulties with executive function.

A systematic overview of the use of mindfulness interventions in schools was conducted by Zenner, Herrnleben-kurz, and Walach (2014). These researchers found that programs focused on mindfulness to be quite popular but varying greatly in the approaches and population sizes involved. They noted that mindfulness-based interventions are helpful to youth in foundational ways to educational and personal development with internal self-regulation skills relating to focusing attention and managing emotions, but also with respect to interpersonal skills such as empathy and compassion. In their overview of some 24 research studies, Zenner et al. (2014) found positive effects on the children with respect to their cognitive abilities as well as respect to improved coping skills for stress and increased resiliency.

Mindfulness-Based Interventions for Developmental Disabilities

Mindfulness skills offer a deepened awareness and presence with both internal and external experiences, contributing to self-compassion that includes self-kindness as well as a sense of commonality with humanity (Burke, 2014, Neff and McGehee, 2010). Such heightened awareness can allow for increased intentionality of attitude and behavior and augment one's ability to self-regulate emotions and reduce tendencies toward automatic overreaction. An essential element of teaching mindfulness skills to youth is adjustment of approaches based on the developmental capabilities of the youth involved (Burke, 2014).

For those with developmental disabilities, research methods have primarily utilized individual instruction to teach mindfulness skills to adolescents and adults (Hwang & Kearney, 2013). Teaching mindfulness skills to subjects with developmental disabilities extended from 12 weeks up to 2 years in consideration of the severity of the disability involved. Studies generally reported positive effects for the chosen objectives that included reduction in aggressive behaviors, obesity, smoking, anxiety, and improvements in social and academic skills. These authors noted that a significant challenge of teaching mindfulness skills to individuals with developmental disabilities is the time-intensive aspect of working individually one-on-one with these individuals for up to six weeks followed by self-practice over months or even years. They note that the mindfulness training practices for those with developmental disabilities show strong promise even as they are undergoing further development (Hwang & Kearney, 2013).

Individual Neurofeedback Interventions for Developmental Disabilities

Neurofeedback (NFB) is yet another type of brain-based neuromodulation. NFB is a noninvasive treatment approach using computerized software and an electroencephalagraph to map some aspect of a client's neurophysiology to assist in self-regulation of certain brainwaves through reinforcements (Swingle, 2010). NFB uses the principles of classical and operant conditioning to train and regulate the brain of its dysregulation, often causing some of the symptoms and concerns for students with exceptionalities. An example of NFB with a child diagnosed with ADHD would consist of a thorough assessment and treatment plan. Then the needed NFB sessions would occur usually with individual, 20-minute sessions where the child would typically watch a movie or play a video game receiving biofeedback for the brain through sounds, music, and/or puzzles to achieve the needed brainwave frequency. This reinforces the child to use the right brainwave for the right task at the right time (Chapin & Russell-Chapin, 2014).

The causes of brain dysregulation stem from just living life, but there are many factors that need to be examined. Dysregulation may occur from a brain trauma such as a concussion, high fevers, substance abuse, genetic predispositions, poor nutrition, or even sleep deprivation. A short screening assessment titled the Neurological Dysregulation Risk Assessment is an easy method towards better understanding the factors causing some brain dysregulation. For the reader, check off each possible factor that may be a source of personal brain dysregulation (Chapin & Russell-Chapin, 2014, pp. 8–9). The complete Neurological Dysregulation Risk Assessment can be viewed and taken in the appendix at the end of this chapter (see Appendix).

NFB as a treatment choice for counseling is a highly efficacious intervention for children with many exceptionalities. The most highly researched is ADHD and has been given an efficacy rating of 4 and 5, "efficacious and efficacious and specific" demonstrated through randomized, controlled, and blind research (Russell-Chapin et al., 2013; Yucha & Montgomery, 2008).

CONCLUSION

As examined in this chapter, counseling services for students with exceptionalities have continued to evolve historically. A discussion of the roles that school and community counselors have to offer demonstrating effective but often underutilized services was presented. A variety of counseling interventions were outlined from career counseling to group counseling to individual counseling, especially focusing on the benefits of brain-based treatments such as mindfulness training and NFB. In addition, keeping a transdisciplinary focus allows counselors in both school and community settings to work and advocate for students with disabilities while empowering and teaching them to become advocates for themselves.

REFERENCES

American School Counselor Association. (2010). *Ethical standards for school counselors.* Retrieved from http://www.schoolcounselor.org/asca/media/asca/Resource%20Center/ Legal%20and%20Ethical%20Issues/Sample%20Documents/EthicalStandards2010.pdf

Antola Crowe, H., Brandes, K., Davison Aviles, B., Erickson, D., & Hall, D. (2013). Transdisciplinary teaching: Professionalism across cultures. *International Journal of Humanities and Social Science, 3*(13), 194–205.

Baskin, T. W., Slaten, C. D., Crosby, N. R., Pufahl, T., Schneller, C. L., & Ladell, M. (2010). Efficacy of counseling and psychotherapy in schools: A meta-analytic review of treatment outcome studies. *The Counseling Psychologist, 38*, 878–893. doi:10.1177/0011000010369497

Bidgood, B. A., Wilkie, H., & Katchaluba, A. (2010). Releasing the steam: An evaluation of the Supporting Tempers, Emotions, and Anger Management (SETAM) program for elementary and adolescent-age children. *Social Work with Groups, 33*, 160–174. doi:10.1080/01609510903366186

Burke, C. (2014). An exploration of the effects of mindfulness training and practice in association with enhanced wellbeing for children and adolescents. In F. A. Huppert & C. L. Cooper (Eds.), *Interventions and policies to enhance wellbeing: Wellbeing: A complete reference guide* (Vol. 6, pp. 141–184). New York, NY: Wiley.

Chapin, T., & Russell-Chapin, L. (2014). *Neurotherapy and neurofeedback: Brain-based treatment for psychological and behavioral problem.* New York, NY: Routledge.

Cherkes-Julkowski, M., Sharp, S., & Stolzenberg, J. (1997). *Rethinking attention deficit disorders.* Cambridge, MA: Brookline Books.

Davison Avilés, R. M., & Skaggs, J. L. (April, 2000). *Career development of exceptional children: Potentials for counseling & advocacy.* A presentation given at the American Counseling Association Conference, Washington, DC.

DO-IT, University of Washington. (2013). *What is the individuals with disabilities education act?* Retrieved from http://www.washington.edu/doit/Stem/articles?48

Duncan, A. W., & Klinger, L. G. (2010). Autism spectrum disorders: Building social skills in group, school, and community settings. *Social Work with Groups, 33*, 175–193. doi:10.1080/01609510903366244

Federal Education Budget Project. (2014). *No child left behind overview.* Retrieved from http://febp.newamerica.net/background-analysis/no-child-left-behind-overview

Flook, L., Smalley, S. L., Kitil, M. J., Galla, B. M., Kaiser-Greenland, S., Locke, J., ... Kasari, C. (2010). Effects of mindful awareness practices on executive functions in elementary school children. *Journal of Applied School Psychology, 26*, 70–95. doi:10.1080/15377900903379125

Hall, T. M., Kaduson, H. G., & Schaefer, C. C. (2002). Fifteen effective play therapy techniques. *Professional Psychology: Research and Practice, 33*, 515–522.

Holcomb-McCoy, C., & Chen-Hayes, S. (2015). Culturally competent school counselors: Affirming diversity by challenging oppression. In B. T. Erford (Ed.), *Transforming the school counseling profession* (6th ed., pp. 173–193). New York, NY: Pearson.

Hwang, Y.-S., & Kearney, P. (2013). A systematic review of mindfulness intervention for individuals with developmental disabilities: Long-term practice and long lasting effects. *Research in Developmental Disabilities, 34*, 314–326. doi:10.1016/j.ridd.2012.08.008

Kiep, M., Spek, A. A., & Hoeben, L. (2014). Mindfulness-based therapy in adults with an autism spectrum disorder: Do treatments last? *Mindfulness, 6*(3), 637–644. doi:10.1007/s12671-014-0299-x.

Myers, R. E., Winton, A. S. W., Lancioni, G. E., & Singh, N. (2014). Mindfulness meditation in developmental disabilities. In N. N. Singh (Ed.), *Psychology of Meditation* (pp. 209–240). Hauppauge, NY: Nova Science Publishers.

National Council on Disability. (1996). *Improving the Implementation of the Individuals with Disabilities Ed Act: Making Schools Work for All of America's Children — Supplement.* Retrieved from http://www.ncd.gov/publications/1996_Publications/04261996

National Council on Disability. (2008). *The No Child Left Behind Act and the Individuals with Disabilities Education Act: A Progress Report.* Retrieved from http://www.ncd.gov/publications/2008/01282008

National Council on Disability. (2014). *National disability policy: A Progress Report.* Washington, DC: National Council on Disability.

National Institute for Early Education Research. (2013). *The state of preschool 2013.* Retrieved from http://nieer.org/yearbook

Neff, K. D., & McGehee, P. (2010). Self-compassion and psychological resilience among adolescents and young adults. *Self and Identity, 9,* 225–240. doi:10.1080/15298860902979307

Niles, S. G., & Harris-Bowlsbey, J. (2013). Career development interventions in the 21st century. Upper Saddle River, NJ: Pearson.

Rock, E., & Leff, E. H. (2015). The professional school counselor and students with disabilities. In B. T. Erford (Ed.), *Transforming the school counseling profession* (6th ed., pp. 350–391). New York, NY: Pearson.

Russell-Chapin, L., Kemmerly, T., Liu, W., Zagardo, M., Chapin, T., Dailey, D., & Dinh, D. (2013). The effects of neurofeedback in the default mode network: Pilot study results of medicated children with ADHD. *Journal of Neurotherapy, 17*(35), 35–42.

Schmidt, J. J. (2010). *The elementary/middle school counselor's survival guide.* San Francisco, CA: Jossey-Bass.

Schmidt, J. J. (2014). *Counseling in schools comprehensive programs of responsive services for all students.* New York, NY: Pearson.

Singh, N. N., Singh, A. N., Lancioni, G. E., Singh, J., Winton, A. S. W., & Adkins, A. D. (2010). Mindfulness training for parents and their children with ADHD increases the children's compliance. *Journal of Child and Family Studies, 19,* 157–166. doi:10.1007/s10826-009-9272-z

Sklad, M., Diekstra, R., De Ritter, M., & Ben, J. (2012). Effectiveness of school-based universal social, emotional, and behavioral programs: Do they enhance students' development in the area of skill, behavior, and adjustment? *Psychology in the Schools, 49,* 892–909. doi:10.1002/pits.21641

Stone, C. B., & Dahir, C. A. (2006). *The transformed school counselor.* Boston, MA: Houghton Mifflin.

Swingle, P. G. (2010). *Biofeedback for the brain.* New Brunswick, NJ: Rutgers University Press.

Trolley, B. C., Haas, H. S., & Patti, D. C. (2009). *The school counselor's guide to special education.* Thousand Oaks, CA: Corwin Press.

U.S. Department of Education. (n.d.). Section 300.8 child with a disability. Retrieved from http://idea.ed.gov/explore/view/p/,root,regs,300,A,300%252E8

Van der Oord, S., Bogels, S. M., & Peijnenburg, D. (2012). The effectiveness of mindfulness training for children with ADHD and mindful parenting for their parents. *Journal of Child and Family Studies, 21,* 139–147. doi:10.1007/s10826-011-9457-0

Ware, J. N., Ort, J. H., & Swank, J. M. (2012). A phenomenological exploration of children's experiences in a social skills group. *The Journal for Specialists in Group Work, 37,* 133–151. doi:10.1080/01933922.2012.663862

Whiston, S. C., Tai, W., Rahardja, D., & Eder, K. (2011). School counseling outcome: A meta-analytic examination of interventions. *Journal of Counseling & Development, 89,* 37–55. doi:10.1002/j.1556-6678.2011.tb00059.x

White, S. W., Koenig, K., & Scahill, L. (2010). Group social skills instruction for adolescents with high-functioning autism spectrum disorders. *Focus on Autism and Other Developmental Disabilities, 25*, 209–219. doi:10.1177/1088357610380595.

Wright, R. J. (2012). *Introduction to school counseling.* Los Angeles, CA: Sage.

Young, J., Ne'eman, A., & Gleser, S. (2011). Bullying and students with disabilities. Retrieved from http://www.ncd.gov/publications/2011/March92011

Yucha, C., & Montgomery, D. (2008). *Evidence-based practice in biofeedback and Neurofeedback.* Wheat Ridge, CO: Association for Applied Psychophysiology and Biofeedback.

Zelazo, P. D., & Lyons, K. E. (2012). The potential benefits of mindfulness training in early childhood: A developmental social cognitive neuroscience perspective. *Child Development Perspectives, 6*, 154–160. doi:10.1111/j.1750-8606.2012.00241.x

Zenner, C., Herrnleben-kurz, S., & Walach, H. (2014). Mindfulness-based interventions in schools – A systematic review and meta-analysis. *Frontiers in Psychology, 5*, 603. doi:10.3389/fpsyg.2014.00603

APPENDIX: NEUROLOGICAL DYSREGULATION RISK ASSESSMENT

Please read each potential source of neurological dysregulation and indicate whether or not it may be a risk factor for you or your child.

	Yes	No
Genetic Influences: Grandparents, parents, or siblings with mental health or learning disorders (including attention deficit hyperactivity disorder), post-traumatic stress disorder, depression, generalized anxiety disorder, substance abuse, personality, or other severe psychological disorders (bipolar or schizophrenia).	_____	_____
Prenatal Exposure: Maternal distress, psychotropic medication use, alcohol or substance abuse, nicotine use, or possible exposure to environmental toxins including genetically modified foods, pesticides, petrochemicals, xenoestrogens in plastics, heavy metals (lead/mercury), and fluoride, bromine, and chlorine in water.	_____	_____
Birth Complications: Forceps or vacuum delivery, oxygen loss, head injury, premature birth, difficult or prolonged labor, obstructed umbilical cord, or fetal distress.	_____	_____
Disease and High Fever: Sustained fever above 104 degrees due to bacterial infection, influenza, strep, meningitis, encephalitis, Reye's Syndrome, PANDAS, or other infections or disease processes.	_____	_____
Current Diagnosis: Of mental health, physical health, alcohol abuse, or learning disorder.	_____	_____
Poor Diet and Inadequate Exercise: Diet high in processed food, preservatives, simple carbohydrates (sugar and flour), genetically modified foods, foods treated with herbicides, pesticides, and hormones, low daily water intake, high caffeine intake, and lack of adequate physical exercise (20 minutes, seven times a week).	_____	_____

Appendix (*Continued*)

	Yes	No
Emotionally Suppressive Psychosocial Environment: Being raised or currently living in poverty, domestic violence, physical, emotional, or sexual abuse, alcoholic or mentally unstable family environment, emotional trauma, neglect, institutionalization, and inadequate maternal emotional availability or attachment.	___	___
Mild to Severe Brain Injury: Experienced one or more blows to the head from a sports injury, fall, or auto accident (with or without loss of consciousness), or episodes of open head injury, coma, or stroke.	___	___
Prolonged Life Distress: Most commonly due to worry about money, work, economy, family responsibilities, relationships, personal safety, and/or health causing sustained periods of anxiety, irritability, anger, fatigue, lack of interest, low motivation or energy, nervousness, and/or physical aches and pains.	___	___
Stress-Related Disease: Includes heart disease, kidney disease, hypertension, obesity, diabetes, stroke, hormonal, and/or immunological disorders.	___	___
Prolonged Medication Use, Substance Use, or Other Addictions: Including legal or illegal drug use, substance abuse, or addiction (alcohol, drugs, nicotine, caffeine, medication, gambling, sex, spending, etc.) and overuse of screen technologies (cell phones, video games, television, computers, Internet, etc.).	___	___
Seizure Disorders: Caused by birth complications, stroke, head trauma, infection, high fever, oxygen deprivation, and/or genetic disorders and includes epilepsy, pseudo-seizures, or epileptiform seizures.	___	___
Chronic Pain: Related to accidents, injury, or a disease process. Including back pain, headache and migraine pain, neck pain, facial pain, and fibromyalgia.	___	___

In general, the greater the number of "yes" responses, the greater the risk of significant neurological dysregulation. However, even one severe "yes" response could cause significant neurological dysregulation and result in serious mental, physical, or cognitive impairment that may benefit from individually designed NFB training

CHAPTER 5

ROLE OF PSYCHOLOGISTS IN INTERDISCIPLINARY RELATIONS IN SPECIAL EDUCATION

Lynda Kasky-Hernández and Gary L. Cates

ABSTRACT

The roles and functions of a school psychologist are multifaceted. School psychologists are traditionally trained in areas of assessment, intervention, consultation, and program evaluation, though they often participate in prevention and crisis intervention efforts and program evaluation (Harvey & Struzziero, 2008). School psychologists work at district, building, and individual student levels to provide comprehensive and effective services to children and families. Despite a wide range of responsibilities, the school psychologist works in conjunction with other school professionals (e.g., general and special education teachers, speech-language pathologists, audiologists, social workers, principals) and parents to foster individual student success. This chapter presents the general roles and responsibilities of the school psychologist, as well as the school psychologist's role within an interdisciplinary team when making appropriate educational decisions.

Keywords: Interdisciplinary team; school psychologist; multitiered system of support; Response-to-Intervention; decision-making

Interdisciplinary Connections to Special Education: Important Aspects to Consider
Advances in Special Education, Volume 30A, 81–94
Copyright © 2015 by Emerald Group Publishing Limited
All rights of reproduction in any form reserved
ISSN: 0270-4013/doi:10.1108/S0270-40132015000030A019

PROFESSIONAL SNAPSHOT

Ms. Francis arrives at the school at 7:30 a.m. on Monday morning. As she sets down her coffee and arranges files for her caseload at the elementary school, she plays back phone messages and responds to emails that she has received over the past three days. Ms. Francis works at two schools, two days in an elementary school and two days in a high school. She also stays busy as a Response-to-Intervention (RtI) specialist for the district and spends one day a week traveling to schools in the district to provide support to staff in their efforts to collect, manage, and interpret school-wide progress monitoring data.

At the top of her list this morning, Ms. Francis has an Individual Education Program (IEP) meeting at 8:05 a.m. for a fourth grade student named Mateo. Mateo is an English Language Learner student and is currently receiving intensive services for reading. Ms. Francis, the interdisciplinary team, and Mateo's parents will together review the information that various members at the school have collected over the past few weeks to (a) determine the educational needs for Mateo in the area of reading and (b) to determine whether those needs warrant eligibility for special education services for more individualized educational programming. Ms. Francis spends the next 35 minutes reviewing data collected from Mateo's educational record, assessment results from the Woodcock Reading Mastery Test (WRMT; Woodcock, 2011), school-wide benchmarking assessment data from the Dynamic Indicators of Basic Early Literacy (University of Oregon, 2015), teacher and student interview transcriptions, and systematic direct behavioral observations she has collected over the past few weeks in preparation for the IEP meeting before greeting Mateo's parents in the main office. After playing the facilitator's role of the meeting, Ms. Francis anticipates that she will likely engage in a variety of interdisciplinary roles related to Mateo's educational future. Specifically she anticipates regardless of outcome that she may play an active role in one or more of the following roles: (a) serve as a parent liaison; (b) coordinate and/or implement intervention services in reading; (c) facilitate intervention data collection, analysis, and interpretation; and (d) provide ongoing systematic support to other team members in the form of consultation.

INTRODUCTION

A school psychologist plays a necessary role in the education system as a trained professional who works with students, families, and school staff to promote student learning and development. The role of the school psychologist is, in part, to ensure that school practices align with recent legislation, including *No Child Left Behind* (NCLB), the *Individuals with Disabilities Education Improvement Act* (IDEIA), and in many states, RtI. As such, the school psychologist plays an integral role in choosing scientifically based interventions, monitoring intervention effectiveness, and contributing to making appropriate data-based decisions for service delivery of all children. In order to provide the most effective services for children and their families, school psychologists work collaboratively with other skilled professionals through a team approach. Together, an interdisciplinary team follows a systematic method for problem solving in order to provide comprehensive and effective services to children and families.

GENERAL ROLES OF THE SCHOOL PSYCHOLOGIST

School psychologists are traditionally trained in many areas of assessment (e.g., cognitive, academic, and social behavior), intervention (e.g., behavioral management and social-emotional intervention), and consultation with parents and school staff (Harvey & Struzziero, 2008). In addition to receiving training in multiple areas, a school psychologist works at various levels within individual schools and districts to provide both direct (e.g., intervention) and indirect (e.g., consultation) academic and mental health services to children and adolescents. These levels include working at a district level or individual schools, as well as working with students at the individual level. Fig. 1 displays common activities of the school psychologist at three levels: district, building, and individual student. We will discuss the various roles individually at each of the major levels.

District-Level Roles

At the district level, a school psychologist may assume responsibilities that affect a large number of schools. As an example, a school psychologist at the district level may be involved in the analysis and interpretation of student data that are collected through an RtI system. Responsibilities may include compiling and managing data related to monitoring student performance for the district. School psychologists at the district level may also train other professionals to collect and manage school and individual class or student data. The data management role is especially important given that federal legislation has placed increasing emphasis on the implementation and monitoring of RtI (Cates, Blum, & Swerdlik, 2011). In addition to involvement in data collection and management, a school psychologist at

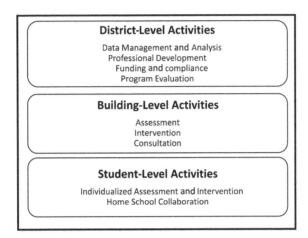

Fig. 1. Common Activities Related to the Role of the School Psychologist at Three Major Levels.

the district level may provide in-service workshops to provide additional training to other educational professionals. Trainings may specifically address a district's needs or may provide helpful educational information on recent topics that benefit the district as a whole, such as assistive technology, supported social-emotional interventions, or other professional development opportunities. These activities are helpful during interdisciplinary meetings such as the one described at the beginning of this chapter as they help with the decision-making process in addition to the understanding and implementation procedures that often follow.

Building-Level Roles

At the building level, a school psychologist supports the efforts of teachers and other school staff in providing educational support to children and their families. School psychologists are frequently called upon to provide expertise in assessment, intervention, and problem solving within interdisciplinary teams for special education decisions. School psychologists are instrumental in identifying and implementing school-wide prevention and intervention programs that are supported by sufficient evidence (Strein, Kuhn-McKearin, & Finney, 2014). For instance, a school psychologist may lead efforts to locate funding, involve families, and monitor the effectiveness of school-wide positive behavior interventions and support strategies

(McKevitt & Fynaardt, 2014). Given their training in evidence-based intervention strategies, school psychologists may lead crisis intervention efforts by developing crisis plans, identifying evidence-based interventions relevant for building-level crisis management, and examining the effectiveness of crisis interventions (Brock, Reeves, & Nickerson, 2014).

Consultation with teachers is also a critical role of the school psychologist. At the building level, a school psychologist may consult with teachers about specific student concerns and provide small-group academic or social-emotional interventions. An important aspect of intervention implementation is the integrity of the intervention. The school psychologist may also conduct treatment integrity checks during class-wide implementation of interventions and are in a position to provide feedback to teachers in order to improve intervention consistency and effectiveness (Cates et al., 2011). Within an RtI framework for service delivery, the school psychologist often participates or even leads universal screening and progress monitoring of students at various grade levels and provides small-group interventions as necessary.

Individual Student-Level Roles

In addition to district- and building-level roles, a school psychologist often works directly with children and their families to identify any academic, behavioral, or social-emotional concerns. Depending on the school's needs, the school psychologist commonly assists in the provision of individualized services. Additionally, school psychologists have specific training in monitoring whether students are responding sufficiently to any interventions that may be in place. School psychologists play a large consultative and communicative role between home and school systems. For instance, a school psychologist may work with parents and teachers to implement a behavioral rewards system that is consistent between the student's home and school settings. In general, school psychologists are in the position to advocate on behalf of individual students and families.

DIRECT SERVICE TO STUDENTS: A MULTITIERED MODEL OF SYSTEM OF SUPPORT

School psychologists interact with students in schools who receive a range of general and special education services. One of the most essential roles of a school psychologist is his/her involvement in the evaluation of children and adolescents' academic skills, cognitive functioning, problem behaviors, and social competencies. The multitiered model of assessment, intervention, and evaluation of outcomes is becoming a useful diagnostic process used to identify student needs that require more specialized educational programming (Greshman, 2014). Within a multitiered system of support such as RtI, the school psychologist interacts with students on all levels to provide appropriate academic and social-emotional support. The number of tiers within a multitiered model typically ranges from two to four, with a three-tiered model being most common. School psychologists play an important role at each level of the model. Tier 1 level services are designed to address the needs of the largest amount of students, targeting approximately 80–90% of the class or school population (Stoiber, 2014). Tier 1 services include class- or school-wide programs, including universal screenings for reading or math, prevention programs, social-emotional learning programs (e.g., Second Step), and the general education curriculum (Cates et al., 2011). The school psychologist may provide assistance at the Tier 1 level by identifying instructional strategies or programs to meet students' needs. School psychologists also provide direct services to students at the Tier 2 level.

At the Tier 2 level, more targeted services are provided in addition to Tier 1 services to a smaller group of students needing more help, time, or support. At the Tier 2 level, the school psychologist may provide consultation and assistance to teachers and other school staff in the identification and implementation of Tier 2 interventions. Identifying the area of concern, selecting evidence-based interventions, and progress monitoring and interpreting data for students in Tier 2 are critical to the success of the multitiered system of support. The school psychologist may also help support students at the Tier 2 level for social-emotional concerns by conducting functional assessments to design more targeted interventions based on student behavior (Stoiber, 2014).

Tier 3 represents the most intensive intervention services for approximately 1–5% of students in a school (Stoiber, 2014). This small group consists of students who are identified by the school psychologist and other members of the decision-making team as not benefiting sufficiently with Tier 1 and Tier 2 services. Tier 3 services are designed to be individualized or small-group intervention and evaluation that supplement Tier 1 and 2 levels of instruction. The school psychologist is highly instrumental at the Tier 3 level through consulting with teachers and other school personnel to determine the specific nature of the student's concerns. The school psychologist is often in a unique position to identify effective intervention strategies for students who exhibit more severe academic, social-emotional, and behavioral concerns (Stoiber, 2014). In general, the school psychologist may also ensure fidelity of Tier 1 and 2 interventions through treatment integrity checks.

In addition to helping identify the necessary level of intervention for the child or adolescent to improve his or her performance to expected levels, the school psychologist also plays a large role in determining student eligibility for special education (Stoiber, 2014). Through a multitiered model of support, a student whose performance does not improve to the expected levels despite intensive levels of support is eligible for evaluation for special education services. The school psychologist is a highly valuable member of the decision-making team that is responsible for addressing student eligibility concerns. The school psychologist's role in the decision-making process is described in more detail below.

DECISION MAKING: AN INTERDISCIPLINARY APPROACH

As a member of an interdisciplinary team, the school psychologist is typically responsible for gathering critical information from teachers, parents, and students in order to facilitate the multidisciplinary team's data-based decision making about children's educational needs. As such, the school psychologist is generally called upon for his or her expertise in areas that are focused on supporting the student both directly and indirectly. School psychologists are traditionally involved in individual assessment (e.g., cognitive and academic assessment), as well as the implementation and monitoring of interventions (e.g., behavior management and counseling). School psychologists also have training in collecting, managing, and interpreting data and student outcomes within multitiered systems of support. Given this wide range of duties, a school psychologist's effectiveness is highly dependent upon the collaboration of a multidisciplinary team.

Decisions about a child's education are made using a problem-solving process in order to collect data from multiple sources of data and multiple informants (e.g., teachers, parents, and the child). The school psychologist often uses data to guide and support decisions. Fig. 2 shows a typical framework that a school psychologist takes during his or her involvement in an IEP meeting. At each stage of the decision-making process (before, during, and after), the school psychologist may use specific strategies to organize data.

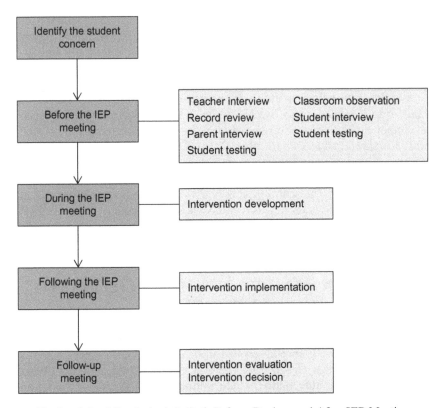

Fig. 2. School Psychologist's Path Before, During, and After IEP Meeting.

During each of these phases, the school psychologist is involved in systematic data collection in order to fully assess the student concern. RIOT is an acronym that provides a blueprint for a best practice approach to assessing student concerns. The methods of assessment involved in the problem analysis fall into four general categories: Reviews, Interviews, Observations, and Tests.

Record Review

A record review includes reviewing such formal school documents such as educational records (e.g., report cards), attendance, suspensions, and medical records. Office referrals and referrals to the school nurse are included within records. Permanent products, or work samples, that inform the specific educational concern can also be collected. For example, completed and graded classroom worksheets can be obtained from the student's teacher to inform decisions about a student who is being assessed for a mathematics concern. If the school is fully engaged in a RtI or other multitiered system of support, data on the student's response to the general curriculum (and potentially more intense services) are also available. Information collected during the record review stage can inform further assessment, as well as help the multidisciplinary team conceptualize the student's concern.

Interviews

Structured, semi-structured, and unstructured interviews can be used to facilitate the data collection process. Interviews can be conducted with the student to obtain more information about him or her. An interview with the student, him/herself, often informs possible rewards and reinforcers that may be used as part of an intervention plan. Students may also be asked directly about their thoughts on instructional strategies that are most effective for them. Interviews also afford the school psychologist with an opportunity to identify the student's strengths, which are important to identify when developing intervention plans and building rapport with the family. Interviews with a parent or parental figure can provide information about the student's development that may contribute to the present concern. Discussing the student's performance in the classroom with the student's teacher(s) also assists the school psychologist in understanding when the teacher first identified the student's concern, strategies the teacher has already attempted, and the result of such strategies.

Observations

In addition to interviewing the student, his or her parent, and/or the student's teachers, school psychologists may also conduct direct observations of the student. Classroom observations can inform the student's academic engagement or on-task behavior during particular subjects in comparison to other subjects. Classroom observations also provide information about the type of instruction that the student is exposed to, the amount of direct feedback provided, and the number of opportunities the student has to respond during a given lesson. Observations across settings help to determine where the student's behaviors are more and less likely to occur.

Testing

Testing is often used in conjunction with a thorough record review, interviews, and observation in order to rule out competing explanations about a student's behavior. Such testing may include specific assessments that target the student's problem in a particular subject (e.g., mathematics or reading). School psychologists are often called upon to assess areas of concern using standardized achievement tests, standardized domain-specific tests, curriculum-based assessments (e.g., comparing a child's performance to peers or a criterion), and curriculum-based evolutions (e.g., observing a student's strengths and weaknesses relative to a curriculum). Rating scales are

	I	C	E	L
R	Review notes from past teachers to find effective instructional techniques	Review a student's permanent products in a particular class (e.g., writing worksheets)	Review a student's old files for previous teachers' recommendations for the best instructional environment for the student	Observe student's self-efficacy for writing by looking at previous writing samples
I	A teacher interview to collect information about effective instruction methods for the student(e.g., large group)	Interviewing the student to learn more about the child's skills in a writing	Speak with the teacher about differences in physical structure of the classroom during writing time	Interview the student to learn more about his or her study habits, attitude towards writing, etc.
O	Conducting a classroom observation to monitor student's on-task behavior during whole class instruction	Observe the nature of various in-class writing tasks and the presentation of those tasks	Conduct a classroom observation of the classroom during writing activities (e.g., proximity of the teacher to students; noisy distractions; disruptive peers)	Teacher ratings of the student's number of attempts on writing-related tasks
T	Academic or cognitive testing; monitoring student's response using a behavioral incentive program	Administration of a diagnostic test using the student's reading curriculum	A behavioral observation of a student's on-task behavior in various desks (e.g., near peers vs. isolated work conditions)	Assessing the student's accuracy on assignments with and without a reward or reinforcement

Fig. 3. ICEL Matrix Example.

also used to identify any concerns teachers have regarding students' behavior, academics, or social performance.

In order to conduct a thorough and informed analysis of the concern, multiple sources of information must also be considered. These sources of information are represented in the acronym ICEL and include the following domains: Instruction, Curriculum, Environment, and Learner. Examples of types of information that can be collected in each domain are listed in in Fig. 3. The use of this matrix can provide insight into the severity of the concern and can initiate a more thorough assessment process (Christ, 2008).

SPECIAL ISSUES RELATED TO SCHOOL PSYCHOLOGISTS AND INTERDISCIPLINARY PROCESS

It is evident that school psychologist play an active role in the mental health and academic success of students in the interdisciplinary process. Because the school psychologist plays many roles and serves many functions, it is helpful to understand the amount of time spent by a school psychologist in the major activities described above. Bramlett, Murphy, Johnson, Wallingford, and Hall (2002) conducted a survey of nearly 800 school psychologists about the amount of time they spent engaged in a variety of activities. The school psychologists reported that 47% of their time was spent in assessment. The remaining time was spent in consultation (16%), intervention (13%), counseling (8%), conferencing (7%), supervision (3%), in-services (2%), research (1%), parent training (1%), and others (3%). It is apparent that roughly 75% of a school psychologist's time is spent in assessment, intervention, and/or consultation.

It is estimated that 20% children will experience a significant mental health issue during their time in school (National Association of School Psychologists (NASP), 2015). Because the school psychologist is an important contributor to the interdisciplinary process, it is also helpful to understand the current status of school psychologists with regard to employment. The NASP recommends a ratio of 1 school psychologist to 1,000 students (NASP, 2015). Currently a ratio of about 1 school psychologist to 1,600 students exists (NASP, 2015). With additional funding decreases and increased levels of accountability with regard to legislation in education, it is apparent that the need for school psychologists to facilitate the assessment, intervention, and consultation process will likely increase. This means that while the student to school psychologist ratio increases, the availability of quality services administered through interdisciplinary teams may decrease.

The shortage of school psychologists is not simply a self-serving point of view of the authors of this chapter. A survey of teachers by Watkins, Crosby, and Pearson (2001) revealed that not only were school psychologists regarded as important to their predominant role of assessment, they were perceived as important to special education input, consultation, and counseling. Specifically teachers were interested in seeing the school psychologist not only maintain their role in assessment but also in seeing them expand their presence in their buildings daily to engage in a variety of activities.

CONCLUSION

The role of the school psychologist is multifaceted. School psychologists are trained in various areas, including assessment (e.g., cognitive and academic assessment batteries, diagnostic testing), intervention (e.g., behavioral intervention, counseling), and consultation with parents and school staff. At the district level, school psychologists are often involved in managing and analyzing data and providing district-wide professional development workshops. At the school and building level, school psychologists spend time exercising their expertise in assessment, as well as intervention and consultation with teachers and parents. At the individual student level, school psychologists often conduct individualized assessment and intervention and collaborate with students' families to promote home—school collaboration and communication. One of the most essential roles of the school psychologist is his or her involvement in the evaluation of students' skills using a multitiered model of assessment, intervention, and evaluation. Through this multitiered system (e.g., RtI), the school psychologist is actively involved in each tier to provide assistance to students identified as requiring varying levels of academic, behavioral, and social support.

Frequently, school psychologists are called upon to participate in the decision-making process regarding students' educational future. The school psychologist uses data to guide important educational decisions using a systematic data collection process (e.g., completion of the RIOT × ICEL matrix) to ensure that an appropriate breadth and depth of information is collected to make such important decisions. Based on a study conducted by Bramlett et al. (2002), school psychologists reported that a large percentage of their role is spent conducting assessments (47% of the school psychologist's time), followed by other activities including consultation (16%), intervention (13%), counseling (8%), conferencing (7%), supervision (3%), in-services (2%), research (1%), and parent training (1%). Thus, school psychologists spend most of their time (75%) engaged in assessment, intervention, and/or consultation activities. The role of school psychologists is increasingly important given the number of students who experience significant mental health issues at some point in their educational career (NASP, 2015). Thus, there is a great need for increased numbers of school psychologists entering the field in order to assist in the necessary assessment, intervention, and consultation to meet students' academic, social, and behavioral needs.

REFERENCES

Bramlett, R. K., Murphy, J. J., Johnson, J., Wallingford, L., & Hall, J. D. (2002). Contemporary practices in school psychology: A national survey of roles and referral problems. *Psychology in the Schools, 39*, 327–335.

Brock, S. E., Reeves, M. A. L., & Nickerson, A. B. (2014). Best practices in school crisis intervention. In A. Thomas & J. Grimes (Eds.), *Best practice in school psychology* (Vol. 3, pp. 211–230). Bethesda, MD: National Association of School Psychologists.

Cates, G. L., Blum, C. H., & Swerdlik, M. E. (2011). *Effective RTI training and practices: Helping school and district teams improve academic performance and social behavior.* Champaign, IL: Research Press.

Christ, T. J. (2008). Best practices in problem analysis. In A. Thomas & J. Grimes (Eds.), *Best practices in school psychology* (Vol. 2, pp. 159–176). Bethesda, MD: National Association of School Psychologists.

Greshman, F. M. (2014). Best practices in diagnosis of mental health and academic difficulties in a multitier problem-solving approach. In A. Thomas & J. Grimes (Eds.), *Best practice in school psychology* (Vol. 1, pp. 147–158). Bethesda, MD: National Association of School Psychologists.

Harvey, V. S., & Struzziero, J. A. (2008). *Professional development and supervision of school psychologists* (2nd ed.). Thousand Oaks, CA: Corwin Press.

McKevitt, & Fynaardt. (2014). Best practices in developing a positive behavior support system at the school level. In A. Thomas & J. Grimes (Eds.), *Best practices in school psychology* (Vol. 1, pp. 165–180). Bethesda, MD: National Association of School Psychologists.

National Association of School Psychologists. (March 1, 2015). *Supporting student success: Remedying the shortage of school psychologists.* Retrieved from http://www.nasponline.org/advocacy/personnelshortages.pdf

Stoiber, K. C. (2014). A comprehensive framework for multitiered systems of support in school psychology. Data-based and collaborative decision making. Best practices in developing prevention strategies for school psychology practice. In A. Thomas & J. Grimes (Eds.), *Best practice in school psychology* (Vol. 1. pp. 41–70). Bethesda, MD: National Association of School Psychologists.

Strein, W., Kuhn-McKearin, M., & Finney, M. (2014). Best practices in developing prevention strategies for school psychology practice. In A. Thomas & J. Grimes (Eds.), *Best practice in school psychology* (Vol. 3, pp. 137–148). Bethesda, MD: National Association of School Psychologists.

University of Oregon. (March 1, 2015). *UO DIBELS Data System.* Retrieved form https://dibels.uoregon.edu

Watkins, M. W., Crosby, E. G., & Pearson, J. L. (2001). Role of the school psychologist: Perception of school staff. *School Psychology International, 22,* 64–73.

Woodcock, R. W. (2011). Woodcock reading mastery tests, revised, examiner's manual. Circle Pines, MN: American Guidance Service.

CHAPTER 6

ROLE OF SCHOOL LEADERS IN INTERDISCIPLINARY CONNECTIONS IN SPECIAL EDUCATION

D. Michael Risen, Jenny Tripses and Anne Risen

ABSTRACT

The chapter examines school administrator responsibilities to special education students and their families from case scenarios based on conflicts between parents and districts regarding services provided by schools to special education students. From these case studies based on real case law, readers are exposed to situations intended to pose questions as to whether administrators met their responsibility to ensure the rights of the special education students. Principals, superintendents, and special education administrators committed to work together to make their school environment and optimal place for children to learn. An equally important role for school administrators is to create and maintain cultures where faculty understand their advocacy role for all children, but in particular, those children most in need of support. Effective administrators hold themselves and other professionals in their district to high standards related to knowledge of school law, particularly special education school

Interdisciplinary Connections to Special Education: Important Aspects to Consider
Advances in Special Education, Volume 30A, 95–117
Copyright © 2015 by Emerald Group Publishing Limited
All rights of reproduction in any form reserved
ISSN: 0270-4013/doi:10.1108/S0270-40132015000030A011

law; communication with parents and other professionals; and collabora-
tions based on the value of what is best for the student. This chapter con-
cludes with a section on ethical leadership or the values underlying
administrative actions affecting individualized education program stu-
dents, their families, and all students who are different whether due to
socioeconomic status, cultural differences, or race.

Keywords: Building administrators; district administrators; special
education administrators; special education school law; ethical
leadership; collaboration between IEP parents and administrators

INTRODUCTION

School administrators wear many hats in their schools and districts. In
many cases, their work is behind the scenes and encompasses many different responsibilities. Those include (a) to create conditions where other educators can develop curriculum and teaching strategies, (b) to ensure
processes as prescribed by law and district policy are followed by both the
spirit and letter of the law for special education students, (c) to support
and evaluate teachers in the classroom, (d) to create effective parent/
teacher/community relationships, (e) to establish and implement universal
codes of behavior for students and others, and (f) other duties as assigned
which typically means making sure other processes of school life such as
the cafeteria, bus, and hall passing are organized and maintained in an
orderly fashion that is generally followed by all. Of all these responsibilities, none is greater than the moral obligation to provide that *all* students
under the care of an administrative team receive quality education, including students whose abilities fall outside the mainstream.

Universal education designed around factory models was instituted at
the beginning of the turn of the last century and was characterized by
bureaucratic methods that included standardization of operation, routine,
and at minimal cost (English, Papa, Mullen, & Creighton, 2012). Special
education students, by definition, test these boundaries. School administrators by the nature of their roles will find themselves in cross paths between
conflicting assumptions, routines, procedures of school business organized
around bureaucratic models created at the beginning of the Industrial Era,
and individualized education program (IEP) students and their families
whose needs and rights frequently fail to fit into standardized methods.

Knowledge of and adherence to school law related to students with IEPs is one of the core foundations upon which all administrative actions be taken (Bateman & Bateman, 2015). Administrators are called to create and support learning environments that support learning needs of diverse students and involve families in all decisions (Sanders & Sheldon, 2009). IDEA provides parents the right to examine children's records, challenge school evaluations, make formal complaints, and pursue due process proceedings when they feel their child's rights have been violated or ignored. Administrators must ensure that regular and special education teachers are well informed and held to high expectations to provide services to students as per their IEPs. In all cases, administrators who are either unaware of or fail to follow the federal guidelines known as the *Individuals with Disabilities Education Act* (IDEA) regulations in the end cause unnecessary difficulties for students, families, their districts, and other educators (Bateman & Bateman, 2015).

Communications with families and other professionals is another critical administrative responsibility. When dealing with differences in opinion related to an IEP student's program, effective administrators act upon the premise that the educators know pedagogy and the parent(s) know their child. When administrators work with those concerned with the outcomes of the education of students with disabilities, administrators create avenues for communication, provide transparent shared decision making, and promote pathways for student progress (Sanders & Sheldon, 2009).

Collaborations with other professionals (such as special education and regular education teachers, paraprofessionals, administrators of other agencies) provide necessary foundations upon which to adopt and implement effective programs for students with an IEP. Consideration must also be given to different roles played by the principal/assistant principal, superintendent, and special education coordinator.

This chapter looks at the work of school administrators from difficult case scenarios when parents were dissatisfied or in disagreement with the services provided by their schools for their child with an IEP. In these three case studies, the reader has to ask whether administrators met their responsibility to ensure the rights of the special education students. In each case, the reader should reflect on the differing circumstances and determine if the administrators met three important leadership functions. These include communication, knowledge of the law, and working cooperatively with educators and other agencies. The cases (all real cases from Illinois due process decisions) are designed to illustrate that administrator responsibilities towards students with an IEP include the requisite technical knowledge of knowing school law as it applies to students with an IEP and their families, strong communications skills, and working well with other educators to comply with those laws. We conclude the chapter with a section on ethical leadership or the values underlying administrative actions affecting students with an IEP, their families, and indeed, all students who are different whether due to socioeconomic status, cultural differences, or race.

COMMON ACRONYMS IN SPECIAL EDUCATION

Special education is a field of specialists governed by a whole host of laws, regulations both federal and state. As a result, this complex field contains numerous acronyms. The complexity of the field and the enormity of the use of acronyms dictate the table below that outlines the most common acronyms utilized throughout the field of special education (Table 1).

Table 1.   Acronyms Defined.

IDEA	*Individuals with Disabilities Education Act* − first passed by Congress in 1975 as Public Act 97-142 − *The Education for All Handicapped Children Act*. Since then, 97-142 has been reauthorized several times with the name changing in 1997 and last reauthorized in 2004.
LEA	Local educational agency or school district (Murdick, Gartin, & Fowler, 2014).
MDT − Multidisciplinary Team	Another name for the local education agency committee that determines whether a student is in need of special education services and, if so, what services. The team members must include at a minimum the parents of the child, the child (when appropriate), a regular education teacher familiar with the child, a special education teacher with knowledge of the child's suspected disability, the local education agency representative (person with authority to authorize resources − usually the principal), a person with knowledge to interpret test results, at the discretion of either party, and other members (Murdick et al., 2014).
	IDEA. The federal law that provides the legal authority for early intervention and special educational services for children from birth to age 21. Part B outlines services for children ages 3 to 21. Part C outlines services for children from birth to age 3.
IEP − Individualized Education Program	A written statement of a child's current level of educational performance and an individualized plan of instruction, including the goals, specific services to be received, the staff who will carry out the services, the standards and timeline for evaluating progress, and the amount and degree to which the child will participate with typically developing peers (Murdick et al., 2014).

Table 1. (*Continued*)

ADHD – Attention Deficit Hyperactivity Disorder	ADHD is a psychiatric disorder of the neurodevelopmental type in which there are significant problems of attention, hyperactivity, or acting impulsively that are not appropriate for a person's age. These symptoms must begin by age 6 to 12 and persist for more than six months for a diagnosis to be made. In school-aged individuals, inattention symptoms often result in poor school performance. However, a diagnosis of ADHD does not ensure IDEA eligibility. The key question is does the child's disability adversely affect educational performance? To be eligible for free appropriate public education (FAPE) under the IDEA, the child must have a disability and must need special education and related services (Wrightslaw).
ODD – Oppositional Defiance Disorder	The *Diagnostic and Statistical Manual of Mental Disorders* (DSM-5), published by the American Psychiatric Association, lists criteria for diagnosing ODD. This manual is used by mental health providers to diagnose mental conditions and by insurance companies to reimburse for treatment. DSM-5 criteria for diagnosis of ODD show a pattern of behavior that: • includes at least four symptoms from any of these categories – angry and irritable mood; argumentative and defiant behavior; or vindictiveness • occurs with at least one individual who is not a sibling • causes significant problems at work, school, or home • occurs on its own, rather than as part of the course of another mental health problem, such as a substance use disorder, depression, or bipolar disorder • lasts at least six months • DSM-5 criteria for diagnosis of ODD include both emotional and behavioral symptoms (DSM-5).
OT – Occupational Therapy	In its simplest terms, OT helps children to participate in the things they want and need to do through the therapeutic use of everyday activities (occupations). Common OT interventions include helping children with disabilities to participate fully in school and social situations (American Occupational Therapy Association).
FAPE – Free Appropriate Public Education	The Supreme Court has determined that school districts meet the requirements of FAPE when the districts can demonstrate they have followed all of the required procedures of the IDEA and that these procedures have produced an IEP for the student that is designed to provide the student with a "floor of opportunity" to receive educational benefit (*Rowley vs. Board of Education of Hendrick Hudson School District*).
IAES – Interim Alternative Educational Setting	The school district's authority to remove a student from the current placement for up to 45 days to a more restrictive placement when the student's behavior involves weapons, drugs, or serious bodily harm (Murdick et al., 2014). The placement that is as close as possible to the general education environment. This educational setting includes providing the IEP

Table 1.   (*Continued*)

LRE – Least Restrictive Environment	student with the greatest amount of opportunity to be educated with the IEP student's nondisabled peers to the maximum extent appropriate for each IEP student. LRE is a requirement under IDEA (Sanders & Sheldon, 2009, pp. 67–68).
IEE – Independent Educational Evaluation	Under the IDEA, parents have a right, under certain circumstances, to request an independent evaluation of the student at public expense. The circumstances include when a hearing officer orders such an evaluation or the parent requests the outside evaluation and the district either agrees to the cost or files a due process notice to defend the district's current evaluation (Murdick et al., 2014).
SLD – Specific Learning Disability	In 2004, the IDEA changed the manner in which students are identified as students with an SLD. Districts are no longer required to utilize the discrepancy model whereby students are tested to determine if there is a significant discrepancy between ability and achievement in the areas of oral expression, listening comprehension, written expression, basic reading skill, reading comprehension, mathematical calculation, or reasoning. Districts now have the option to consider whether the child responds to scientific, research-based interventions. Those who do not can be considered to be eligible for special education as a child with an SLD (Osborne, 2006).

CASE 1 – CONTINUUM OF SERVICES

Background

This case study involves an eight-year-old male student born prematurely. Parents reported the student underwent numerous serious surgeries and now suffers from cognitive deficits, attention deficit hyperactivity disorder (ADHD), oppositional defiance disorder (ODD), gastroesophageal reflux disease, and chronic lung disease. The student received early intervention services to address issues with walking, talking, eating, self-regulating, accepting touch and affection, and understanding the world around him. The student's parents provided private education for the student from early childhood through the first grade.

During the middle of the student's first grade school year, the parents met with the private school staff due to increasing concerns with the student's deteriorating behaviors and the ability of the private school to provide an effective program in light of those behaviors. The staff described the student's behaviors as increased anger towards the student's peers, which precipitated anger from his peers in return. The student disrupted the class and could not work independently or calm himself down.

The student displayed vocal and physical outbursts during class and circle time. The student demonstrated difficulty with sitting and reading quietly on an individual basis. Overall, the student had considerable difficulties with dysregulation. Thus, the private school staff indicated to the parents they could not provide effective programming for the upcoming second grade year. The private school staff recommended that the parents provide the student with a smaller class size, a reduced teacher to student ratio, and recommended a classroom staffed by highly trained special education teachers to meet the needs of the student.

When the parents enrolled the student in the public school district where the parents and student resided, the district explained they had recently adopted a full inclusion policy for all grade school students. As a result, the district administration determined the student would be served in a regular division classroom of 19 students with two teachers and a paraprofessional. The teachers included a certified second grade teacher and a certified special education teacher. The district made the determination based on a review of the student's records and prior to conducting a full IEP team meeting to review the student's records and consider placement options appropriate for the student's individual needs. As a result, the parents placed the student unilaterally in a private therapeutic day school, filed a due process complaint, and sought tuition reimbursement from the district.

During the due process proceedings, evidence included the following facts. As a result of the district's decision to pursue a concept of full inclusion, the district failed to offer any district programs for students with specific learning disabilities (SLDs) or emotional concerns, the district's director determined the student's placement in the inclusion classroom prior to the IEP team meeting, and the IEP team failed to consider alternate placements for the student, but rather affirmed the administration's decision to offer the needed services within the structure of the regular classroom. Additionally, at least one other student in the student's proposed regular education classroom also displayed special needs. This student displayed significant levels and degrees of behaviors related to complex disabilities and caused regular disruptions to the classroom. Once the IEP team finally met, the team members only focused on the single issue of the student's need to be with typically developing peers, but failed to demonstrate any meaningful consideration for the significantly complex and varied academic, speech/language, occupational therapy (OT), vision, and social emotional development needs of the student. The student's lengthy and substantive school records reflected the student's significant and complex needs. Despite this, the IEP called for delivery of many of the student's related services in the second grade regular classroom environment.

The IEP team recommended this placement in spite of the universal view of the educated professionals who worked with the student for the previous five years. This universal view of the student's dysregulation issues included the view of the current district staff who served him during the early childhood program a few years earlier. The student's records from the previous five years reflected that the student required a smaller and more controlled classroom environment to succeed.

Requirements of the IDEA and the Courts

Among other requirements, the IEP must reflect "how the child's disability affects the child's involvement and progress in the general education curriculum ..., articulate measurable educational goals, and must specify the nature of the special services that the school will provide" (See 34 CFR 300.320(a)(1)(i)). The IDEA further requires that students first be assessed in all areas of expected disability. Next, and based on the assessment and other required factors for consideration, develop an appropriate and timely IEP. The IEP team, in conjunction with parental input, should then determine the most appropriate program of services and supports and the location or "placement" for those programs and services. When considering the "appropriate placement," IDEA requires schools and districts to "ensure that a continuum of alternative placements is available to meet the needs of children with disabilities for special education and related services" (34 CFR 300.320(a)(1)(i)).

The IDEA also requires "The continuum required in paragraph (a) of this section must include the alternative placements listed in the definition of special education under Sec. 300.38 (instruction in regular classes, special classes, special schools, home instruction, and instruction in hospitals and institutions); and make provision for supplementary services (such as resource room or itinerant instruction) to be provided in conjunction with regular class placement" ((34 CFR §300.115(a)(b)). Courts have also affirmed these requirements. The DC Court in *Gellert* ruled for the parents in a due process proceeding and stated "finding a denial of FAPE where district insisted that small class size was not required for student with emotional disturbance, yet failed to show that [the student in the case] could receive FAPE without the specific accommodations of small class size and a quiet, calm learning environment" (*Gellert v. D.C. Pub. Sch.*).

The student's records clearly detailed and documented the student's varied needs. Because the student displayed significant and complex impairments, that required specialized instruction, or modifications and supports, in all academic areas, including speech/language, OT, social/emotional development, and vision, the IDEA expects and requires that the student receive services in a more specialized approach than offered by the district.

The district in this instance chose to focus on the single issue of the student's purported need to be with his typically developing peers. This "one-size-fits-all" policy required the student to adapt to the District's program. This is a clear mistake since IDEA demands the opposite. The statutes require districts adapt programs and services to meet the needs of the student. As a result, this district failed to ensure a continuum of placement options that the IEP team could consider in order to meet the complex needs identified in the student's records and previous IEPs. As a result, the parents won the due process complaint and they were awarded full tuition reimbursement for the remainder of second grade and all of third grade. The reviewing court affirmed the award and ruled "that the district's strategy of assigning all students with disabilities to general education classrooms '[took] mainstreaming a step too far'" (*Evanston vs. Luca J. et al.*).

Implications for School Leaders

The principal of this student should have worked cooperatively with the special education administrator and invited key staff from the student's private school to attend the student's placement IEP. The private school staff could then have informed the principal and special education administrator and other IEP team members of the student's complex disabilities and how those disabilities manifested in the classroom. If the principal and special education administrator had a better understanding of the legal requirements of the IDEA, they would have recognized that the student's complex needs could not be met in an inclusion classroom.

By involving the parents and private facility staff in the IEP decision-making process, the principal and special education administrator would have enabled the IEP team to make a placement decision that was more consistent with the requirements of the IDEA. The process would have likely made arrangements to place the child in a smaller, more self-contained classroom with specialized staff and services designed to meet the unique needs of the student, rather than asking the student to adjust or adapt to a district policy. By communicating with the parents and private

facility staff who knew the student best, and either seeking legal advice earlier in the process, or researching the issues independently, the school leaders could have avoided a lengthy and costly due process experience that
would then have saved the district tens of thousands of dollars in man
hours and legal fees.

CASE 2 – THE IDEA ILLINOIS REGULATIONS AND SERVICE ANIMALS

Background

This case involves an eight-year-old girl and her new service dog. At young
age, the doctors diagnosed the student with epilepsy. On at least one occa-
sion, the student experienced a seizure and stopped breathing. As a result,
the student's condition was considered life threatening. Thus, the parents
sought out and secured a service dog for the student. The service dog's primary function was to alert adults around the student when the dog sensed
the student was about to experience a seizure.

The parents notified the district towards the end of the first semester of
second grade that the student would have the service dog at the start of the
second semester. The parents and training organization brought the dog to
school for an all school assembly to explain to students and faculty that the
student's service dog was working whenever at school. The assembly fully
explained to the students and faculty the proper way to interact with the
student's service dog. The parents attended school with the student and service dog on two half-day sessions to observe how the student handled the
service dog and to see if there were any problems when at school. There
were none. The bus driver also reported the student and service dog performed well while riding the bus.

The conflict developed when a part-time faculty member (who also had
a physical disability and her own service dog) expressed concerns to the
principal that the student's service dog had not been properly trained. The
disabled teacher was also a service dog and attack dog trainer. The parents
asserted the teacher was upset that the student's service dog had not been
secured through the disabled teacher's training service. The conflict esca-
lated when the student's service dog barked at the teacher's wheelchair
when startled outside of the teacher's classroom. From that point, the
teacher made continuous demands with the school's principal that the

student's service dog be banned from the facility. At one point, the teacher threatened to call the police if the dog came on the school's premises again. As a result of the controversy and the inability of the school's administrators to secure a resolution, the faculty also became divided with one camp supporting the teacher with the disability and the other camp supporting the student and her service dog.

While the district administration (principal, special education coordinator, and superintendent) had interactions with the parents, teacher, student, and service animal, they were unable to put into place a plan to resolve the issues. Even though the parent had provided the district with prior notice of the service animal's arrival, the district did not convene an IEP team to discuss how the service animal should be treated as part of the student's specialized programming and services. Additionally, the district did not have a policy in place to guide the administration on the integration of a service animal into the school setting. As a result of the conflict, the parents unilaterally enrolled the student in a private school and demanded through a due process complaint that the district pay for the costs of the private placement. The impartial hearing officer awarded the student and the parents the requested tuition payments and ordered the district to reimburse the parents accordingly.

Requirements of the IDEA and the Courts

As described by the U.S. Supreme Court, the IEP is a comprehensive statement of the educational needs of a child with a disability and the specially designed instruction and related services a district will employ to meet those needs (*Burlington Sch. Comm. v. Massachusetts Dept. of Educ.*). As part of providing a student with FAPE, the IDEA defines when a school must provide a student with appropriate accommodations and modifications in the IEP; Illinois statutes define a student's eligibility to have a service dog; and the Illinois Criminal Code defines what qualifies as a service animal:

> Review and revision of IEPs—(1) General. Each public agency must ensure that, subject to paragraphs (b)(2) and (b)(3) of this section, the IEP Team—(i) Reviews the child's IEP periodically, but not less than annually, to determine whether the annual goals for the child are being achieved; and (ii) Revises the IEP, as appropriate, to address ... (C) Information about the child provided to, or by, the parents, as described under §300.305(a)(2); (D) The child's anticipated needs; or (E) Other matters (34 CFR §300.324(b)).

With regard to providing appropriate accommodations and modifications, the IDEA requires "(4) A statement of the special education and related services and supplementary aids and services, based on peer-reviewed research to the extent practicable, to be provided to the child, or on behalf of the child, and a statement of the program modifications or supports for school personnel that will be provided to enable the child – (i) To advance appropriately toward attaining the annual goals; (ii) To be involved in and make progress in the general education curriculum in accordance with paragraph (a)(1) of this section, and to participate in extracurricular and other nonacademic activities; and (iii) To be educated and participate with other children with disabilities and nondisabled children in the activities described in this section" (34 CFR §300.320). Finally, the IDEA provides that districts provide students with "related services" which means transportation and such developmental, corrective, and other supportive services as are required to assist a child with a disability to benefit from special education (*34 CFR §300.34*).

The IDEA also defines each of the listed related services and describes what those services include. The list of related services spelled out in *34 CFR §300.34* is illustrative and is not exhaustive. Related services may include other developmental, corrective, or supportive services if they are required to assist a child with a disability to benefit from special education (34 CFR §300.305(a)(i-iii)).

The statutes of Illinois (where this case was reviewed) require that "Service animals such as guide dogs, signal dogs or any other animal individually trained to perform tasks for the benefit of a student with a disability shall be permitted to accompany that student at all school functions, whether in or outside the classroom. For the purposes of this Section, 'service animal' has the same meaning as in Section 48-8 of the Criminal Code of 2012" (ILCS 105/14-6.02). The Illinois Criminal Code defines service animal as "a dog or miniature horse trained or being trained as a hearing animal, a guide animal, assistance animal, a seizure alert animal ..." (ILCS 720 5/48-8). Additionally, the Code of Federal Regulations requires that "a public entity shall modify its policies, practices, or procedures to permit the uses of a service animal by an individual with a disability" (28 CFR §35.136).

The Court in *Rowley* (*Board of Educ. Of the Hendrick Hudson Cent. Sch. Dist. v. Rowley*) established a two-prong test for the provision of FAPE for a student. The first prong stipulates that schools and districts must first follow the rules of the IDEA. If the finding includes such a determination, then the school or district must provide a program and specialized services that are reasonably calculated to enable the student to receive educational benefit. Furthermore, the Seventh Circuit has ruled that any finding of procedural error can only constitute a denial of FAPE if the error(s) (1) impeded the child's right to FAPE; (2) significantly impeded the parents' opportunity to participate in the decision making process regarding the provision of FAPE to the parents' child; or (3) caused a deprivation of educational benefits (*Board of Educ. Of Township High School District No. 211 v. Ross*).

Finally, the Seventh Circuit decided a similar case and ruled: "A single provision in the Illinois School Code undermined a district's efforts to keep a 6-year-old boy with autism from bringing his dog to school. Determining that the dog qualified as a 'service animal' despite its alleged failure to respond to commands or provide the child with necessary assistance, the Illinois Appellate Court held that the child could bring the dog to all school functions. The court indicated that the decision turned on the plain language of Section 14-6.02 of the school code. That provision states that a district must permit service animals such as guide dogs, signal dogs, or any other animal trained to perform tasks for the benefit of a student with a disability to accompany the student at all school functions, whether inside or outside of the classroom."

"Despite the inevitable impact a service animal's presence at school will have on a student's individualized education program, the School Code requires school districts to admit the service animal with the student so long as the animal meets the definition set forth in Section 14-6.02" (*K.D., by and through his Parents v. Villa Grove CUSD #30*). As a result, the district failed to implement Illinois regulations and failed to develop an IEP that included appropriate provisions for integrating the child's service dog in the school and the child's IEP specialized programs and services.

Implications for School Leaders

The school administrators in this case included the principal, superintendent, and special education administrator. The principal failed to get out in front of the controversy that ensued when the part-time faculty member expressed concerns about the student's service dog. In essence, there were two distinct disability rights knocking against each other. The part-time music teacher's *Americans with Disabilities Act* rights and the student's IDEA rights conflicted in this situation. While some provisions were made to prepare students for the addition of a service dog to the school, none were made for teachers and paraprofessionals. Because the district failed to convene an IEP team to discuss how the service animal should be treated as part of the student's specialized programming and services, teachers had no basis upon which to evaluate the part-time teacher's complaints or concerns about the student's service dog. Administrators did not have appropriate leverage when dealing with the complaining part-time music teacher because provisions for the student's service dog were not included in the IEP.

The resulting controversy could have been avoided if the principal had worked with the special education administrator and other educators involved in the student's program. Additionally, the district did not have a policy in place to guide the administration on the integration of a service animal into the school setting. The superintendent and special education administrator would have better served the district by providing the necessary conditions for the board of education to develop and adopt a policy on service animals. Such a policy could have also provided the principal with the necessary administrative procedures needed to deal effectively with the integration of the student's service animal into the school setting.

As it happened, the court of public opinion created conditions that the parents believed were detrimental to the child. The district then suffered the resulting liability by not meeting both appropriate legal standards and implementing those standards in a manner that gave direction for both the part-time music teacher's concerns and the integration of the student's service animal into the school setting.

CASE 3 – THE IDEA AND THE MULTIDETERMINATION REVIEW PROCESS

Background

This case involved a student aged 16 years and 7 months who was a junior in high school. The IEP team identified the student as having an SLD and other health impairment due to ADHD. The student expressed concern over a big test that had been approaching and talked with some classmates who also had ADHD. They told him that their prescription for Ritalin helped them focus on test day. So he asked if he could borrow one tablet for the upcoming test. His classmate gave him two tablets. He took the prescribed one tablet on test day and gave the other one away to another student who also had a test coming up.

The student performed satisfactorily on the test. However, during the exchange at school, a teacher observed him giving the pill to the other student. The school suspended him for distributing drugs on campus and the district's no tolerance policy meant he would be recommended to the board of education for expulsion. In the meantime, the district placed the student on homebound instruction for the remaining four weeks of the school year and provided the student with a computerized curriculum. The student's special education teacher visited the home each day for one hour of specialized services consistent with the student's current IEP.

Shortly after the homebound instruction began, the student experienced a severe emotional episode that required a two-day hospitalization. After being discharged from the hospital, the medical team recommended that the school meet with the discharge nurse, the parents, and student to discuss best practice for returning the student to school and addressing his emotional concerns. On the morning of the student's return to school, the parents were informed that they were to first meet with the assistant principal about the drug incident to hear the student's side of the story. The student readily admitted what he had done and explained he was only trying to ensure his performance on the math exam. He further explained that he had wanted his parents to try medication to help with his ADHD, but they had been resistive to any medications. He acknowledged giving the additional pill to the other student but also thought he was simply helping that student as he believed he had been helped.

The school authorities then met with the parents and hospital discharge nurse (the nurse attended the meeting via telephone) to discuss the hospital's recommendations for the student's emotional health. Then, the district informed the parents they would move right into the manifestation determination review (MDR) to discuss whether the drug incident was a manifestation of the student's disability prior to recommendation for expulsion. At the MDR, the attendees included the parents and the student (who again confirmed his responsibility and reasons for his behavior), the assistant principal, the school nurse, and the guidance counselor. The district did not provide any prior notice of the meeting, and the parents testified they thought the meeting was just a continuation of the hospital transition meeting due to the presence of the nurse and the lack of any other teacher participants. The MDR determined the student's behaviors were not a manifestation of his disability and, over the parents' objections, recommended the student's expulsion. The parents filed a due process complaint thereby effecting stay put during the duration of the due process proceedings.

Requirements of the IDEA and Illinois Regulations

The statutes and case law that cover this decision include those related to the interim alternative educational setting (IAES) (34 CFR §300.530(g)), MDR (34 CFR §300.530), proper notice as it relates to IEP team meetings to consider a change of placement, proper notice to provide parents the opportunity to prepare to participate (34 CFR §300.503(a)(1)), and the makeup of an IEP team (34 CFR §300.321). The IDEA provides that school personnel may remove a student to an IAES for not more than 45 school days without regard to whether the behavior is determined to be a manifestation of the child's disability, if the child (1) carries a weapon to or possesses a weapon at school, on school premises, or to or at a school function under the jurisdiction of an state educational agency (SEA) or an LEA; (2) knowingly possesses or uses illegal drugs, or sells or solicits the sale of a controlled substance, while at school, on school premises, or at a school function under the jurisdiction of an SEA or an LEA; or (3) has inflicted serious bodily injury upon another person while at school, on school premises, or at a school function under the jurisdiction of an SEA or an LEA (34 CFR §300.530(g)). The hearing officer ruled that the district correctly followed the procedures for providing the student with an IAES.

The MDR is an evaluation of a child's misconduct to determine whether that conduct is a manifestation of the child's disability. It must be performed when a district proposes disciplinary measures that will result in the change of placement for a child with a disability (34 CFR §300.530(e)). The MDR analysis must be performed within 10 school days of "any decision to change the placement of a child with a disability because of a violation of a code of student conduct" (34 CFR 300.530(e)). A change in placement occurs when the removal is for more than 10 consecutive school days, the child has been subjected to a series of removals that constitute a pattern of behaviors because the series of removals total more than 10 school days in a year; the child's behavior is substantially similar to the child's behavior in previous incidents that resulted in the series of removals; and such additional factors as the length of each removal, the total amount of time the child has been removed and the proximity of the removals to one another (34 §CFR 300.536). The MDR should be conducted by the district, the parent, and relevant members of the IEP team (as determined by the parent and the district) (34 §CFR 300.530(c)).

The district failed to provide the appropriate members of the MDR team. Pursuant to 34 CFR 300.530(e)(1), conduct must be found to be a manifestation of the child's disability if (1) the conduct in question was caused by or had a direct and substantial relationship to the child's disability or (2) the conduct in question was the direct result of the (district's) failure to implement the IEP. The MDR must involve a review of "all the relevant information in the (child's) file, including the child's IEP, any teacher observations, and any relevant information provided by the parents" (34 §CFR 300.530(e)).

If the MDR reveals that the conduct was a manifestation of the child's disability, the IEP team must (1) conduct a functional behavioral assessment,... or, if a behavioral intervention plan already has been developed, review the behavioral intervention plan, and modify it, as necessary, to address the behavior; and (2) return the child to the placement from which the child was removed, unless the parent and the district agree to a change of placement as part of the modification of the behavioral intervention plan (34 §CFR 300.530(f)). The IDEA requires districts to notify parents anytime an IEP meeting is to be conducted and the notice must indicate the purpose, time, and location of the meeting and who will be in attendance (*34 CFR 300.321*). Illinois regulations require districts provide a notice to parents at least 10 days prior to the implementation of any IEP (Ill Admin Code §226.220(a)).

Finally, the IDEA requires that districts ensure that an IEP team for a child with a disability includes (1) the parents of the child; (2) not less than one general education teacher of the child (if the child is or may be participating in the general education environment); (3) not less than one special education teacher of the child, or, where appropriate, not less than one special education provider of the child; (4) a district representative who (i) is qualified to provide, or supervise the provision of, specially designed instruction to meet the unique needs of children with disabilities, (ii) is knowledgeable about the general education curriculum, and (iii) is knowledgeable about the availability of district resources; (5) an individual who can interpret the instructional implications of evaluation results, (6) at the discretion of the parent or the district, other individuals who have knowledge or special expertise regarding the child, including related services personnel as appropriate; and (7) whenever appropriate, the child (*34 CFR 300.321*(a)).

Since the district erred in the MDR determination, failed to provide the appropriate IEP team participants, failed to provide the parent with proper notice regarding the purpose of the meeting and those who would be in attendance, and failed to include the child's special education teacher and a regular education teacher with knowledge of the student, the district could not possibly make an accurate determination as to the antecedent of the student's behavior. Thus, the district erred in determining the student's behavior was not a manifestation of the student's disability. Therefore, the recommendation for an expulsion was voided and the hearing officer ordered the student returned to the child's stay put placement. The district was also required to complete a functional behavior assessment and develop a behavior intervention plan for the student.

Implications for School Leaders

The assistant principal in this case clearly did not follow the requirements of IDEA rules and procedures required for all students with an IEP in the disciplinary process. The meeting with the hospital representative to discuss the student's social emotional needs from the perspective of the student's most recent hospitalization was conducted appropriately. At that point, the assistant principal should have informed the parents of the need to conduct the MDR, identify which staff members would be most appropriate to participate, and schedule the MDR meeting for another day. If time was of the essence, the assistant principal could have sought a waiver of the 10-day notice requirement and scheduled the MDR meeting within the next several days provided the parents were in agreement. The assistant principal also should have identified a regular educator and special educator familiar with the student and his needs so the team completing the MDR could have considered important information about the student from the perspective of these educators.

The student suffered from ADHD. Students who are impacted by ADHD frequently act on impulse and fail to consider the consequences of their actions. It is likely that both the regular educator and special educator would have raised this fact during the MDR. Doing so would have provided the MDR team the information needed to conclude the student's disability likely caused him to both use the drug on campus as well as distribute the drug to the other student before the student fully considered the consequences of his actions. Thus, the MDR team should have concluded the student's behaviors were directly related to the student's disability and discipline of any type was not appropriate for this particular student.

If in doubt, the assistant principal should have collaborated with the district's special education administrator and/or deferred the handling of the MDR to the special education office. It is likely the special education administrator would have provided the parent with the proper notice or secured the required waiver of the 10-day notice before conducting the MDR. It is also likely the special education administrator would have included the appropriate MDR team members thereby increasing the likelihood that the MDR team functioned appropriately. Once the MDR team determined the student's conduct was a manifestation of the student's disability, the MDR team could have referred the matter to the full IEP team for the completion of a functional behavior analysis and development of a behavior intervention plan based on that analysis and implemented the same for the student.

Collaboration between the assistant principal and special education administrator would have avoided the messy expulsion, lost educational time for the student, and significant attorney's fees incurred by the board of education as a result of losing the due process complaint. The district had to pay the board of education legal team to defend the administrator's decision making and had to pay the parent's legal costs as a result of the parent prevailing at the due process hearing. In this case, the district's legal costs for both sets of attorneys exceeded a quarter of a million dollars.

ADMINISTRATOR RESPONSIBILITIES FOR STUDENTS WITH DISABILITIES AND THEIR FAMILIES

As demonstrated in these three cases, knowledge of the law related to special education students and their families, clear communication skills, and effective collaborations with educators and agencies involved with students with an IEP are absolutely essential. The consequences for the student, his/her family, the school community, and school district are detrimental to all in terms of lost educational opportunities for the student, distraction from the processes of teaching and learning by educators, and often significant financial reparations incurred by districts when an IEP student's rights are violated. We turn now to illustrate how effective administrators handle responsibilities with students with an IEP, their families, and programs.

Knowledge of special education law, effective communication, and collaboration are absolutely necessary but not sufficient for school administrators who lead excellent special education programs. Ethical responsibilities compel principals, special education coordinators, and superintendents to hold high expectations for themselves and others so that all students with IEPs receive the requisite opportunities to achieve to the maximum extent appropriate.

"Increasingly, value conflicts have become a defining characteristic of school administration, thereby promoting interest in the study of values and ethical decision-making" (Begley, 1999, p. 318). It is precisely these conditions under which administrators distinguish themselves as either compliance driven or ethically driven. The values and ethics of leaders centers on the moral purpose of leadership (Fullan, 2003; Sergiovanni, 1992) which in turn is concerned with right and wrong, serving the common good, and developing a common sense of purpose (Furman, 2003; Sergiovanni, 1992, 1994). "Moral leadership involves much more than compliance towards bureaucratic rules or authorities. Moral leadership requires thoughtful consideration of the value, meaning, and purpose of schooling to meet increasingly diverse and complex challenges in a pluralistic society" (Lyman, Ashby, & Tripses, 2005, p. 119).

Moral leadership or ethics can seem esoteric and fine for scholarly discussion but unrealistic in the complex world of school administrators. However, those administrators whose moral compass and integrity are grounded in strong beliefs that all children deserve an education that meets their needs will employ values when working with others to resolve conflicts related to providing services to students with an IEP. In practical terms, this means that an administrator who is ethically grounded will not only be knowledgeable about laws related to special education, but will also seek out other professionals who take seriously their responsibility to keep up to date on school law.

A strong ethical foundation compels an administrator to ensure that everyone involved with special education students is well informed about legal requirements and local efforts to meet those requirements. The principal, special education administrator, and superintendent then would ask subordinates to share the processes of communication including newsletters, notices of IEP meetings, and parent involvement efforts.

The principal in most cases is the administrator most familiar with students with an IEP, educational environment in the classroom, and families. This familiarity provides ample opportunities to hold high expectations for classroom instruction, quality of IEP meetings, problem solving as inevitable issues arise, and expectations that other faculty members engage fully in providing appropriate learning conditions for the student. Responsible principals will proactively model partnerships with parents based on high expectations and mutual respect grounded upon the principle that educators know how to provide the best educational program and parents know their child. Other educators will also be expected to develop and maintain partnerships with parents. Responsible principals establish clear expectations with all educators and support staff about necessary adaptations for IEP students and follow up to ensure plans put in place are implemented with integrity. Finally, the responsible principal recognizes his/her responsibility to consult with and work closely with the special education administrator. The principal's responsibility to consult with the superintendent immediately at the first sign of a conflict with other faculty or families regarding a placement, discipline, or services involving a student with an IEP cannot be overestimated.

The special education director is frequently the "problem solver" when it comes to addressing the most complex and thorny issues that frequently present themselves when educating children with disabilities. Typically, the special education director leads one or more service teams (i.e., school psychologist and social worker) who then work directly with the special education teachers and related service providers (i.e., speech and language pathologist, occupational therapist, physical therapist, and assistive technology specialist) to provide services to students with an IEP and their families.

The superintendent is critical to establish a strong culture of high expectations for all students and educators. The superintendent's role in most cases is to ensure that processes are in place to hire and oversee other administrators who are knowledgeable about special education law and practices and who hold themselves and others to high standards of providing each student with a quality education. The superintendent is the focal leader and, as such, must also ensure that students with an IEP receive the programs and services they are entitled to by federal and state regulations. Superintendents who understand this responsibility think in terms of doing what is best for the student rather than what is best for the organization. Anytime a school leader makes a decision that is in the best interest of the student, it is difficult to make the wrong decision.

The ideal organizational model includes a superintendent of schools, principal(s), and special education director (or other special education administrator) who are all well versed in both the requirements of the law and the pedagogy of teaching children with disabilities. The key components are the principal(s) and special education director. The special education administrator leads and coordinates the regular education and special education staff and administrators in the process of identifying, developing, and implementing programs for students with disabilities.

Successful administrators ensure that procedures and policies are followed for students with an IEP. Collaborations with others involved with special education students will be nurtured in order to meet the needs of such students. In practical terms, it means the administrators will work together and stay the course in situations when parents and educators have differing opinions about a child's IEP. In the words of the now retired superintendent Carol Struck, "All people have valuable input. They have a different perspective that can help you view a problem from a different angle, from different life experiences. Rarely ever is input worthless" (Lyman et al., 2005, p. 135).

Successful administrators strive to work with all constituents to achieve the vision "What can we do together to make this school the best possible place for children to learn and faculty to work?" Making this vision a reality requires the special education director and special education coordinators (special education administrator similar to a principal) to work collaboratively with school principals and unit office administrators to advocate for those students with IEPs who cannot advocate for themselves.

The most important responsibility for the team is to ensure the appropriate data and best practices are consistently shared with the IEP team members to provide a lawful IEP to each student that provides that the student receives some educational benefit. This problem-solving and collaboration approach is critical to the success of any administrator (Leithwood & Steinbach, 1995). It becomes even more important for the special education administrator or director as the students these administrators oversee are very typically the students who cannot self-advocate, who are dependent on others for their own individual success, and who are frequently shunned or shut out by the mainstream population of the school if efforts are not made to provide for these students with an IEP.

CONCLUSION

Principals, superintendents, and special education administrators committed to the vision to make their school the best possible place for children to learn and faculty to work understand their advocacy role for all children, but in particular, those children most in need of support. Quality education happens when administrators are well qualified in their particular area and grounded in the moral obligation to provide that *all* students under the care of an administrative team receive quality education, including students whose abilities fall outside the mainstream. Equally important are the capacity and commitment to respect contributions of other professionals and the family while at the same time holding self and others to high standards of accountability. Gone are the days when principals would say a special education teacher "really cares about those kids" with little to no consideration given to whether or not the students learned. Often behind the scenes, effective administrators work together to ensure that care for IEP students and their families involves also ensuring the student learns to his/her potential. Nothing less will do.

REFERENCES

Bateman, C., & Bateman, D. (2015). Special education's hotspot: The principalship. *Principal Leadership, 15*(6), 19–21.

Begley, P. (1999). Values, preferences, ethics, and conflicts in school administration. In P. Begley (Ed.), *Values and educational leadership* (pp. 237–254). Albany, NY: State University of New York Press.

English, F., Papa, R., Mullen, C., & Creighton, T. (2012). *Educational leadership at 2050: Conjectures, challenges, and promises.* New York, NY: Rowman & Littlefield Education.

Fullan, M. (2003). *The moral imperative of school leadership.* Thousand Oaks, CA: Corwin Press.

Furman, G. (2003). The 2002 UCEA presidential address. *UCEA Review, 45*(1), 1–6.

Individuals with Disabilities Education Act 20 USC 1400 (IDEA).

Leithwood, K., & Steinbach, L. (1995). *Expert problem solving: Evidence from school and district leaders.* Ontario: Ontario Institute for Studies in Education.

Lyman, L., Ashby, D., & Tripses, J. (2005). *Leaders who dare: Pushing the boundaries.* Lanham, MD: Rowman & Littlefield Education.

Murdick, N., Gartin, B., & Fowler, G. (2014). *Special education law.* Boston, MA: Pearson.

Osborne, A. G., Jr. (2006). *Special education and the law.* Thousand Oaks, CA: Corwin Press.

Sanders, M. G., & Sheldon, S. B. (2009). *Principals matter: A guide to school, family, and community partnerships.* Thousand Oaks, CA: Corwin Press.

Sergiovannis, T. (1992). *Moral leadership: Getting to the heart of school improvement.* San Francisco, CA: Jossey Bass.

Sergiovanni, T. (1994). *Building community in schools.* San Francisco, CA: Jossey Bass.

CHAPTER 7

ROLES OF RELATED PROFESSIONALS IN SPECIAL EDUCATION

Stacey Jones Bock and Christy Borders

ABSTRACT

Roles of special education-related service professionals have changed since the passage of P.L. 94-142. Many children are spending a majority of their day in the general education classroom, however services can be delivered in a variety of settings ranging from the general education classroom to a one-on-one setting. Professionals deliver services based upon the educationally necessary model, which is determined by members of the Individualized Education Program team. Regardless of where services are delivered, when there are multiple related service professionals on a child's educational team, there is a great deal of collaboration and communication required. A basic framework for ensuring this occurs includes selecting a key communication person or case manager, striving for clarity in communication, setting a schedule for consistent check-ins, removing discipline jargon, and communicating what is important to parents.

Keywords: Related service; educationally necessary; collaboration

Interdisciplinary Connections to Special Education: Important Aspects to Consider
Advances in Special Education, Volume 30A, 119–129
Copyright © 2015 by Emerald Group Publishing Limited
All rights of reproduction in any form reserved
ISSN: 0270-4013/doi:10.1108/S0270-40132015000030A005

ROLES OF RELATED PROFESSIONALS IN SPECIAL EDUCATION

The landscape of special education has changed over the past 40 years. The roles of related professionals have also changed, with the majority of children with disabilities spending the majority of their day in the general education classroom (OSERS, 2014). Initial integration of related service professionals involved a pullout model where the child would leave the special education classroom and go to a further segregated setting for therapy. Today, related service professionals are often integrated throughout the child's day. This level of integration in educational programming warrants intensive collaboration among all educational team members. This chapter will review the law that provides the foundation for related services, cover broadly defined roles of related service professionals, discuss issues related to educational necessity, and provide a framework for collaboration and communication of the educational team.

RELATED SERVICE MANDATES

Related services were first mandated when the Education for All Handicapped Children's Act (P.L. 94-142) was signed into law in 1975. P.L. 94-142 specifically assured that all children with disabilities had available to them a free and appropriate public education. It included the concept of related services; other services determined educationally necessary in order to benefit from special education. At that time, the term related service was defined as "transportation and such developmental, corrective, and other supportive services (including speech pathology and audiology, psychological services, physical and occupational therapy, recreation, and medical and counseling services, except that such medical services shall be for diagnostic and evaluation purposes only) as may be required to assist a handicapped child to benefit from special education, and includes the early identification and assessment of handicapping conditions in children" (P.L. 94-142).

Current law, the Individuals with Disabilities Education Improvement Act (2004), kept the core structure of P.L. 94-142 in place; however, there were a few additions that reflect changes in society. For instance, there have been several technological advances in society that have directly impacted the disability community. One such societal change that is reflected in the mandate is the clarification of supports related to cochlear implants. Cochlear implants were rudimentary and only initially studied when P.L. 94-142 was passed but now there are over 200,000 individuals in the United States implanted with cochlear devices. Thus, cochlear implants are specifically addressed within the revised definition and examples of supports are specifically covered as well some areas such as medical costs are excluded (Apling & Jones, 2005).

> Related services means transportation and such developmental, corrective, and other supportive services as are required to assist a child with a disability to benefit from special education, and includes speech-language pathology and audiology services, interpreting services, psychological services, physical and occupational therapy, recreation, including therapeutic recreation, early identification and assessment of disabilities in children, counseling services, including rehabilitation counseling, orientation and mobility services, and medical services for diagnostic or evaluation purposes. Related services also include school health services and school nurse services, social work services in schools, and parent counseling and training. Exception; services that apply to children with surgically implanted devices, including cochlear implants. Related services do not include a medical device that is surgically implanted, the optimization of that device's functioning (e.g., mapping), maintenance of that device, or the replacement of that device. (Individuals with Disabilities Education Improvement Act, 2004, § 2658)

The law does not define or describe the scope and practice of a related service; rather it merely provides a list of services. It is up to the child's Individualized Education Program (IEP) team to decide which related services are necessary. Professionals that have extensive education, licensure, and expertise in the related service area often provide the services. However, in some states, law provides for trained and supervised paraprofessionals or assistants to provide the related service. Table 1 provides a list related service professionals and examples of services that might be provided in a school setting.

Some related service areas such as speech-language pathology, audiology, and physical therapy have specific professional organizations outlining recommendations and, in some cases, guidelines for service provision and specific responsibilities related to the roles in educational settings. Most related service providers' licensures allow for service delivery across the life span. For example, an audiologist can serve young children all the way through adulthood. Therefore, provision within the school setting is often guided by recommendations put forth by the professional organization.

Inclusive practices in educational settings have led to more inclusive practices with related services. However, related service professionals still provide services on a continuum as provided for by law (see Fig. 1). Professionals may provide services in a pullout setting through one-on-one therapy all the way to dual therapies with a small group in the inclusive environment. An example of dual therapy with a small group would

Table 1.   Related Service Professionals and Functions.

Related Service Provider	Example Services
Speech-Language Pathology (SLP)	Provide services to individuals or small groups of students who exhibit delays or disabilities related to speech or language
Audiology Services	Perform hearing screenings and tests; set-up audiological equipment for students with hearing loss; monitor progress of students who are deaf/hard of hearing
Interpreting Services	Translate spoken language of the teacher into a visual form of sign language for a student who is deaf/hard of hearing
Psychological Services	Perform tests of achievement, intellectual, social/emotional and/or behavioral ability as a component of diagnosis or for progress monitoring
Physical Therapy	Provide services to individuals in order to allow them to move as independently as possible in the school environment and participate in classroom activities
Occupational Therapy	Provide services to individuals or small groups of students in order to improve their performance of activities throughout the school day, often through building strength related to fine and gross motor skills
Recreation/Therapeutic Recreation	Assess students and create plans to ensure they have the skills necessary to participate in leisure activities
Counseling Services/ Rehabilitation Counseling	Provide guidance to students related to decision-making and self-knowledge as well as assisting students to recognize strengths to guide goal setting for the future
Orientation and Mobility Services	Instruct students with low vision or blindness to safely maneuver through their school environment and to orient to new environments they encounter
Medical Services	Diagnosis or evaluate a student for specific medical conditions
School Health/School Nurse Services	Perform required medical care that may be necessary in order for a student with a disability to attend school
Social Work Services	Group or individual counseling for students who may be struggling in their home or school environment
Parent Counseling and Training	Assist and/or counsel parents to obtain the skills necessary to help carry out the goals in a student's IEP outside of the school environment
Transportation	Provide transportation to and from school, between schools, and in or around schools for all students including those that require specialized equipment

be where the speech-language pathologist and the occupational therapist would come into the classroom during snack time to address all common goals for a child that stretch across both service areas. A benefit of this type of therapy is that the child can practice the skill in the natural environment.

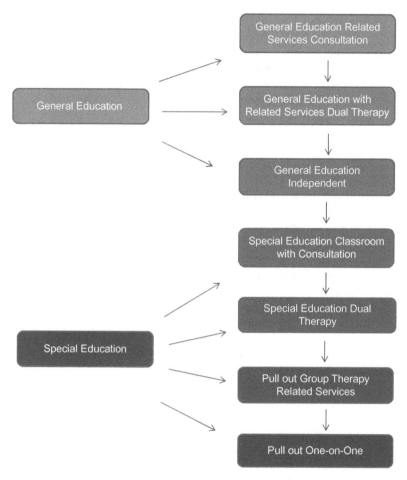

Fig. 1. Continuum of Locations in Which Individuals Can Receive Related Services in the School Setting.

EDUCATIONALLY NECESSARY

The question of whether a related service should be provided can be difficult. The law provides little guidance for the determination or the provision of related services. In fact, the wording used in the law has led to great debates within professional communities and conflicts between parents and their local school districts. Although the report does not indicate the specific area disagreed upon, the *Thirty-sixth Annual Report to Congress on the Implementation of the Individuals with Disabilities Education Act, 2014* reported a large number of complaints recorded for the 2011–2012 school year with 5,013 signed complaints, 17,109 signed due process complaints, and 9,212 mediation requests recorded across the United States. It is likely that some of these conflicts arose due to requests for additional services.

One area of the law that professionals and parents often struggle with is whether the service is *educationally necessary*. Whether a related service is deemed medically necessary or educationally necessary has been the focus of several disputes (U.S. General Accounting Office, 1989). The imprecision of legislative language leaves this difficult determination up to interpretation by the members of the IEP team. Letters from well-meaning physicians requesting additional services from the schools can further complicate the determination. The physicians are often well versed in medical treatments but are often lacking in their knowledge of special education services and law. They may request services for children that they deem medically necessary but those services may not be necessary for a child to benefit from special education.

Leiter and Krauss (2004) conducted an in-depth examination of parental requests for additional related services. While parents are considered a core member of the team, parent participation on the team can be limited by feelings of intimidation (Silverstein, Springer, & Russo, 1992) or fears that questioning will impact services for their child or their relationship with the school (Engle, 1991). Leiter and Krauss (2004) examined data from a national survey and found that only 15% of parents had requested additional services (after the IEP had been established) in the 12 months prior to the survey. The majority of parents surveyed were satisfied (83%) with their child's special education services. Of those parents requesting additional services, a startling 80% reported problems in obtaining those services. "For parents who reported problems obtaining additional services, 60% had children with multiple disabilities, 13% had children who received services in a special setting at school, and 27% had children who received special education services outside of school" (p. 140). Also noted was an association between those parents who pay out of pocket for services and those who reported problems.

COLLABORATION AND COMMUNICATION AMONG EDUCATIONAL TEAM MEMBERS

Special education teachers possess knowledge and skills across a wide range of disabilities, instructional practices, and curricula. However, sometimes the needs of students are beyond the scope of special education training. When a student exhibits a specific need that falls outside the scope of the teacher's skill, it becomes necessary to involve an expert. The expert is the related service professional and children may have multiple related services provided for in their IEP. With the focus of services on incorporation of a student within the inclusive environment, there is a great deal of collaboration and communication required among all the professionals on the team. This can also create an additional challenge when communicating and collaborating with parents.

FRAMEWORK FOR COLLABORATION AND COMMUNICATION

There are many different approaches to collaboration and a variety of different terms used to illustrate nuances in the overall concept. Different terms that may be used include *multidisciplinary*, *cross-disciplinary*, or *collaborative teaming*, to name a few. This chapter will not delineate the differences between the terms but readers should be aware that there are several different frameworks and terms used to express the concept of everyone working together in special education. In order to address the challenges inherent in collaboration and communication, we will present a basic framework that could be easily implemented to ease communication across the team, including with parents and related service professionals. While there are countless strategies that could be employed, we will outline an initial five steps teams should consider taking to improve communication across the team.

SELECT A KEY PERSON FOR COMMUNICATION AMONG ALL TEAM MEMBERS

Case management is large role for special education teachers. In the case of students with complex or multiple learning needs, there may be several team members on the IEP team. It is imperative that the selection of one individual to provide case management occurs so each and every member of the team knows whom to contact with questions and concerns. The most logical person to assume this role is the special education teacher; however, teams may choose a different professional based upon a variety of factors. For instance, if the student spends 80% or more of the day in the general education classroom, then the general education teacher would likely assume the role.

ENSURE CLARITY IN COMMUNICATION

It is often the role of the special education teacher to gather educational updates from related service professionals and share that information with parents. When sharing information from related service professionals with families, teachers should focus not only on transmission of message but also clarity. A few extra minutes spent with the families can assure understanding or enlighten questions the teacher can then express back to the overall team. In many cases, the related service providers may send a report home to the parents. The special educator, as a case manager, cannot simply see this as compliance and move on. They must reach out and contact the parents to check their understanding of the content. The collaboration piece comes into play as the special educator also reads the report and makes connections related to who else on the team could benefit from this same information. For example, if the speech-language pathologist has been working on words ending in "−ly," the general and special educator could be sure to highlight these words during instruction. The occupational and physical therapists could also quite easily add the use of adverbs into their lessons since they are often focusing on having the child perform a task. One can easily see how this collaboration could lead to additional opportunities to respond for the student. Increasing opportunities to respond is a simple approach that often leads to efficiency in meeting goals. This approach also leads to an increased chance that the student will generalize information across settings and individuals. Therefore, not only is communication clear but instruction is enriched across the child's day.

CONSISTENT CHECK-BACKS

Bock, Michalak, and Brownlee (2011) pointed out that one key to successful collaboration is to set guidelines for the team. One such guideline is setting a schedule for meetings and check-ins. Unfortunately, there are many cases in which the IEP team develops a great plan and everyone leaves the meeting only to have communication across the team cease until the next meeting. In order to best meet the needs of the student, the special education teacher has a role of checking back with each provider on the IEP on a consistent schedule. This can lead to the collaboration mentioned above. Time is noted to be one of the most detrimental barriers to effective collaboration (Conderman & Johnston-Rodriguez, 2009; Cook & Friend, 1993; Worrell, 2008). By setting a regular time frame for check-back, the team can ensure ongoing, consistent communication. While a once-per-month check-back may likely be sufficient for most students and teams, it is important to remain flexible with this time line. If a student is struggling in one particular area, that related service provider may need to be contacted more than one time per month. For example, if a child who is deaf changes amplification devices from a hearing aid to a cochlear implant, the audiologist, speech-language pathologist, and teacher of the deaf will need to be contacted more frequently as the child adjusts to new auditory input. Another example of a situation in which increased communication may be required is if a child displays inappropriate behavior. It is important to be aware that difficult situations may lead to professionals or parents shying away from communication. Teams need to approach difficult situations with problem-solving strategies in order to keep the lines of communication consistently open. Problem-solving strategies range from opening team meetings with guidelines that require the meeting to end with meaningful solutions to keeping track of communication using a structured team collaboration report. Difficult situations can often serve to strengthen the bonds of the team when the team handles the situation with open, honest, and consistent communication.

DE-JARGON THE JARGON

Bock et al. (2011) suggested that teachers and professionals simplify the language they use with each other and with the parents. By using jargon in communication with parents and other professionals, isolation of those who do not understand occurs. The purpose behind collaboration is to eradicate confusion and isolation thus making the use of jargon counterproductive. The field of special education and all related professions is full of acronyms and field-specific jargon. While this eases communication among those individuals in that field, it can become a cause of miscommunication or confusion for others. Teachers and related service professionals must strive to remove the jargon. One role the special educator can play is one of the copyeditor in which they ask related service providers to first explain the acronyms in all reports and read reports with the eye of parents in mind. They can read for terms that may be confusing for unfamiliar readers.

CONSIDER AND COMMUNICATE WHAT IS IMPORTANT TO THE PARENTS

Parental perspectives are more readily understood and considered when the relationship established between the parent and teacher is grounded in trust and respect. While a related professional may be focused on the development of a specific skill, the parents' focused energy may be on additional areas or skills, short-term or long-term. The case manager must discuss with each team member the importance of not only communicating progress on discipline-specific goals but also items the parents have mentioned as important to their specific family. This will help to further develop trust across the team and generalization of prioritized skills across environments. Often times, concerns and goals of the parents are not initially explicitly stated. Active listening, appropriate body language, and clear verbal communication can help facilitate clear understanding among team members (Fulk, 2011). Teachers can also spend time and energy learning about the family and their unique desires and dreams for their child (Nabors, 2011).

CONCLUSION

The roles of related service professionals vary by expertise and discipline. Their services are mandated by law and are required, or educationally necessary, for some students with disabilities to benefit from special education. In some states, trained and supervised paraprofessionals can deliver related services such as occupational therapy. Today, many children receive their related services in the inclusive environment, however a continuum is still provided for by law. A child may receive services from one related service professional or more; therefore, it is important to have a case manager in charge of communication among the team and with the family members. If there is a lack of communication among the team members then there is likely a lack of collaboration. Related service professionals should strive for consistent communication with their case managers and the families of the students they serve.

REFERENCES

Apling, R. N., & Jones, N. L. (2005). *Individuals with Disabilities Education Act (IDEA): Analysis of changes made by P. L. 108–446* (Vol. 1). Washington, DC: Congressional Research Services.

Bock, S. J., Michalak, N., & Brownlee, S. (2011). Collaboration and consultation: The first steps. In C. G. Simpson & J. P. Bakken (Eds.), *Collaboration: A multidisciplinary approach to educating students with disabilities* (pp. 3–15). Waco, TX: Prufrock Press.

Conderman, G., & Johnston-Rodriguez, S. (2009). Beginning teachers' views of their collaborative roles. *Preventing School Failure, 53*, 235–244.

Cook, L., & Friend, M. (1993). Educational leadership for teacher collaboration. In B. S. Billingsley, D. Peterson, D. Bodkins, & M. B. Hendricks (Eds.), *Program leadership for serving students with disabilities* (pp. 421–444). Blacksburg, VA: Virginia Polytechnic Institute and State University.

Education for All Handicapped Children Act of 1975, Pub. Law 94-142 (November 29, 1975).

Engle, D. (1991). Law, culture, and children with disabilities: Educational rights and the construction of difference. *Duke Law Journal, 166*, 166–205.

Fulk, B. (2011). Effective communication in collaboration and consultation. In C. G. Simpson & J. P. Bakken (Eds.), *Collaboration: A multidisciplinary approach to educating students with disabilities* (pp. 19–30). Waco, TX: Prufrock Press.

Individuals with Disabilities Education Improvement Act, 20 U.S.C. § 400 et seq. (2004).

Nabors, D. (2011). Working collaboratively with families. In C. G. Simpson & J. P. Bakken (Eds.), *Collaboration: A multidisciplinary approach to educating students with disabilities* (pp. 33–45). Waco, TX: Prufrock Press.

Silverstein, J., Springer, J., & Russo, N. (1992). Involving parents in the special education process. In S. L. Christenson & J. C. Conoley (Eds.), *Home-school collaboration: Enhancing children's academic and social competence* (pp. 383–407). Washington, DC: National Association of School Psychologists.

U.S. Department of Education, Office of Special Education and Rehabilitative Services, Office of Special Education Programs. (2014). *Thirty-sixth annual report to congress on the implementation of the individuals with disabilities education act.* Retrieved from http://www2ed.gov/about/reports/annual/osep/2014/parts-b-c/index.html#download

U.S. General Accounting Office. (1989). *Special education: The attorney fees provision of Public Law 99–372.* Washington, DC: Government Printing Office.

Worrell, J. L. (2008). How secondary schools can avoid the seven deadly sins of inclusion. *American Secondary Education, 36*, 43–56.

CHAPTER 8

ROLES OF PARENTS/FAMILIES/ GUARDIANS

Julia B. Stoner

ABSTRACT

Strong relationships between parents and education professionals benefit all, especially children with disabilities. Parents of children with disabilities were integral to the development of special education, are their children's best advocate, and are the members of the Individual Education Plan team who know the child the best. As education professionals we must strive to develop and maintain a strong relationship with parents and involve them in all aspects of their children's education. This chapter provides an overview of parental rights and the Individuals with Disabilities Education Act (IDEA). The theoretical foundations of parental engagement is discussed and explored. Finally, recommendations are provided for developing and maintaining strong relationships with parents of children with disabilities.

Keywords: Parents of children with disabilities; relationships between parents and education professionals; effective communication with parents of children with disabilities

Interdisciplinary Connections to Special Education: Important Aspects to Consider
Advances in Special Education, Volume 30A, 131–150
Copyright © 2015 by Emerald Group Publishing Limited
All rights of reproduction in any form reserved
ISSN: 0270-4013/doi:10.1108/S0270-40132015000030A006

INTRODUCTION

I clearly remember a very young mother as she entered the room and con-
fronted a strange new world. It was her son's first individualized education
program (IEP) meeting. She was scared, and understandably, seemed reluc-
tant to participate. She spoke hesitatingly and cried. Most striking, she
appeared to be completely overwhelmed by all the information that flew
around the table, as three therapists, a special educator, general educator,
social worker, and the coordinator of the program shared their input and
perspective. Although we tried to make her comfortable we could have
done so much more.

We had her son in our program for 17 years. It was a period of growing
trust, increasingly candid exchanges, and focused engagement around an
accepted, common purpose − the best interests of her son. At the last IEP
meeting, I couldn't help but reflect on how this young mother had changed.
Her confidence had increased. She was knowledgeable about all her son's
therapies, and questioned what she didn't understand. Perhaps most critical
she provided information that was relevant to establishing appropriate
goals and objectives for her son. In short, she had fulfilled her role as an
important member of her son's team. Unfortunately, not all relationships
evolve so positively. Effective communication can give way to stilted
exchanges laden with suspicion and cynicism. Barriers, erected by both the
parent and education professionals, can thwart the path of progress.
Fortunately, with knowledge and implementation of best practices, these
important relationships can strengthen and ultimately benefit children with
disabilities.

I want to be very clear at this point; I am not a parent of a child with a
disability, and I will always have a limited view of that role. However,
much of my research has focused on the relationships between parents/
guardians/families and education professionals. Throughout this chapter I
will refer to the primary caregiver as parent unless the relationship is specifically stipulated (e.g., mother, father, sibling, etc.). I have been privileged
to have spent a large amount of time with parents due to my work in the
public schools, research and consulting. My experiences and research have
provided a glimpse into parents' reality and needs, and has fostered foundational perspectives on how education professionals can forge bonds with
parents.

This chapter is organized to provide a brief overview of parental rights
and the Individuals with Disabilities Education Act (IDEA); the theoretical
foundations of engagement with parents of children with disabilities; and

a summary of recommendations for collaborating with parents. Supporting research will be discussed throughout the chapter.

A BRIEF OVERVIEW OF PARENTAL RIGHTS
AND THE IDEA

Special education exists today because of parents of students with disabilities. In 1972, parents of students with intellectual disabilities, along with the Pennsylvania Association of Retarded Citizens, sued the State of Pennsylvania, requesting a "free and appropriate education" for their children (Pennsylvania Association for Retarded Citizens (PARC) v. Commonwealth of Pennsylvania, 1971, 1972). Following the success of this lawsuit, parents in almost every state won similar suits, thereby guaranteeing their children an education (Turnbull, Turnbull, Erwin, & Soodak, 2006). These lawsuits, along with parental advocacy, led to the passage of The Education for All Handicapped Children Act of 1975, known as Public Law 94-142. Today we refer to this legislation as IDEA. One of the most important aspects of the IDEA is the acknowledgment of parents as educational decision makers (Turnbull et al., 2006). Reviewing the amendments to the IDEA and the specific rights of parents are beyond the scope of this chapter; however the entire IDEA is available online at http://idea. ed.gov/explore/home. In 1997, amendments made to the IDEA focused on strengthening the role of parents and expanding opportunities for parents and key public agency staff (i.e., special educators and related services) to work in new partnerships (Wright & Wright, 1999). The IDEA clearly states that "the parents of a child with a disability are expected to be equal participants along with school personnel, in developing, reviewing, and revising the IEP for their child" (Wright & Wright, 1999, p. 213).

Furthermore, the IDEA stipulated that parents must be involved as team members in *all aspects* of their children's education. This included identifying and evaluating their children for special education; setting goals and making service delivery choices; and making any educational decisions that affected their children (Office of Special Education and Rehabilitation Services [OSERS], 2006). In essence, the IDEA legitimized parents' role in the education of children with disabilities (Turnbull, Turnbull, Shank, & Leal, 1999). Furthermore, parents were identified as serving a key role in effective intervention strategies (Feinberg & Vacca, 2000; Lord & McGee, 2001; Stoner, Meadan, & Angell, 2013). Many see parental involvement as a basic tenet of the special education system (e.g., National Center for Learning Disabilities Inc, 2005; Turnbull et al., 2006). Consequently, education professionals have a legal obligation to foster partnerships with parents of students with disabilities.

THEORETICAL FOUNDATION FOR FOSTERING ROLES WITH PARENTS OF STUDENTS WITH DISABILITIES

The rationale for including parents in their children's education goes beyond compliance with IDEA. In fact, research has indicated that students with disabilities experienced more positive outcomes when parents played a role in their education. Much of this research is based on common theoretical foundations – "a particular perspective or lens, through which to examine a topic" (Trent University, n.d.). Specifically, there are three underlying theoretical foundations for parent role engagement: (a) the family systems theory, (b) the family-centered approach to service provision, and (c) the effect of parental involvement with education professionals.

Family Systems Theory

Family systems theory is based on general systems theory, which was initially proposed by Kenneth Boulding (1956). Turnbull and colleagues (2006), the primary proponents of family systems theory in special education, have emphasized three systems theory assumptions: (a) inputs and outputs, (b) wholism, and (c) boundaries. The first of these assumptions deals with the relationship between inputs and outputs. For example, characteristics of the family, such as age of family members, number of family members, and type of disability, interact to produce idiosyncratic outcomes or outputs. Turnbull et al. specify these outputs as family functions such as affection, education, recreation, economic status, self-esteem, etc. In applying this assumption to families of children with disabilities, education professionals must understand the unique characteristics of the disability and the effect the disability has on the family. While not all children with a specific disability will be exactly the same, there are some commonalities due to the nature of the disorder. For example, parents of children with autism spectrum disorders (ASDs) must deal with uneven, inconsistent intellectual development and/or disruptive behavior (Moes, 1995) whereas parents of children with dyslexia will be far less likely to deal with these issues. The implication is that as education professionals we must have or gain knowledge of the specific disability, and recognize that parents are coping with the effects of the disability on their entire family.

The second assumption of family systems theory is that of wholism; the family must be "understood as a whole and cannot be understood by examining only its component parts" (Turnbull & Turnbull, 2001, p. 109). The family system is comprised of both individuals and a set of subsystems. These include the marital, parental, sibling, and extended family subsystem. Further, each of these family subsystems has a set of rules for interaction, cohesion, and adaptability. As such, education professionals should not focus solely on the child with the disability when interacting with parents. The family system, including interactions among various family members, siblings, work schedules, resources, and more, contributes to how the family will interact with education professionals. Indeed, "simply understanding the child does not mean that you will understand the family, understanding the family is necessary to understanding the child" (p. 109).

The third assumption of family systems theory is that of boundaries, which vary to the degree they are open or closed. A family may have open boundaries, which can facilitate collaboration with professionals; or closed boundaries, which may limit collaboration. Logically, the family's previous interactive experiences will powerfully affect the degree of openness of these boundaries. For example, if a parent had conflict with her son's kindergarten teacher, and that conflict was not addressed, and affected the trust the parent had in the teacher, then the parent will probably enter the relationship with the first grade teacher with trepidation and the first grade teacher will have to work hard at establishing trust with the parent.

So what is the importance of family systems theory? Education professionals should approach the family as a system of members who establish roles and relationships while interacting with others both within and outside the family. Consequently, it is not just the presence of a disability, but all that the disability entails (i.e., cost, time, energy expenditure, increased knowledge, increased collaboration skills) including interactions with education professionals, that affect the family and the student with a disability.

Families are unique. They have different levels of openness, and these levels change due to circumstances and experiences. Of course, education professionals cannot control or even influence the vast majority of factors that affect the family. However, by establishing effective communication with families, building trust, and staying informed of changes in the family education professionals are better prepared to understand and interact with families. Perhaps more importantly, you can be one of the positive inputs.

Meadan and colleagues (2015) completed a program evaluation of an early intervention project that was aimed at teaching social-pragmatic communication strategies to parents of young children who were essentially nonspeaking. One parent spoke of how the success of the intervention affected the entire family, "It's just a lot happier lifestyle that she has so many words and can be a part of all of the communication that goes on because we are a talking family"(p. 20). Family members learned the strategies that worked with the child and this also enhanced the child's communication. Consequently, all family members were positively affected.

Family-Centered Approach to Service Provision

A family-centered approach (Dunst, Trivette, & Deal, 1988; Turnbull & Turnbull, 2001) to providing education and related services to a child with a disability is based on "the premise that the health and well-being of the family as a whole greatly influences the quality of life of the family member with a disability" (Thompson & Stoner, 2000, p. 1). When families fully participate in the education of their children with disabilities, they are empowered, which has been defined as "increasing control over one's life and taking action to get what one wants" (Turnbull & Turnbull, 2001, p. 41). Consequently, when families are viewed as the center of service provision there is an obligation to interact with families in a positive and proactive manner that recognizes and utilizes their individual strengths. The family-centered approach is a foundation of early intervention and parents typically respond positively to this approach.

The following quote is from a parent of a student with autism, explaining the benefits of early intervention services, which included her as a participant.

> And they [early interventionists] were kind of teaching me while they were teaching him. They would go through things. And give me maybe two or three suggestions of what to work on during the week. And you would do that and you will report back on how that went. And then they will give you more things and kind of keep building on their skills. (Stoner et al., 2005, p. 43)

However, once the child, at the age of three, enters the special education system, the focus changes to a child-centered approach. During early intervention, individualized family support plans (IFSPs) are developed with the goals and objectives focused on the family, providing assistance to the family (such as contacting audiologists who specialize in pediatric audiology) and not just to the child. Individualized education programs (IEPs) are developed in special education and essentially the goals focus only on the individual child. This transition time from early intervention to special education can be quite challenging for parents (Stoner et al., 2005). The implication for education professionals is to realize that when you take into account the needs of the family, it benefits parental engagement and ultimately the child.

Parental Engagement

The benefit of parental engagement with their children's education is well documented for all children (Mundshenk & Foley, 1994; Sheridan & Kratochwill, 1992; Snodgrass, 1991), as well as children with disabilities (e.g., Aigne, Colvin, & Baker, 1998; Conderman & Katsiyannis, 1996; Dunlap, 1999; Lambie, 2000; Mahoney & Kaiser, 1999; Mundshenk & Foley, 1994; Sheridan & Kratochwill, 1992; Snodgrass, 1991). In a perfect world all parents would be fully engaged in their children's education, and it can be frustrating when parents do not engage. The lack of parental involvement hinges on a number of factors. As described in our opening story, some parents are intimidated at an IEP meeting, which involves listening to five or six education professionals. Some parents have had negative experiences at school themselves and consequently, are hesitant even entering the school again. Other parents may not have the means to attend meetings, may have other children who need care during meeting times, or may be working shifts that do not allow them to attend. This list is certainly not exhaustive – there are certainly as many reasons for lack of parental engagement as there are parents.

However, since research has strongly indicated that parental engagement leads to better student outcomes, education professionals must put aside judgment. Education professionals must reach out to parents, welcome them, and look to the research on how to foster the parental role as outlined by the IDEA. Perhaps the most important and at times the most difficult behavior that education professionals must do is set aside judgment of all parents, regardless of their involvement.

Here is a situation that occurred with a close friend of mine, a general education teacher whom I walked with daily. One morning, after she started a new job at an inner city elementary school, she was bemoaning the fact that no parents attended her parent-teacher conferences. She talked about how horrible it was that the parents didn't care enough to partici- pate, and she emphasized how this negatively affected their children's impressions of the importance of school. She concluded, "this just shouldn't happen". And then she shifted and declared, "I am going to change this!" Five years, yes, five years, later at 5:30 in the morning, she was jumping with joy as we began our walk. Why? She had 100% atten- dance at her parent-teacher conferences.

What did she do? She changed her perspective toward the parents and looked at what they needed. For example, she made introductory and wel- coming phone calls at the beginning of the year. She called parents when their children had done something good, she wrote notes home praising the children. At parent-teacher conferences she provided snacks and even encouraged parents to bring other children they couldn't leave at home. She offered to stay late or come in early to meet parents' work schedules. About a week before the conferences she made up special baskets contain- ing shampoo, hair conditioner, body lotion (obtained from her friends' stays at hotels), and a children's book. As her students queried her about the baskets they would be told that when their mom, dad, grandma, or older brother or sister came for the parent-teacher conferences they would receive the basket.

Time passed and her reputation as an excellent teacher, who authenti- cally cared about her students grew. She also did not judge parents. She changed her perspective from "how awful parents don't come to parent- teacher conferences" to "what can I do to encourage parental engage- ment?". That perspective made the difference in her behavior; increased parental engagement; and ultimately benefited her students.

Although research supports the benefit to students of parental engage- ment, reports of parental involvement have not been encouraging. Two early studies (Goldstein, Strickland, Turnbull, & Curry, 1980; Yoshida, Fenton, Kaufman, & Maxwell, 1978) investigating parental engagement in special education found that parents of children with disabilities reported attendance at IEP meetings, but claimed they had little or no involvement in developing objectives, interventions, or methods of evaluation. In more recent studies, parents of children with disabilities have reported no invol- vement with IEP or IFSP plans, lack of choices in services, or lack of effec- tive services (Kohler, 1999; McWilliams, Young, & Harville, 1995; Osher, 2005; Spann, Kohler, & Soenksen, 2003). In summary we know that families are affected by our actions with their students (family systems theory); that a family-centered approach benefits the family and the student; and that parental engagement fosters student outcomes.

THE IMPORTANCE OF TRUST AND COMMUNICATION

Trust between parents and education professionals has emerged as a critical factor in improving student achievement (Bryk & Schneider, 2003; Tshannen-Moran, 2004). Bryk and Schneider found that trust was associated with greater and longer lasting gains in student achievement. Trust may influence student achievement because of its role in creating and maintaining collaborative relationships, as it shapes parents' attitudes toward educational systems and influences their participation in their children's educational programs (Stoner & Stoner, 2014; Tshannen-Moran, 2004).

Hoy and Tschannen-Moran (1999) proposed that trust is "an individual's or group's willingness to be vulnerable to another party based on the confidence that the latter party is benevolent, reliable, competent, honest, and open" (p. 189). Parents of children with disabilities have a great need to trust education professionals since their children are particularly vulnerable.

Numerous researchers have emphasized the importance of trust between parent and education professionals (Angell, Stoner, & Shelden, 2009; Blue-Banning, Summers, Frankland, Nelson, & Beegle, 2004; Dominque, Cutler, & McTarnaghan, 2000; Hoy & Tschannen-Moran, 1999). In a study by Angell and colleagues, parents of children with varying disabilities who were interviewed regarding their relationships with education professionals. Not surprisingly, parents sought and desired a strong bond of trust, especially if they felt such a relationship would benefit their children. Unfortunately, many parents had experienced negative interactions with professionals in general (from the medical and educational arenas) prior to entering the special education system. Each negative interaction reduced their trust, and increased their skepticism and caution toward all professionals (Stoner et al., 2005).

Interpersonal relationships are the primary avenue for building trust (Angell et al., 2009; Hoy & Tschannen-Moran, 1999). Trust is built incrementally through personal interactions, encounters, and exchanges (Rousseau,

Sitkin, Burt, & Camerer, 1998) and it is incumbent on education professionals, using effective communication to build a strong, trusting relationship.

Ongoing, respectful communication is vital to establish and maintain trust between parents and education professionals. Not surprisingly, the significance of effective communication has been the focus of numerous papers and reports covering a range of issues and disabilities (e.g., Mathur & Smith, 2003; Montgomery, 2005; Munk et al., 2001). For example, parents desire and expect frequent communication, a need that is intensified when problems are present (Stoner & Angell, 2006). In fact, evidence has indicated that the vast majority (75%) of mothers of children with disabilities desired communication from their children's teachers (Singh, 2003).

Teacher responses to parents' communication strategies had the potential to develop, maintain, enhance, reduce, or even destroy trust. Evidence (Stoner & Angell, 2006) has indicated that parents adopted particular communication strategies based on the content of the communication. When the content was about everyday topics, mothers employed a dialogic communication strategy and the communication itself was more relaxed. Parents expected a response from teachers but there was no sense of urgency with dialogic communication.

However, when an issue arose, a problem-focused communication strategy was preferred and parents expected an immediate teacher response. Teacher responses did not have to be in agreement with the parents' desires, but they needed to be respectful; demonstrate authentic caring for students; and they needed to acknowledge the parents' perspectives on problems. Communication that was not respectful, had no aspect of authentic caring, or was dismissive of the mothers' concerns was detrimental to trust. In addition, if mothers perceived inaction by teachers, the mothers' trust was reduced or destroyed. This perspective is consistent with research that has focused on conflict between parents of children with disabilities and education professionals (Lake & Billingsley, 2000).

A recent study has indicated the majority of parents preferred communicating through email. While email may improve efficiency it may not enhance the overall quality of communication (Thompson, 2008). As such, it is critical to understand parental preferences. For example, one mother desired phone communication to resolve a problem since resolution could be attained during the conversation. And another preferred daily progress notes. Regardless of the mode of communication, a quick response time is especially important during problem-focused communication. Parents primarily want the initial response to acknowledge their concern and do not necessarily expect immediate resolution.

PARENTAL PERSPECTIVES OF THEIR RELATIONSHIPS WITH EDUCATION PROFESSIONALS

Fiedler's (2000) research investigating parental participation in IEP meetings indicated that IEP meetings tend to function as a formal, legal process that presented parents with a previously developed IEP for their information and signature. The predetermined nature of this exchange undermines the value of parental involvement and diminishes foundations of trust. In their discussion of parent-school collaborative efforts, Turnbull and Turnbull (2001) concluded that "the dominant theme of all the research and testimony is that schools try to comply with the legal mandates and procedures but do not make an effort to foster empowerment through collaboration" (p. 231). Further while education professionals are following the legal "mandates" of IDEA, they are missing the "intent" of the law — to give parents opportunities to be "collaborative partners" in planning their children's education.

Fishman and Nickerson (2015) conducted a survey of parents of children with disabilities to ascertain predictors of parental engagement. They found that while a number of variables contributed to parental involvement, only one variable was significant — receiving a direct, personal invitation from a teacher. However, we must remember that "... parents of students of students in special education are influenced by multiple, complex factors when making decisions about their involvement practices" (p. 523). Basically, parents of children with disabilities are unique and education professionals must approach them as such; parents are unique individuals with their own levels of involvement. Education professionals must listen to what parents want, encourage them to participate, and practice strategies that have the potential to increase their engagement in parental roles.

Here the nature of parental roles is especially helpful. Roles may be viewed as a comprehensive pattern of behaviors and attitudes, constituting a strategy for coping with a recurrent set of situations (Turner, 1990). Studies on role theory have indicated that engagement in multiple roles may have a definite advantage by attenuating the stressful impact of any single role (e.g., Kandel, Davies, & Ravies, 1985; Marks, 1977). Marks postulated that human resources of time and energy are flexible and can be personally constructed and controlled depending on the level of commitment to a certain role. Numerous quantitative studies have found that the more roles an individual holds, the better the individual's psychological well-being (e.g., Adelmann, 1994; Miller, Moen, & Dempster-McClain, 1991). The implication of the research on role theory clearly indicates that engaging in multiple roles may be an effective coping strategy.

Stoner and Angell (2006) reported on their findings of the roles parents of children with ASD engaged in as they interacted with education professionals. The findings of this study revealed a comprehensive analysis of parent perspectives on four distinct roles: (a) negotiator, (b) monitor, (c) supporter, and (d) advocate.

The Roles of Negotiator, Supporter, Monitor, and Advocate

Initial IEP meetings were pivotal in the parents' development of the role of negotiator. Many of the parent participants felt that their first IEP was very difficult, they did not know what to expect, listened to many professionals whom they did not know, and at times felt totally lost. As one parent stated:

> No, I think I was just lost, I was totally lost. I don't know why but it seemed that I was inside a glass wall and I couldn't hear. I mean I was hearing everything but I couldn't process it.

However, as parents engaged more with education professionals, the role of negotiator began to develop and solidify. Parents gained knowledge of their children's disability through an intense process of self-education, often augmented by parent support groups. They learned it was essential and necessary to negotiate to obtain all services that their children needed. This was exemplified by the following quote.

> Like last year I asked for summer school. And everybody was saying no, no, no, there is nothing like that. Summer school is a month or two for the kids, and a few hours a day that they can go. That's it. And I contacted the State Board of Education. I had an email, and they told me if the kid tends to regress they have to provide it. And I put that in a letter to the special education director. And I said "Well, this is what they are telling me." And we ended up having summer school for 10 weeks.

Another parental role identified is that of monitor. Monitoring involved both formal and informal aspects. Parents who monitored their children's education through informal means relied on communication notebooks, volunteering in classrooms or schools, and their children's work. However, formal monitoring occurred during IEP meetings and parent-teacher conferences. Consider the following example of a parent in the study, who had conflict with the school in obtaining services for his son. The parent even described his monitoring participation as policing.

> Policing. Definitely. It was one of the first roles we took. We left them alone for two years, you remember the story I told you. They screwed up so bad. They wasted two golden years of this child's life. And then we wasted another two years, so they can come around, and finally learn or figure out what it is they are finally doing or they are supposed to do. Yes, definitely policing.

Monitoring increased when parents perceived problems, and it decreased when no problems were perceived.

Another role that parents identified was the role of supporter, and the recipient of this support was most frequently their children's teacher. The supporter role was demonstrated through various actions, such as buttressing requests between teachers and administrators, sending materials to teachers, and/or assisting teachers in their classrooms.

> Even though the teacher knows that if they need any kind of help, let's say they need somebody to laminate things for them, or to do copying. There is a lot of stuff that I have at home that the Board of Education doesn't even have it in their classrooms. If they ask me I will not even hesitate. I will send it right away. I have this CD with pictures, the teachers want. And it cost 60 bucks but the school doesn't want to order it. It doesn't matter, and I can send it to you. And you can pull out all the picture things and send it back.

These types of support ultimately benefited the children, and that was the parents' prime motivation for this type of support. Previous research in the area of support has focused on professional support to families (e.g., Fiedler, 2000; Turnbull et al., 2006) and not family support to professionals. However, the parent participants in this study were actively engaged in the role of supporter. Furthermore, the intensity of role engagement was mediated by perceived positive dispositions of the teachers.

The role of advocate varied among participants; however, all parents engaged in some form of advocacy. Parents' advocacy efforts did not focus solely on their own children. Some spoke to university classes; some talked with parents of newly diagnosed children; and others attended the IEPs of other children to support their parents. One parent developed a handbook of information about ASD.

The most active advocates in this study were the mothers, who were not working outside the home. The following quote is from the husband of one of the participants,

> And she is really on this crusade to educate herself and be an advocate for the disability and that kind of thing. And she is not working, and she focuses on the child and everything she can do. And she really puts her heart and soul into it. And it is fortunate that she has that attitude because I don't have the time to deal with it, to tell you the truth.

Stoner and Angell (2006) clearly identified the parental role of advocate and how assuming this role benefited parents.

This study obtained the self-reported roles of parents of children with ASD and generalization to other parents of children with varying disabilities is cautioned. However, the findings indicate parental involvement in multiple roles may be a coping mechanism and should be encouraged and cultivated.

BEST PRACTICES FOR FOSTERING THE ROLE OF PARENTS OF STUDENTS WITH DISABILITIES

The following recommendations are based on research, previous literature, the professional experiences of the author, and, perhaps most importantly, perspectives articulated by parents of children with disabilities. We must always keep in mind that parents have lived the experience.

Parent Roles

Recognize the benefit of parents' assuming multiple roles and encourage parents to be fully engaged in their children's education. Let's start with a central assertion. Most parents know their children best. They are the experts on their own child. Educational professionals should empower parents by recognizing, valuing, and learning from parental expertise. Special educators need to directly acknowledge that expertise by communicating frequently and consistently with parents throughout the school year.

Acknowledge the fact that parents may want to be engaged in their children's education at varying levels. Regardless of the extent to which parents want to get involved, it is incumbent upon professionals to welcome them, keep them informed, and allow them to be as participative as they desire. Recognize that parents are as individual as their children and as such take time to get to know them. Each and every interaction with parents has the potential to foster parent engagement. Try meeting parents at the door and walking them into IEP meetings; make name tags for everyone if parents don't know the professionals at the meeting; and ask the parent to speak first instead of last. Give the parent plenty of opportunities to ask questions and answer in everyday language, rarely using the acronyms so prevalent in special education. Provide parents with information about the disability, refer them to local support groups, and ask them what they need. Thank the parent with a note for attending. Respect and honor parent input.

Communication

Communicate with parents about services that would benefit their children, inform them of options, and encourage them to be fully functioning members of IEP teams. Communication with parents of children with disabilities must be perceived as important, must be cultivated early in the school year in a positive and proactive manner, and, when parents communicate with teachers, appropriate responses should be forthcoming. Trust is built incrementally over time and, unfortunately, can be destroyed much faster. Numerous researchers have found a positive relationship between parental involvement and communication by teachers (Ames, De Stefano, Watkins, & Sheldon, 1995; Epstein, 1990; Shirvani, 2007). Ask parents specifically *how* they want you to communicate, *when* they want communication, and *how frequently* they want communication.

However, communication is of heightened importance at the beginning of the school year. Teachers should contact parents before the school year begins, meet with them to learn about the child, and if possible invite the child into the classroom before the first day of school. Communication must be open and honest. Problems should be discussed as they emerge and parental concerns should not be dismissed. The special educator must recognize that many parents are monitoring their children's behavior. The parents strongly believe their child's behavior will indicate when problems arise in the classroom.

Sensitivity

Be sensitive to parents' need to monitor their children's education. Recognize that it is parents' right and responsibility to monitor the quality and content of their children's educational programs. Some parents may choose to do this on a regular, ongoing basis. Others may monitor less closely or not at all. Parents' engagement in formal or informal monitoring as members of their children's IEP teams can help professionals provide appropriate, quality services. Furthermore, monitoring is a functional role that can alleviate parents' stress and increase their support for education professionals. Invite parents into your classroom. Offer opportunities when parents may come and observe their child in settings such as field trips, library visits, or on the playground. Let parents know that they are welcomed to observe their child and your interaction with their child.

Open your doors, communicate daily, and give information freely to parents. Parents want to know about their children's day at school and education professionals must assume that responsibility when students cannot recount their day's happenings. Remember that especially with a non-speaking student, the typical communication between the child and parent is missing, and parents will need to fill that gap.

Parental Trust

Understand that parental trust can be affected by previous interactions with medical and education professionals. Professionals may have to rebuild trust that has been undermined by perceived negative experiences. This recommendation focuses on building trust between parents and special educators. Trust is either enhanced or reduced with every interaction between parents and special educators. Special educators should develop sensitivity to the opportunities they have to create trust with parents and should maximize those opportunities to build trust. Trust is created by communicating with parents, listening and respecting parental views, and following through on promises. Promises may be those made by individual teachers or may be implied in promises of effective intervention and service delivery. Regardless of who makes the promises, they must be kept. When there is a perceived breach of trust, it affects the interaction between parents and educators. Breaches of trust also require time to mend. Education professionals must realize that building trust with parents is well worth the cost of time and effort. Trust may alleviate or reduce future conflicts and even lead to avoidance of costly litigation. Most importantly trust is necessary to a relationship that values parents and their significant role in the education of their children.

While it may take a great number of positive interactions to build trust, it can only take one or two negative interactions to undermine trust. View each interaction with parents as an opportunity to build or increase trust. Education professionals should establish a relationship of *trust* from the very beginning. The relationship between parents of children with disabilities and the school is long-term. Investing in the quality of this relationship will serve both parents and school districts well.

Best Practices

Use best practices during IEP meetings, especially the first IEP meeting. Reach out to parents before the IEP meeting, offer to explain the structure of the meeting, and ask for input on any goals parents may have for their children. Meet the parents at the school or classroom door. Walk into the meeting with them. Sit them next to the person who is writing the IEP or better yet, have the IEP projected so that all IEP team members can view it. Give the parent the full time allotted. Do not begin shuffling papers or packing up notes before the IEP has concluded. As noted previously, follow up with a short note, thanking the parents for participating and acknowledging the time and energy they are giving.

Finally, special educators should recognize how much parents of children with ASD value them. Most parents value the work of education professionals. The parents are with the child the majority of the time. They know how difficult it can be to deal with their child. Most parents sincerely appreciated the effort and commitment education professionals gave to their child.

CONCLUSION

In conclusion, theoretical foundations help us understand the necessity and benefit of parental involvement. Evidence indicates that families function as a system. Therefore, to understand children with disabilities we must understand their families. Using a family-centered approach to the education of children with disabilities enhances parental engagement and leads to better outcomes for the child.

In addition, education professionals should respect and welcome parents and the roles play in the education of their children. As professionals, educators should cultivate, enhance, and value parental engagement. Both professionals and parents have a common goal — the best education for their children.

REFERENCES

Adelmann, P. K. (1994). Multiple roles and psychological well-being in a national sample of older adults. *Journal of Gerontology: Social Science, 49*, 277–285.

Aigne, D., Colvin, G., & Baker, S. (1998). Analysis of perceptions of parents who have children with intellectual disabilities: Implications for service providers. *Education and Training in Mental Retardation and Developmental Disabilities, 33*, 331–341.

Ames, C., De Stefano, L., Watkins, T., & Sheldon, S. (1995). *Teacher's school-to-home communications and parent involvement: The role of parent perceptions and beliefs.* Report No. 8. East Lasing, MI: Michigan State University. Center of Families, Schools, and Children Learning. (ERIC Document Reproduction Service No. ED 383451).

Angell, M. E., Stoner, J. B., & Shelden, D. L. (2009). Trust in education professionals: Perspectives of mothers of children with disabilities. *Remedial and Special Education, 30*(3), 160–176.

Blue-Banning, M., Summers, J. A., Frankland, H. C., Nelson, L. L., & Beegle, G. (2004). Dimensions of family and professional partnerships: Constructive guidelines for collaboration. *Exceptional Children, 70*, 167–185.

Boulding, K. (1956). General systems theory: The skeleton of a science. *Management Science, 12*, 197–208.

Bryk, A. S., & Schneider, B. (2003). Trust in schools: A core resource for school reform. *Educational Leadership, 60*(6), 40–44.

Conderman, G., & Katsiyannis, A. (1996). State practices in serving individuals with autism. *Focus on Autism & Other Developmental Disabilities, 11*, 29–36.

Dominque, B., Cutler, B., & McTarnaghan, J. (2000). The experience of autism in the lives of families. In A. M. Wetherby & B. M. Prizant (Eds.), *Autism spectrum disorders: A transactional developmental perspective* (pp. 369–394). Baltimore, MD: Brookes Publishing.

Dunlap, G. (1999). Consensus, engagement, and family involvement for young children with autism. *The Journal of the Association for Persons with Severe Handicaps, 24*, 222–225.

Dunst, C., Trivette, C., & Deal, A. (1988). Strengths-based family centered intervention practices. In *Family systems intervention monograph* (Vol. 2, No. 3). Morganton, NC: Family, Infant, and Preschool Program, Western Carolina Center.

Epstein, J. (1990). School and family connections: Theory, research, and implications for integrating sociologies of education and family. In D. G. Unger & M. B. Sussman (Eds.), *Families in community settings: Interdisciplinary perspectives* (pp. 99–126). New York, NY: The Haworth Press.

Feinberg, E., & Vacca, J. (2000). The drama and trauma of creating policies on autism: Critical issues to consider in the new millennium. *Focus on Autism & Other Developmental Disabilities, 15*, 130–138.

Fiedler, C. (2000). *Making a difference: Advocacy competencies for special education professionals.* Boston, MA: Allyn and Bacon.

Fishman, C. E., & Nickerson, A. B. (2015). Motivations for involvement: A preliminary investigation of parents of students with disabilities. *Journal of Child and Family Studies, 24*, 523–535.

Goldstein, S., Strickland, B., Turnbull, A. P., & Curry, L. (1980). An observational analysis of the IEP conference. *Exceptional Children, 46*, 278–286.

Hoy, W. K., & Tschannen-Moran, M. (1999). Five facets of trust: An empirical confirmation in urban elementary schools. *Journal of School Leadership, 9*(3), 181–208.

Kandel, D. B., Davies, M., & Ravies, V. (1985). The stressfulness of daily social roles for women: Marital, occupational, and household roles. *Journal of Health and Social Behavior, 26*, 67–78.

Kohler, F. K. (1999). Examining the services received by young children with autism and their families: A survey of parent responses. *Focus on Autism and Other Developmental Disabilities, 14*, 150–158.

Lake, J. F., & Billingsley, B. S. (2000). An analysis of factors that contribute to parent-school conflict in special education. *Remedial and Special Education, 21*, 240–251.

Lambie, R. (2000). Working with families of at-risk and special needs students: A systems change model preview. *Focus on Exceptional Children, 32*(6), 1–22.

Lord, C., & McGee, J. P. (2001). *Educating children with autism.* Washington, DC: National Academy Press.

Mahoney, G., & Kaiser, A. (1999). Parent education in early intervention: A call for a renewed focus. *Topics in Early Childhood Special Education, 19*, 131–141.

Marks, S. R. (1977). Multiple roles and role strain: Some notes on human energy, time and commitment. *American Sociological Review, 42*, 921–936.

Mathur, S., & Smith, R. M. (2003). Collaborate with families of children with ADD. *Intervention in School and Clinic, 38*, 311–315.

McWilliams, R., Young, H., & Harville, K. (1995). Satisfaction and struggles: Family perceptions of early intervention services. *Journal of Early Intervention, 19*, 43–60.

Meadan, H., Stoner, J. B., & Angell, M. E. (2015). Parent perspectives on home-based intervention for young children with developmental disabilities: The Parent-Implemented Communication Strategies (PiCS) Project in Illinois, USA. *Journal of the American Academy of Special Education Professionals*, (Spring/Summer). Retrieved from http://aasep.org/aasep-publications/journal-of-the-american-academy-of-special-education-professionals-jaasep/jaasep-springsummer-2015/parent-perspectives-on-home-based-intervention-for-young-children-with-developmental-disabilities-the-parent-implemented-communication-strategies-pics-project-in-illinois-usa/index.html

Miller, M. L., Moen, P., & Dempster-McClain, D. (1991). Motherhood, multiple roles, and maternal well being: Women of the 1950s. *Gender and Society, 5*, 565–582.

Moes. (1995). *Office of Special Education and Rehabilitation Services [OSERS]*, 2000.

Montgomery, D. J. (2005). Communicating without harm: Strategies for enhancing parent-teacher communication. *Teaching Exceptional Children, 37*(5), 50–55.

Mundshenk, N., & Foley, R. (1994). Collaborative relationships between school and home: Implications for service delivery. *Preventing School Failure, 39*, 16–21.

Munk, D. D., Bursuck, W. D., Epstein, M. H., Jayanthi, M., Nelson, J., & Polloway, E. A. (2001). Homework communication problems: Perspectives of special and general education parents. *Reading and Writing Quarterly, 17*, 180–203.

National Center for Learning Disabilities, Inc. (2005). *Annual report: Awareness, advocacy, action.* (ERIC Document Reproduction Service No. ED495 880), 1–28.

Office of Special Education and Rehabilitation Services [OSERS]. (2006). *Building the legacy: IDEA 2004.* Retrieved from http://idea.ed.gov/static/modelForms

Osher, T. W. (2005). *Opportunities for parental involvement in special education afforded by the Individuals with Disabilities Education Act Amendments of 1997.* Retrieved from http://www.elc-pa.org/Opps4ParInvSpEd.htm

Pennsylvania Association for Retarded Citizens (PARC) v. Commonwealth of Pennsylvania, 1971, 1972.

Rousseau, D. M., Sitkin, S. B., Burt, R. S. & Camerer, C. (1998). Not so different after all: A cross discipline view of trust. *Academy of Management Review, 23*(3), 393–404.

Sheridan, S., & Kratochwill, T. (1992). Behavioral parent-teacher consultation: Conceptual and research consideration. *Journal of School Psychology, 10,* 117–130.

Shirvani, H. (2007). Effects of teachers' communication on parents' attitudes and their children's behaviors at school. *Education, 28*(1), 34–47.

Singh, D. K. (2003). Let us hear the parents. *Journal of Instructional Psychology, 30*(2), 169–173.

Snodgrass, D. (1991). The parent connection. *Adolescence, 26,* 83–87.

Spann, S. J., Kohler, F. W., & Soenksen, D. (2003). Examining parents' involvement in and perceptions of special education services: An interview with families in a parent support group. *Focus on Autism and Other Developmental Disabilities, 18*(4), 228–237.

Stoner, C. R., & Stoner, J. B. (2014). How can we make this work? Understanding and responding to working parents of children with autism. *Business Horizons, 57,* 85–95.

Stoner, J. B., & Angell, M. E. (2006). Parent perspectives on role engagement: An investigation of parents of children with ASD and their self-reported roles with education professionals. *Focus on Autism and Other Developmental Disabilities, 21*(3), 177–189.

Stoner, J. B., Bock, S. J., Thompson, J. R., Angell, M. E., Heyl, B., & Crowley, E. P. (2005). Welcome to our world: Parent perspectives of interactions between parents of young children with ASD and education professionals. *Focus on Autism and Other Developmental Disabilities, 20,* 39–51.

Stoner, J. B., Meadan, H., & Angell, M. E. (2013). A model for coaching parents to implement teaching strategies with their young children with language delay or developmental disabilities. *Perspectives on Language Learning and Education (ASHA Journal), 20*(3), 112–119.

Thompson, B. (2008). Characteristics of parent-teacher e-mail communication. *Communication Education, 57*(2), 201–223. doi:10.1080/03634520701852050.

Thompson, J. R., & Stoner, J. (2000). *Family support: Meeting the challenge in Illinois 12 years later.* Springfield, IL: Illinois Council on Developmental Disabilities.

Trent University. (n.d.). *Theoretical frameworks.* Retrieved from http://trentu.ca/history/workbook/theoreticalframeworks.php

Tshannen-Moran, M. (2004). *Trust matters: Leadership for successful schools.* San Francisco, CA: Jossey-Bass.

Turnbull, A., Turnbull, H. R., Shank, M., & Leal, D. (1999). *Exceptional lives: Special education in today's schools* (2nd ed.). Upper Saddle River, NJ: Merrill/Prentice Hall.

Turnbull, A., Turnbull, R., Erwin, E., & Soodak, L. (2006). *Families, professionals, and exceptionality: Positive outcomes through partnerships and trust* (5th ed.). Upper Saddle River, NJ: Merrill/Prentice Hall.

Turnbull, A. P., & Turnbull, H. R. (2001). *Families, professionals, and exceptionality: Collaborating for empowerment* (4th ed.). Columbus, OH: Merrill/Prentice Hall.

Turner, R. H. (1990). Role change. *Annual Review of Sociology, 16,* 87–110.

Wright, P. W. D., & Wright, P. D. (1999). *Wrightslaw: Special education law.* Hartfield, VA: Harbour House Law Press.

Yoshida, R. K., Fenton, K., Kaufman, M. J., & Maxwell, J. P. (1978). Parental involvement in the special education pupil planning process: The school's perspective. *Exceptional Children, 44,* 531–533.

CHAPTER 9

THE ROLE OF COMMUNITY IN SPECIAL EDUCATION: A RELATIONAL APPROACH

Kate Warner, Karla Hull and Martha Laughlin

ABSTRACT

This chapter addresses the importance of community in fostering transformative learning and living environments for children with special needs. Community is conceptualized as a special kind of relationship between people, who, regardless of geography, share common values, concerns, interests, or experiences. This understanding of community as relationship is linked to the importance of empowering family involvement and decision making as children with special needs navigate the educational system that seeks to help them grow and thrive. This theoretical frame is used to analyze the ways in which the wisdom families have about their children and the wisdom educators have about teaching children who have special needs can be used to nurture life-changing educational experiences.

Keywords: Community; family therapy; special education; family therapy in schools; relational therapy; communities of care

Interdisciplinary Connections to Special Education: Important Aspects to Consider
Advances in Special Education, Volume 30A, 151–166
Copyright © 2015 by Emerald Group Publishing Limited
All rights of reproduction in any form reserved
ISSN: 0270-4013/doi:10.1108/S0270-40132015000030A008

THE ROLE OF COMMUNITY IN SPECIAL EDUCATION

It should, indeed be our goal in all of education to produce caring, moral persons, but we cannot accomplish this purpose by setting an objective and heading straight toward it. Rather, we approach our goal by living with those whom we teach in a caring community through modeling, dialogue, practice, and confirmation.

–Noddings (1984, p. 502)

For decades special education school programs have provided millions of children, particularly those with severe disabilities, much needed equipment, specially trained teachers, tutors, interpreters, computer-assisted technology, rehabilitation therapists and doctors, and opportunities to grow and be educated with children without disabilities. In addition, huge strides have been made in reducing discrimination for employment opportunities. Commonplace in most large cities are automatic doors, parking for the disabled, wheelchair mobility via ramps, aisles, and check-out lines, accessible bathrooms, audio loops in offices and theaters, Braille signage inside elevators and stairwells, kneeling buses, accessible train cars, and trained staff. Yet, a 2010 survey conducted for the Kessler Foundation and the National Organization on Disability show that Americans with disabilities continue to report low life satisfaction as compared with people without disabilities – 34% versus 61%, the same 27 point gap reported in 2004 (Taylor, Krane, & Orkis, 2010). How do we make sense of this?

While we do not claim to have a definitive answer to this very large question, we do think that a new way of thinking, and a different set of questions would point us in the direction of the answer. The question that has been asked to this point has been, what laws need to be passed to provide *"equality of opportunity, full participation, independent living, and economic self-sufficiency"* (IDEA, 2004). We continue to think linearly about disability as a "thing," something separate and apart from ourselves that we can "fix" by getting rid of barriers to education and providing technological advances that enable people with disabilities to live more manageably. Our national approach to disability reflects a business and marketing orientation: figure out how much capital to invest, improve the product, make it more marketable, more able to compete in the open market, and less expensive to maintain later. Problem solved.

However, disability is not an instrumental phenomenon, a problem pragmatically solved through technology and education. It is a relational phenomenon with many fingers that touch all aspects of personal, family, and community life. In short, it is not a problem *for* the community but a problem *of* community.

As educators and therapists, we have found commonality of purpose and intent in our work with children and families, and we believe that as a collaborative team, we have something to offer that neither therapists, teachers, families, or students alone can achieve. This idea — that neither of us can work without the other — reflects the well-used but still relevant proverb that it takes a village to raise a child (Clinton, 1996; Rattigan-Rohr, 2012), a notion that lies at the heart of any chapter about the role of community in special education. However, it is not just the notion of working as a collaborative team that is important, it is our focus on a family-centered, systemic approach to building our community of care for students with disabilities and their families that will challenge schools to move forward.

WHAT IS COMMUNITY?

The idea that it takes many hearts and hands to raise a child has become commonplace — almost a cliché. Nonetheless, this is not a trivial idea, and it is a heavily researched idea. There are many studies that give validity to the now common understanding that children are less likely to get into trouble with the law or get involved with drugs (Weiss & Stephen, 2009) and more likely to generally do better in life when they live in stable, family-school communities (Chetty, Hendren, Kline, & Saez, 2013).

Iyer (2013) notes that there are 220 million people living in countries not their own, a "floating tribe" of deeply multi-cultured people: Children born of parents who, themselves, come from different countries in which their children have never lived or even visited. Children and their parents may have been educated in more than one country, none of which were their own place of birth or that of their parents. Given our ability to move about the globe, both physically and as "stationary" participants in social media and virtual communities, and the plethora of people with multi-cultural backgrounds and experiences, a definition of community cannot be restricted to people living in common association with each other. Talk of community has long ago dropped the assumption that people are living in face-to-face physical proximity to one another. "Home," Iyer (2013) concludes, "has really less to do with a piece of soil than, you could say, with a piece of soul" (para 2, p. 50), and as a result, he suggests that now we often "choose our sense of home, create our sense of community, fashion our sense of self" (para 4:03) Community, then, is simply a special kind of relationship between people, who, regardless of geography, share common values, concerns, interests, or experiences.

Parents do not raise children in isolation, without relationship to other people and institutions. Although children, families, communities, and whole societies are often thought of as discrete, localizable entities, they are more usefully seen as interwoven relationships of reciprocity: Children bloom under the care of their families, families flourish when communities have their best interests at heart, and communities − families and children − thrive when society looks to the well-being of its state and local communities. For parents of children with special needs it takes doctors, teachers, clergy, business people, and therapists. It takes local leaders, legislators, and those responsible for protecting our health and safety − it takes community. This is a given.

COMMUNITY LOST

In the early 1900s, most public school systems excluded children with severe disabilities − some by law (IDEA, 2004). Children with less severe disabilities might attend special schools, which did not include children without disabilities, but often dropped out because they required accommodations that were not available. The inclusion of students with disabilities took root when the national community − the American public and government − recognized that children with disabilities were, like all children, people with value:

> Disability is a natural part of the human experience and in no way diminishes the right of individuals to participate in or contribute to society. Improving educational results for children with disabilities is an essential element of our national policy of ensuring equality of opportunity, full participation, independent living, and economic self-sufficiency for individuals with disabilities. (IDEA, 2004)

Since Gallup began asking Americans their views on public education 25 years ago, the public has seen a steady, 25-year downward trend in opinion about public education (Lopez, 2010). In 1985, 58% of Americans gave public education a C or lower; in 2010, it was 79% (PDK/Gallup, 2014). As of 2012, children are being educated in an educational system that ranks 36th among 65 nations (PISA, 2012). When the children now in this system reach adulthood, they will compete in global markets with multi-cultured, often multi-lingual people educated in superior educational systems from at least 29 different nations.

In 1983, Schön published *The Reflective Practitioner*, in which he suggested that the professions were suffering a loss of public confidence so severe that he thought we were suffering a "crisis of confidence in professional knowledge." This crisis of confidence continues today. The public has watched as government officials commit crimes, researchers write articles using invented data, school shootings become a standard event, teachers go to jail for changing students' answers on tests that risk school closure and the drop-out rate in our schools remains high. These things produce a distrustful public that is wary of "experts" claiming to have superior knowledge, people in authority, and public information in general.

In the field of education, Schon's (1983) crisis of confidence has appeared as a rift in school-community relations. Poor student performance is often viewed as the result of poor teaching, so in recent decades, as US education has fallen in the international rankings (PISA, 2012), parents accuse teachers of failing to do their jobs. In turn, teachers blame parents for failed parenting as well as failing to value education at home. As John Sculley put it, the public "expect[s] teachers to handle teenage pregnancy, substance abuse, and the failings of the family. Then we expect them to educate our children" (Paterson, 2010, p. 78). As parents blame teachers and teachers blame parents for failures that are systemic and beyond either parents or teachers alone, the parent-school community divide widens, and Schön's crisis of confidence worsens.

THE EROSIVE NATURE OF ROLES

Special education requires the effort of a variety of professionals completing independent and overlapping tasks. As such, our disciplinary emphasis in training and development has largely focused on the knowledge and skill set of our profession and identifying our "role" in the community of care. It is commonly recognized that collaborative efforts between professionals results in positive interdependence that assists in achieving a common, agreed-upon goal (Villa & Thousand, 1988). Welch and Sheridan (1995) describe collaboration as

> a dynamic framework for educational efforts which endorses collegial, interdependent, and co-equal styles of interaction between at least two partners working jointly together to achieve common goals in a decision making process that is influenced by cultural and systemic factors. (p. 11)

Although most schools have developed a variety of collaborative teams to serve students with disabilities, those teams tend to be driven by individual professionals with roles and skill-sets placing the family and/or student in passive roles on the team. Team members may communicate and collaborate but typically do not put the importance of building a community of care at the top of our list. Identifying who does what is obviously an important task but we continue to fail in our efforts to integrate all of the moving parts in our community and ensure that families are active in the community and their children remain the pivotal point for our actions.

Family participation became a central tenet in the IDEA (2004) focusing on securing parents as active partners throughout the special education process from assessment to delivery of services. Research on parent-professional collaboration continues to identify a significant power imbalance resulting in less than perfect family-school partnerships (Harry, 2008). In spite of the emphasis on active parent participation in IDEA (2004), researchers continue to report parents of students with disabilities feeling lonely, confused, powerless, and overwhelmed (Conroy, 2012; Turnbull, Turnbull, Erwin, & Sodak, 2006).

Spann, Kohler, and Soenksen (2003) cite studies showing that many parents involved with early intervention services did not collaboratively develop Independent Family Service Plans (IFSP) with professionals, which consequently failed to reflect families' existing views and priorities. Other studies show that while parents attend their child's individualized education program (IEP) meeting, they are not involved in developing objectives, interventions, or methods of evaluation. And yet other studies suggest that school personnel often view parents as adversarial, dysfunctional and not credible as sources of information (Spann et al., 2003). Clearly, parents continue to experience schools as holding the real reins of power while expecting them to stay on the sidelines and follow directions. This might suggest that more education for parents would be helpful. Or, it might suggest that schools' notion of community remains incomplete — perhaps parents correctly perceive that often, schools want parents to be involved when and in the manner the school deems it necessary or helpful, but otherwise, schools want parents to stay out of the way.

Each side — parent and school — draw a line in the sand between child rearing and education and then accuse the other side of failing at its job while claiming success at its own. Neither "side" is correct because the two are not separable. They are the two complementary sides of a single coin, connected and shaping one another. Education and growing up transpire together, each informing the other, each occurring in both school and home.

FAMILY-CENTERED COMMUNITIES OF CARE IN SPECIAL EDUCATION

Although it is important to have the right individuals at the table, it is not so much the *who* is involved in the community of care for students with disabilities and their families, it is the *how* they are involved. If we look at the family-centered practices that are considered a practice-of-choice in early intervention, we can gain insight into the critical components of an effective community of care. Family-centered practices are characterized by treating families with dignity and respect; information sharing so families and students can make informed decisions; and choice regarding involvement in the provision of services (Dunst, Trivette, & Hamby, 2006). Most school teams believe they do treat families with respect and give them information to make choices, but the reality is the way in which they accomplish those goals is often perceived very differently by families.

Dunst et al. (2006) describe a practice-based theory of family-centered help as including relational and participatory practices. Relational refers to practices such as active listening, compassion, empathy, and respect. Participatory refers to practices that are "individualized, flexible, and responsive to family concerns and priorities, and which involve informed choices and family involvement in achieving desired goals and outcomes" (Dunst, Trivette, & Hamby, 2007, p. 371). Of these two, participatory practice emerges as the most distinctive. Listening well, showing empathy, and being "nice" are important, but when the service remains professional-centered despite these, families experience the difference (Espe-Sherwindt, 2008).

As professors and researchers in special education and family therapy, we have noticed that while we have quite different jobs, we often work with the same people — kids, parents, and families — and deal with the same problems — school difficulties. While the family therapists among us do not consider themselves experts on education, they nonetheless get frequent and detailed accounts from parents and their children about what happens in the classroom as well as at home and how these events shape one another, and how their responses to such events, in turn, shape how they are in the classroom. We hear what is said in meetings between parents and

teachers, as well as what parents think about what was said in those meetings. We hear what parents and children think of their teachers as well as
what they assume teachers think of them. Similarly, while the educator
among us does not regard herself a therapist, she nonetheless finds herself
frequently seeking solutions that will have a "therapeutic" effect on problems that extend well beyond education. We think that a well-structured
collaboration between special educators and family therapists could provide an enhanced level of care for families with special needs children. To
explain this, we will describe how family therapists think and orient themselves to problems. We begin with an illustration.

CLIENT-CENTERED THERAPY IN THE FIELD OF FAMILY THERAPY

When Marge brought her son, Kyle, into our family therapy clinic, she was
frantic about his grades. He wasn't living up to his IEP; he was barely passing the 9th grade. He wouldn't do his homework, and, when he did, he
would not turn it in, for some inexplicable reason that drove Marge crazy.
Over the years, Marge had spent hours on emails, phone calls, and conferences with the guidance counselor and Kyle's teachers, but they seemed
only to offer the same solution: Marge and her husband need to figure out
a way to just make Kyle do his homework. This was a great frustration to
Marge: What they offered as a solution was, to her, a restatement of the
problem. If she knew how to "make-Kyle-do-his-homework," there would
be no problem.

Marge knew Kyle was smart. She thought his problem was his passivity:
He was apathetic about his life and his future. He just didn't care about
school or grades. She was frantic with worry that Kyle would flunk the 9th
grade, get left behind by his friends, then get discouraged, maybe even drop
out of high school, and never make it to college. She envisioned him living
as a bum on the street. Kyle said he didn't care if he didn't make it into college. She wanted us to make him care.

Marriage and Family Therapy is a systemic orientation to facilitating
change in individuals, couples, and families. A systemic orientation means
that we bring to our work two basic assumptions. First, we assume that
people are always in the process of "making sense." To "make sense" is to
order our worlds, to bring organization, categorization, and meaning to
what we experience, perceive, and believe. People simply do not hold beliefs

or opinions that do not make sense to them. They don't make decisions or act on ideas that do not make sense to them.

A second, but closely related idea is our view that the world is most usefully understood as relationally organized. We perceive the world as an interwoven, interconnected web of relations, rather than as a series of discrete objects causing and effecting one another. We are in continual relationship with language and ideas ("I love systems theory"), language and material objects ("I hate my old car"), language and emotions ("I love my teacher!"), language and behaviors (I hate when I act like that), and, of course, ourselves ("Self, look at that scale! You have got to quit eating chocolate"). The therapy world in which we work is a world of words, language, and meaning, which is quite different than the world of *objects*, the world of physical matter, where one piece of matter can change another piece of matter by energistically colliding with it. In the material world, change is brought about by force (Bateson, 2000; Keeney, 1983). Our work — the art and science of human change — belongs to the world of *relationship*, where change is brought about by information (Bateson, 2000).

When someone comes to us for therapy, we do not hear her[1] problem as a-thing-to-be-gotten-rid-of but rather as a relationship to be disentangled (Flemons, 2002). We listen for the various ways that her problem is a tangle of various relationships, whether with abstract ideas, with herself, with someone else, or with physical objects. This is not always easy to do, since language, by its very nature, separates and particulates, blinding us to connections. When Marge asks us to "make Kyle care," she is saying that she cannot see how his "not caring" makes sense. And, given how unproductive, even destructive "not caring" is, it only makes sense to get rid of it, the "thing" (not caring) that is causing all the trouble. Unable to "see relationally," Marge cannot perceive the various ways that Kyle's "not caring" is connected to his relationship to himself, his mom, and his ideas about his future. So, from her point of view, the solution was to yank the "not caring" out of him. This, she had been trying to do for years. But nothing seemed to work, and as Kyle grew and Marge's attempted solutions seemed to be less and less effective, Marge's worry deepened and grew, and she intensified her efforts, applying "more of the same" with ever greater intensity and attention to detail. Still, nothing worked. Kyle had barely made it out of the 7th and 8th grades. Now in the 9th grade but still with the same indifferent work and study patterns, Marge, in desperation, brought him to the "big guns" — therapists, people who understood the human mind and could get inside his head, making him succeed where she had failed. When we asked, "What have you done to solve this problem?" Marge told story after story, each one detailing her efforts since Kyle was a small boy to make him care about his future.

THE ROLE OF FAMILY THERAPY IN FAMILY-CENTERED COMMUNITIES OF CARE

It is a well-established principle of systems theory that a part of a system cannot control the whole of which it is a part (Bateson, 2000; Keeney, 1983). Language, however, inclines us to believe otherwise. Language breaks the world into pieces and sets the pieces over and against one another, giving the illusion that one piece can control another (Flemons, 1991).

During our initial session with Marge, we asked her a number of questions about Kyle's learning disability. One of the important pieces of information to immerge concerned how Marge and her husband, Ken, responded to Kyle's diagnosis at 5 years of age by a school psychologist, who described Kyle as a very intelligent but "impaired" learner. As they talked about it, the psychologist made the off-hand comment that Marge and Ken would always have to work very hard to keep Kyle in school and up to grade level. This put both of them, but particularly Marge, on high alert. From that moment on, she organized her life and her family's life around doing what was necessary to keep Kyle from stepping into this invisible pool of quicksand that would suck him under. She made sure that he succeeded in school. Of course, the more Marge collaborated with his teachers, supervised and monitored homework, coached, guided, and handled his academic life, the more passive Kyle became. After all, why reach out your own arms and legs for help when someone else with deep concern for your life will do that for you? Once we had established how, given the context, it made sense for Kyle to be so passive about his life, we asked Marge to continue helping Kyle — but in a different way. As Kyle's rescuer, Marge's efforts would be aimed less at a preventing him from stepping into the mire and more at letting him experience for himself the seriousness of his situation and the actual possibility that he could get sucked under. This required that she clear space for him to feel the danger and to turn back to himself, to discover his strength and capabilities as an older, stronger, more knowledgeable young man. With some considerable trepidation, Marge did this. And Kyle responded accordingly. When he flunked a course, he was concerned, a response Marge had never seen in him. When he flunked a second course, he was upset. But with this second failure, as with the first, Marge did not let loose with her own anxiety. Instead, she empathized with Kyle's fear that he might not graduate with his class. She supported him with simple comments that indicated that she would not rescue him from his disappointment but that she was willing to help, such as, "if you want to do something differently and I can help, just let me know." But she continued to give him the freedom (and the responsibility) to make his own way. When we checked back with the family three years later, Kyle was about to graduate from high school and head off to college in another state.

Parents, teachers, and other authoritative adults often attempt to facilitate change in a child (or each other) by applying a material-world kind of thinking that seeks to get rid of problems by the "force" of words. Viewing problems as localizable "things," adults throw words at them as if the words will crash into the problem, and it will crumble into a thousand harmless pieces. As we've noted, words, being abstractions and having no actual "force" to them, rarely work on problems the way we hope they will, which is to make them go away. So, we do something that exacerbates the problem: We do the same thing again. We throw more words at the problem, only this time we do it more loudly or more menacingly, maybe adding such game-changers as, "And I mean it!", "I'm serious this time!" or, "There is going to be real trouble, if you don't do what I say!" We learn early in life that the solution to the non-resolving solution is to try it again: Common sense tells us that when attempted solutions don't work, reapply them with more force.

All of us have seen a child yank on a toy or a tricycle that is wedged on something, and we've observed that the more she yanks, the tighter the wedge becomes. When we see this, we are seeing a child apply her learned problem solving principle — when an attempted solution does not resolve the problem, apply more of the same solution (Watzlawick, Weakland, & Fisch, 1974). Children learn this from adults. When words don't have their intended effect, an adult often says them more emphatically, more intensely, more forcefully, with more volume or for a longer duration. As the speaker gets more frustrated at the failure of her words to achieve compliance, she may begin to handle her words like projectiles, hurling them with more volume, rapidity, or threat.[2] But words, whether those of a teacher, a parent, or a therapist, sent as mortar, cannot control behavior or *make* children acquiescent, nor can they inject hope or demolish unwanted feelings or behaviors. Words-sent-as-objects cannot physically command action or control behavior and symptoms; they cannot resolve confusion, vanquish an urge, dissolve rage, or banish fear. Words (and problems) are not localizable objects subject to the laws of physics, but part of complex relationships that include linguistic, paralinguistic, cultural, and contextual factors. They cannot be used instrumentally to remove a problem as though it were a cancer to be excised.

Language gives the illusion of control. A mother brought her 15 year old daughter, Cloe, to us when the school threatened to kick her out if she didn't see someone for her "anger problem." The way Cloe used language to describe her anger gave us clues about how she thought about herself and how she thought about anger. In short, we could "see" her relationship with anger. She complained, for example, that anger "gets the best of me," words that give anger a location, as though it were a concrete entity, and putting it somewhere outside of her "self" where it robs her of something (the best of her). Her "self" and her "anger" are discrete entities, different experiences of one person. When Cloe declared that she is, "never going to let myself get angry like that again," her language implies that one part of her (her will, perhaps) can control the rest of her, including the "part" in which her anger resides.

Cloe's choice of words is not a problem with Cloe. This is the nature of reflexivity and language: We stand outside and look back in to observe and reflect back on ourselves (as in, "Oh! I can't believe I said that to him."). Yet the "I" doing the contemplating is the same person as the "myself" being contemplated. Any part of ourselves that seems in need of control (anger, depression, procrastination, anxiety, etc.) is as much our "self" as the part trying to control (Laughlin & Warner, 2007). Language and the reflexive nature of being successfully fool us into the perception that portions of the self are separate and apart, rather than complementary parts of a larger whole (Flemons, 1991). It is impossible to *not* be simultaneously embedded in multiple connections. The *experience* of learning and a child's subsequent response to that experience are not material "things" that act mechanistically on the student. These things are all relational, belonging to the non-material world of relationship.

SPECIAL EDUCATION-FAMILY THERAPY CREATED COMMUNITY OF CARE

In a mobile all the pieces, no matter what size or shape, can be grouped together and balanced by shortening or lengthening the strings attached or rearranging the distance between the pieces. So it is with the family. None of the family members is identical to any others; they are all different and at different levels of growth. As in a mobile, you can't arrange one without thinking of the other. (Satir, 1972, pp. 119–120)

Special educators have explored the importance of building teams, or communities, in a variety of ways over the years. We have experimented with multi-disciplinary teams, inter-disciplinary teams, and trans-disciplinary teams. But our efforts at creating a community of care for students with disabilities and their families were more focused on creating a community of professionals to *help* families and students and less focused on looking at special education from the inside out − from the perspective of the family and the student. Even as we found ways to invite families into the process, our extension of an "invitation" denoted our authority over the process.

However, focusing on the work of Dunst et al. (2007), early intervention specialists have been growing in their understanding of building a community of care that places families at the center of the process. Having learned that ensuring family voice and choice are the drivers of a successful process, they have pioneered a process that empowers family decision making. The results have been transformational beyond special education outcomes. Although schools would be wise to adopt some of these ways of thinking and behaving to transform their teams into communities of care, family-centered practices are difficult to implement as a best practice model, not because educators do not know how to work with children with disabilities, but because they do not know how to work with families in a family-centered way (Healy, Keesee, & Smith, 1989).

Given that family therapists' training and epistemological orientation, as described above, consists of those elements that educators recognize as crucial to developing family-centered practice (Espe-Sherwindt, 2008), a collaborative effort between special educators and family therapists could provide a solution. Specifically trained to work with families, family therapists could train teachers and other school personnel ways of approaching families that avoid persuasion, infusion of guilt or fear, cajoling, selling, threatening, or begging, all of which are, at best, fruitless, and at worst, set up defensiveness, anger, and embattle participants. By training teachers in the following seven points, teachers would learn the art of family-centered practice:

1. assume parent, student, and teacher viewpoints are valid
2. learn how to make sense of viewpoints that do not seem logical
3. learn a slower-paced disentanglement orientation rather than a rapid fire "getting rid of"
4. orient toward conversational evolution rather than control

5. look for how "more of the same" maybe entrenching the problem
6. learn to recognize (and avoid) language as a force designed to physically change someone or something
7. learn to see the connections between ideas, perceptions, relationships, people, and things.

The theoretical frame that informs the MFT discipline would inform all conversations. The notion that families, teachers, and students are always in the process of "making sense" of their worlds would apply. This would mean that all perspectives would be heard and valued. Whether student, teacher, or parent, each has a valid but different way of making sense of the issues at hand. Each has a different task and each has different information that shapes his or her perception. Given this, no participant is viewed or treated as the bad person, in the wrong, or crazy – no one is pathologized. Given that all viewpoints are respected and balanced with those of others, no single view stands in opposition or judgment, thus making family-student-teacher collaboration authentic and, most importantly, useful. Using a family therapy theoretical frame, we can critically analyze the way in which we work together as a community of caregivers and, importantly, the way in which families and students are supported to be in the driver's seat of the educational community team. The role of community in special education is one of the most important concepts we could transform and in doing so, we could collectively and positively impact the life's journey for the families and students we encounter.

CONCLUSION

Community is often viewed as a bricks-and-mortar concept, a matter of physically bringing people together in time and space. In this chapter, we suggest that community is more usefully thought of as a way of thinking, an orientation. When teachers view parents as resources, avenues open up that can help make their task easier. They can reach out to parents in a different way, one that is truly collaborative and contains a spirit of mutual helpfulness. When parents help teachers – making the teacher's jobs easier – and teachers help parents – making parents' jobs easier, the consequent benefits to the student are enormous. Family therapists, trained to see the way that people make sense of their worlds, themselves, and their problems are able to help parents and teachers make better sense, have clearer understandings of a student's behaviors and failures, and to act as translators of a student's seemingly nonsensical behavior. When teachers recognize that parents can help them provide a higher quality service, and work with parents in a family-centered, rather than professional-centered way, the spirit of the 2004 IDEA is realized as a true special education community emerges.

NOTES

1. To honor gender equality and for the sake of simplicity and clarity, we have chosen in this chapter to randomly switch between the use of female and male pronouns.
2. Some adults reach the upper boundary of the obedience that can be wrung from language. Often feeling there are no other options, they ultimately, inflict bodily harm, even death.

REFERENCES

Bateson, G. (2000). *Steps to an ecology of mind.* Chicago, IL: University of Chicago Press.
Chetty, R., Hendren, N., Kline, P., & Saez, E. (2013). The equality of opportunity project. *Summary of Project Findings,* July. Retrieved from http://obs.rc.fas.harvard.edu/chetty/website/IGE/Executive%20Summary.pdf
Clinton, H. R. (1996). *It takes a village.* New York, NY: Simon & Schuster.
Conroy, P. (2012). Collaborating with cultural and linguistically diverse families of students in rural schools who receive special education services. *Rural Special Education Quarterly,* *31*(3), 20–24.
Dunst, C. J., Trivette, C. M., & Hamby, D. W. (2006). *Family support program quality and parent, family and child benefits.* Asheville, NC: Winterberry Press.
Dunst, C. J., Trivette, C. M., & Hamby, D. W. (2007). Meta-analysis of family-centered help giving practices research. *Mental Retardation and Developmental Disability Research Reviews,* *13*(4), 370–378.
Espe-Sherwindt, M. (2008). Family-centred practice: Collaboration, competency and evidence. *Support for Learning,* *23*(3), 136–143.
Flemons, D. (1991). *Completing distinctions.* Boston, MA: Shambhala.
Flemons, D. (2002). *Of one mind: The logic of hypnosis, the practice of therapy.* New York, NY: W. W. Norton.
Harry, B. (2008). Collaboration with culturally and linguistically diverse families: Ideal vs. reality. *Exceptional Children,* *74*(3), 372–388.
Healy, A. L., Keesee, P. D., & Smith, B. S. (1989). *Early services for children with special needs: Transactions for family support.* Baltimore, MD: Brookes.
IDEA. (2004). *Title I, part A, section 601.* Retrieved from http://idea.ed.gov/explore/view/p/%2Croot%2Cstatute%2CI%2CA%2C601%2C
Iyer, P. (2013). *Where is home? TedTalk.* Retrieved from http://www.ted.com/talks/pico_iyer_where_is_home

Keeney, B. (1983). *Aesthetics of change*. New York, NY: Guilford.

Laughlin, M., & Warner, K. (2007). Re-membering: A relational approach to sexual abuse. In S. Green & D. Flemons (Eds.), *Quickies: The handbook of brief sex therapy* (pp. 280–303). New York, NY: W. W. Norton.

Lopez, S. J. (2010). *Americans' views of public schools still far worse than parents'*, August 25. Retrieved from http://www.gallup.com/poll/142658/Americans-Views-Public-Schools-Far-Worse-Parents.aspx

Noddings, N. (1984). *Caring: A feminist approach to ethics and moral education*. New York, NY: Teachers College Press.

Paterson, K. (2010). *Teaching in troubled times*. Markham, Ontario: Pembroke Publishers.

PDK/Gallup. (2014). *The PDK/Gallup poll of the public's attitudes toward the public schools*, September. Retrieved from http://pdkpoll.pdkintl.org/#9

PISA. (2012). Retrieved from http://www.oecd.org/pisa/keyfindings/pisa-2012-results-overview.pdf

Rattigan-Rohr, J. (2012). *It takes a village: A collaborative assault on the struggling reader dilemma*. Rotterdam: Sense Publishers.

Satir, V. (1972). *Peoplemaking*. Palo Alto, CA: Science and Behavior.

Schon, D. A. (1983). *The reflective practitioner: How professionals think in action*. New York, NY: Basic Books.

Spann, S. J., Kohler, F. W., & Soenksen, D. (2003). Examining parents' involvement in and perceptions of special education services: An interview with families in a parent support group. *Focus Autism other Developmental Disabilities, 4*(18), 228–237. doi:10.1177/10883576030180040401

Taylor, H., Krane, D., & Orkis, K. (2010). *The ADA, 20 years later: Executive summary*, July. Retrieved from http://nod.org/assets/downloads/2010_Survey_of_Americans_with_Disabilities_GAPS_Full_Report.pdf

Turnbull, A., Turnbull, R., Erwin, E., & Sodak, L. (2006). *Families, professionals, and exceptionality: Collaborating for empowerment*. Upper Saddle River, NJ: Prentice-Hall.

Villa, K., & Thousand, J. (1988). Enhancing success in heterogeneous classroom and schools: The power of partnerships. *Teacher Education and Special Education, 11*, 144–154.

Watzlawick, P., Weakland, J., & Fisch, R. (1974). *Change: Principles of problem formation and problem resolution*. New York, NY: W. W. Norton.

Weiss, H. B., & Stephen, N. (2009). From periphery to center: A new vision for family, school, and community partnerships. In S. Christenson & A. Reschley (Eds.), *Handbook of school–family partnerships* (pp. 448–472). New York, NY: Routledge.

Welch, M., & Sheridan, S. M. (1995). *Educational partnerships: Serving students at risk*. Fort Worth, TX: Harcourt Brace.

CHAPTER 10

ROLE OF GOVERNMENT AGENCIES IN ENHANCING SPECIAL EDUCATION

Sunday Obi

ABSTRACT

Education is primary a state and local responsibility in the United States. It is states and communities, as well as public and private organizations of all kinds, that establish schools and colleges, develop curricula, and determine requirements for enrollment and graduation. The appropriate roles for state in the education of all children continue to be an issue of urgent concern. The Individuals with Disabilities Education Act *mandates cooperating and reporting between state and federal educational agencies. State educational agencies, in turn, must ensure that local schools and teachers are meeting the state's educational standards. The importance of this responsibility creates controversy on how public education should be implemented and what policy directions state and local governments should take. It is apparent that enhancing public education programs to benefit all students requires a process of system change, as opposed to isolated programs and invalidated instructional practices often common with programming in some school districts. This*

Interdisciplinary Connections to Special Education: Important Aspects to Consider
Advances in Special Education, Volume 30A, 167–184
Copyright © 2015 by Emerald Group Publishing Limited
All rights of reproduction in any form reserved
ISSN: 0270-4013/doi:10.1108/S0270-40132015000030A020

chapter discusses the role of government agencies in enhancing special education and problems associated with it.

Keywords: Education; agencies; policymakers; accountability; reauthorize; monitoring

Education is primarily a state and local responsibility in the United States. It is states and communities, as well as public and private organizations of all kinds, that establish schools and colleges, develop curricula, and determine requirements for enrollment and graduation. The appropriate roles for state in the education of all children continue to be an issue of urgent concern. The importance of this responsibility creates controversy on how public education should be implemented and what policy directions state and local governments should take (Engel, 1999). It is apparent that enhancing public education programs to benefit all students requires a process of system change, as opposed to isolated programs and invalidated instructional practices often common with programming in some school districts. This chapter discusses the role of government agencies in enhancing special education and problems associated with it.

The U.S. Department of Education was created in 1867 to collect information on schools and teaching that would help the states establish effective school systems. While the agency's name and location within the Executive Branch have changed over the past 130 years, this early emphasis on getting information on what works in education to teachers and education policymakers continues down to the present day. The antipoverty and civil rights laws of the 1960s and 1970s brought about a dramatic emergence of the Department's equal access mission. The passage of laws such as Title VI of *the Civil Rights Act* of 1964, Title IX of *the Education Amendments* of 1972, and Section 504 of *the Rehabilitation Act* of 1973, which prohibited discrimination based on race, sex, and disability, respectively, made civil rights enforcement a fundamental and long-lasting focus of the U.S. Department of Education. In 1965, *the Elementary and Secondary Education Act* launched a comprehensive set of programs, including the Title I program of Federal aid to disadvantaged children to address problems of poor urban and rural areas. And in that same year, *the Higher Education Act* authorized assistance for postsecondary education, including financial aid programs for needy college students. Despite the growth of the Federal role in education, the Department never strayed far from what would become its official mission: to promote student achievement and preparation for global competitiveness by fostering educational excellence and ensuring access. While education is primarily a state and local responsibility in the United States, the U.S. Department of Education plays a leadership role in the ongoing national dialog over how to improve results of our education system for all students.

CRITICAL ISSUES FACING GENERAL AND SPECIAL EDUCATION

Recently, there has been growing concern about the role of federal, state, and community agencies in enhancing education for all children. Understandably, everyone responsible for the education of all students work collectively to ensure that they are successful in their endeavors at school. Critics of public education have become extremely good fishermen in the river called "accountability." These fishermen have hooked a number of red herrings: zero tolerance, No Child Left Behind, vouchers, grade-level testing, and all children can learn. While these schemes and slogans are partly political and partly nonsense, together they are rapidly being established as criteria for evaluating school effectiveness (Thomas & Bainbridge, 2000). According to Thomas and Bainbridge (2000), the late Ronald R. Edmonds who was acknowledged as the "father of the effective-schools movement" suggested that all children can learn the basic curriculum of the school" (pp. 34–35). They argued that all children can learn if the following happens:

- State legislatures provide adequate financial support for schools as required by a number of current State Supreme Court decisions.
- Every child has adequate health care, as required for appropriate cognitive development.
- A certified teacher with adequate salary staffs every classroom.
- Every child attends a school that meets the life safety codes established by the states.
- Every child is cared for in high-quality child care facility.
- Each child has the opportunity to learn according to his or her developmental needs.

All children can learn the basic curriculum of the school *if given equal opportunity to do so* and if provided the opportunity to learn in accordance with standards written into the Goals 2000: Educate America Act of 1994

(U.S. Department of Education, 1994). Unfortunately, most states do not provide these fundamental conditions. Hill (1999) contended that many children with special health care needs, including those who would be considered by many to have "profound" problems and who in the past would have been cared for in hospitals and other institutions, are living at home and being integrated at school with their "normal" peers. A strong public education system is vital to America's well-being. While we are committed to the elaboration of the American public education, we support effective schools that provide educational excellence so that *all* children will have the opportunity to achieve academically at the highest level. The hope is help these children to become responsible citizens, attain economic self-sufficiency, and maintain a sense of self through their own cultural heritage. Clearly, when parents, school personnel, community members, and government officials work together, they ensure that *all* children have an opportunity to receive quality education. More specifically, federal, state, and community agencies must influence the quality of schools, and these supports must be consistent over time and across communities.

Special education programs in the United States were made mandatory in 1975 when the U.S. Congress passed the *Education for All Handicapped Children Act* (EAHCA) in response to discriminatory treatment by public educational agencies against students with disabilities. More specifically, before Congress passed the EAHCA (Public Law 94-142) in 1975, more than one million children with disabilities were excluded from school. Initially, the law focused on ensuring that children had access to an education. Again, due to a series of advocacies, litigations, and legislations in the United States, the well-being of exceptional students was enhanced. For example, Public Law 99-457 of 1986, an amendment of PL 94-142, was an asset in addressing special education concerns of children from birth to five years of age. In 1990, the *Individuals with Disabilities Education Act* (IDEA, PL 101-476) was instituted to respond to the incessant needs of exceptional individuals. With this law, the term "handicap" became a taboo — at least, there is a real understanding that individuals can be disabled or impaired and not be handicapped. This law attempted to revisit the traditional categories of exceptionalities and reiterate fundamental concepts embedded in the EAHCA (PL 94-142). In addition, it addresses the issues of "who," "why," and "how" to admit exceptional individuals into school programs by (a) referral and identification, (b) nondiscriminatory assessment, (c) parental consent, (d) procedural safeguards, (e) placement in the least restrictive environment, and (f) individualized education programming

(IEP). These concepts have impacted not only special education programs but also all aspects of professional training, including related services.

Furthermore, when Congress reauthorized IDEA in 1997, accountability and improved outcomes were emphasized while maintaining the goals of access and due process. In other words, the 1997 amendment included (a) annual goals and benchmarks or objectives on the IEP, (b) expansion of the IEP team to include a general education teacher, (c) inclusion of students with disabilities in state and school district assessment of achievement, and this decision-making process became part of the IEP, and (d) specific discipline procedures to protect the rights of students with disabilities and to maintain safety and security in schools. In fact, IDEA clearly stipulated that school officials may remove students with disabilities who violate school rules to appropriate interim alternative settings, or other settings, or can suspend them for up to 10 school days. Even so, educators could implement such measures only to the extent that they used similar punishments when disciplining students who are not disabled. In addition, students may be removed to interim alternative educational setting for up to 45 days under specified circumstances, without regard for whether their misbehavior was a manifestation of their disabilities. Under IDEA, school officials were required to conduct functional behavioral assessments and implement behavioral intervention plans for students placed in interim alternative settings. Similarly, some of these provisions codified existing case law, while others clarified some of the gray areas, and some even settled disagreements that had existed between and among the courts.

As indicated earlier, special education is governed by state statutes as well as the federal laws in order to provide opportunities or access to millions of individuals with disabilities. One of those laws is the *No Child Left Behind Act* (NCLB) that was enacted in 2001. The NCLB, an extension of the original *Elementary and Secondary Education Act* of 1965, has impacted the delivery of special education services (Zirkel, 2004). The key elements in the NCLB are to (a) improve the academic achievement of students who are economically disadvantaged; (b) assist in preparing, training, and recruiting highly qualified teachers (and principals); (c) provide language instruction for children of limited English proficiency; (d) make school systems rely on teaching methods that are research based and that have been proven effective; and (e) afford parents better choices while creating innovative educational programs, especially where local school systems are unresponsive to parents' needs (Wenkart, 2003). As part of the process of complying with the revised IDEA and the NCLB, school officials must take measurable steps to recruit, hire, train, and retain highly qualified school personnel to provide special education and related services to students with disabilities. To continue the progress in the field of special education, Congress passed the *Individuals with Disabilities Education Improvement Act* (IDEIA) of 2004, which requires schools to use "proven methods of teaching and learning" based on "replicable research." This law, IDEIA 2004, ensures that all children and youth with disabilities have the right to free, appropriate public education. In addition, this law defines special education as specially designed instruction that meets the unusual needs of an exceptional student (Huefner, 2006) and which might require special materials, teaching techniques, or equipment and/or facilities. Clearly, to meet the needs of all students with disabilities, a range of educational agencies must be in place in all 50 states, with the federal agency leading the way.

EDUCATION AND GOVERNMENT AGENCIES

The passage in 1965 of Title V of the *Elementary and Secondary Education Act*, which provided federal funds to bolster the professional staff of state education agencies, greatly increased state-level educational activity. It led, for example, to increased research, media, and consulting services to local school districts, and administration of federal funds for compensatory education. State monitoring of local graduation standards and instructional quality are essential and reinforced by regional accrediting agencies. During the nineteenth century, secondary school courses were so diverse that universities had no way of knowing what and how much their incoming students knew. They therefore established the practices of certifying the curricula of given schools and then accepting their students without entrance examinations. Eventually, these certification practices were institutionalized, and the resulting agencies visited high schools to approve their curricula, certify their students, and "accredit" their programs. These agencies have made secondary school course offerings more uniform, at least for college-preparatory programs, and they have created an external watchdog function, which reduces the autonomy of schools and districts (Bennett & LeCompte, 1995).

In most states, the board is elected and the chief state school officer (CSSO) is either elected or appointed by the governor. Usually, as is the case on the local level, the CSSO is expected to assume policy leadership with the cooperation and under the supervision of the board. The administrative details are attended to by the staff of the State Department of Education (Engel, 1999). State officials must guarantee that local officials operate within the limits of state law. In matters such as teacher certification, school accreditation, and special and vocational education, most states exercise a great deal of control. Indeed, state mandates have become especially significant in the education of students with special needs. Similarly, federal mandates have become significant in the education of special needs population.

The State Legislature

The legislative branch of the state exercises two kinds of power. One is to enact rules and regulations that are binding on the jurisdiction of the created agency. The other is the power to enforce the laws passed by the legislature or the regulations passed by some other body. State regulations take precedence over the policies of local school districts, and the school district policies must conform to the regulations of the State Board.

State Board of Education

Most states have created a state agency to make regulations governing education within the state. One of the major reasons for such an agency is to take pressure off of the legislative branch to continually pass legislation and to provide some overall direction for schooling in the state through the adoption of statewide regulations affecting all school districts within the state. These bodies are given rule-making power by their creators. Under the powers delegated to it by the General Assembly, the State Board promulgates and adopts rules and regulations concerning educational programs in areas such as certification of school personnel, curriculum, pupil attendance and transportation, and special education.

State Departments of Education and CSSOs

Many states have created some agency to provide administrative supervision for the public schools. The exact nature of this agency differs from state to state. Most states also have a CSSO who is in charge of the state agency. This agency can be an independent agency or a part of the executive branch of the state government, and the CSSO can be elected or appointed. These government personnel can legally exercise the powers granted them by the state constitution or statutes. The State Boards of Education partners with school districts to provide programs and services for students with specialized educational needs. Special Education Services assure that these programs and services meet state and federal requirements and involve both compliance and technical assistance functions. Compliance functions include monitoring least restrictive environment compliance, administering due process system, providing mediation services, conducting compliant investigations, approving policies and procedures, conducting focused and comprehensive reviews, and approving nonpublic special education facilities. Technical assistance functions involve providing information and guidance on promising practices in educating students with disabilities, including the operation of numerous statewide training and technical assistance initiatives, administering the comprehensive system of personnel development for special education, and management of grant programs to schools for special education service delivery.

School Districts

In the history of public education, school districts and school boards were created quite early because in most states schooling was first established and controlled by the local community. School districts are the state agencies with which most citizens are familiar, and they are local agencies created by the General Assembly, which have been given various powers by the legislature. Some of the more important duties of school district boards are:

- adopt rules and regulations governing teachers and students;
- determine the school budget and set the millage to be levied on assessed valuation of property in the district, which provides most of the local tax monies to fund the schools;
- hire teachers and contract for various services, including the maintenance and construction of buildings;
- choose textbooks and establish the curriculum; and
- serve as the local agency in the first level of adjudication for teachers and students in matters such as teacher dismissal or student expulsion.

In doing the above, the school district board must conform to the regulations of the State Board of Education and the statutes of the General Assembly.

The Special Education Cooperative Agency

IDEIA (2004) stipulates that there must be collaborative partnerships fostered, and why states have taken this order seriously. For example, in the State of Kentucky, all 173 local school districts and the Kentucky Schools for the Blind and Deaf are members of a special education cooperative. The Special Education Cooperative Network is intended to assist local school districts in meeting the needs of its member districts. Services range from technical assistance, trainings, professional development, specialized services, research, and other needs identified by member districts and the Kentucky Department of Education. Kentucky's Special Education Cooperatives enhance the educational opportunities and outcomes of students by providing effective leadership and delivering specialized services in partnership with the Kentucky Department of Education, local school districts, institutes of higher education, and other service providers.

THE U.S. OFFICE OF SPECIAL EDUCATION: THE PILLAR FOR ENHANCING SPECIAL EDUCATION

The Office of Special Education (OSEP) is dedicated to improving results for infants, toddlers, and children with disabilities from birth age through 21 years by providing leadership and financial support to assist states and local districts. OSEP is committed to ensure that students with disabilities are an integral part of all aspects of P-12 education policy development and program implementation. Also, the OSEP works to promote educational equity and excellence for students with disabilities by:

- overseeing the implementation of federal and state laws and policy for students with disabilities;
- providing general supervision and monitoring of all public and private schools serving New York State preschool and school-age students with disabilities;

- establishing a broad network of technical assistance centers and providers to work directly with parents and school districts to provide current information and high-quality professional development and technical assistance to improve results for students with disabilities;
- ensuring a system of due process, including special education mediation and impartial hearings; and
- meeting with stakeholders through the Commissioner's Advisory Panel for Special Education Services.

In fact, the OSEP's mission is to promote student achievement and preparation for global competitiveness by fostering educational excellence and ensuring equal access. In an effort to accomplish its mission, it has created many other services including:

1. *Association of Service Providers Implementing IDEA Reforms in Education* (ASPIRE) and IDEA Local Implementation by Local Administrators (ILIAD) – The ASPIRE and ILIAD Partnership Projects involve professional organizations working together to provide needed information, ideas, and technical assistance to implement the *Individuals with Disabilities Education Act* of 1997 (IDEA '97).
2. *Center for Effective Collaboration and Practice* (CECP) (http://cecp.air. org/) – It is the mission of the Center to support and to promote a reoriented national preparedness to foster the development and adjustment of children with or at risk of developing serious emotional disturbance. To achieve that goal, the Center is dedicated to a policy of collaboration at federal, state, and local levels that contributes to and facilitates the production, exchange, and use of knowledge about effective practices.
3. *Center for Positive Behavioral Supports* (http://www.pbis.org/) – The Center's purpose is to give schools capacity-building information and technical assistance for identifying, adapting, and sustaining effective schoolwide disciplinary practices.
4. *Center for Special Education Finance* (CSEF) (http://www.csef-air.org/) – The CSEF was established in October 1992 to address fiscal policy questions related to the delivery and support of special education services throughout the United States.
5. *Center of Minority Research in Special Education* (COMRISE) (http:// curry.edschool.virginia.edu/go/comrise/) – COMRISE is designed to enhance the capacity of researchers in special education from historically Black colleges and universities and other minority institutions of

higher education (IHEs) to build and pursue research agendas focused on minority issues in special education.

6. *The Center on Accelerating Student Learning* (CASL) (http://kc.vanderbilt. edu/casl/) – The CASL is designed to accelerate learning for students with disabilities in the early grades and thereby to provide a solid foundation for strong achievement in the intermediate grades and beyond.

7. *Consortium for Appropriate Dispute Resolution in Special Education and Support* (CADRE) (http://www.directionservice.org/cadre/) – CADRE's mission is to provide technical assistance and serve as an information clearinghouse on dispute resolution in special education.

8. *Consortium on Inclusive Schooling Practices* (CISP) (http://ruralinstitute. umt.edu/Community/cisp.asp) – The CISP represents a collaborative effort to build the capacity of state and local education agencies to serve children and youth with and without disabilities in school and community settings.

9. *CPB/WGBH National Center for Accessible Media* (NCAM) (http:// ncam.wgbh.org/) – The CPB/WGBH NCAM is a research and development facility that works to make media accessible to underserved populations such as disabled persons, minority-language users, and people with low literacy skills.

10. National Information Clearinghouse on Children Who Are Deaf-Blind (DB-LINK) (http://www.tr.wou.edu/dblink/) – The DB-LINK is a federally funded information and referral service that identifies, coordinates, and disseminates (at no cost) information related to children and youth who are deaf–blind (ages 0–21 years).

11. *Descriptive Video Service* (http://main.wgbh.org/wgbh/pages/mag/) – Making television and movies more accessible to people who are blind or have low vision.

12. *Families and Advocates Partnership for Education* (FAPE) (http://fape. org/) – The FAPE is a new project which aims to inform and educate families and advocates about the *Individuals with Disabilities Education Act* of 1997 (IDEA '97). The Partnership helps to ensure that the changes made in IDEA are understood by families and advocates and are put into practice at local and state levels.

13. *Family Center on Technology and Disability* (http://www.fctd.info/) – The purpose of the Family Center is to assist organizations and programs who serve families of children with disabilities by providing information and support on accessing and using assistive technology.

14. *The Federal Resource Center for Special Education* (FRC) (http://www.dssc.org/frc/) – FRC seeks to respond quickly to the needs of students with disabilities, and the families, professionals, and communities who are associated with these students, and encourages the development of programs for students with disabilities that will lead to the educational results needed for employment, a good family life, and positive participation in the community.

15. *HEATH Resource Center* (http://www.heath.gwu.edu/) – National Clearinghouse on Postsecondary Education for Individuals with Disabilities. The HEATH Resource Center of the American Council on Education is the national clearinghouse on postsecondary education for individuals with disabilities.

16. *The National Center on Education, Disability, and Juvenile Justice* (http://www.edjj.org/) – The National Center on Education, Disability, and Juvenile Justice is a collaborative research, training, technical assistance, and dissemination program designed to develop more effective responses to the needs of youth with disabilities in the juvenile justice system or those at risk for involvement with the Juvenile Justice System.

17. *National Center on Educational Outcomes* (NCEO) (http://ced.umn.edu/nceo/) – The NCEO was established in 1990 to provide national leadership in the identification of outcomes, indicators, and assessments to monitor educational results for all students, including students with disabilities.

18. *National Clearinghouse for Professions in Special Education* (NCPSE) (http://www.special-ed-careers.org/) – The NCPSE is committed to enhancing the nation's capacity to recruit, prepare, and retain well-qualified and diverse educators and service personnel for children with disabilities.

19. *The National Early Childhood Technical Assistance System* (NEC*TAS) (http://www.nectac.org/) – NEC*TAS is funded by the Office of Special Education and Rehabilitative Services (OSERS) to support the development of policies, programs, and practices for young children with disabilities and their families.

20. *The National Information Center for Children and Youth with Disabilities* (NICHCY) (http://www.nichcy.org/) – The NICHCY provides information on disabilities and disability-related issues, links people with others who share common concerns, publishes newsletters and issue papers, and generally helps information flow between people who have it and people who need it.

21. *The National Institute on Disability and Rehabilitation Research* (NIDRR) (http://about/offices/list/osers/nidrr/index.tml) – The NIDRR provides leadership and support for several programs related to the rehabilitation of individuals with disabilities.

22. *The National Rehabilitation Information Center* (NARIC) (http://www.naric.com/) – The NARIC is funded by the Department of Education to disseminate information on spinal cord injury, head injury, assistive technology, the *Americans with Disabilities Act*, independent living, return to work, vocational rehabilitation, etc.

23. *National Technical Assistance Consortium for Children and Young Adults Who Are Deaf-Blind* (NTAC) (http://www.tr.wou.edu/ntac/) – The NTAC provides technical assistance to families and agencies serving children and young adults who are deaf–blind.

24. *OSERS Regional Resource and Federal Centers* (RRFC) (http://www.dssc.org/frc/rrfc.htm) – The Regional Resource Centers are Office of Special Education Programs-funded programs that provide technical assistance services to state education agencies in the 50 states and 7 U.S. jurisdictions. They are specifically funded to help states improve programs and services for children and youth with disabilities, their families, and the professionals who serve them.

25. *The Policy Maker Partnership for Implementing IDEA '97* (PMP) (http://ideapolicy.org/pmp.htm) – The PMP is one of four linked projects funded by the U.S. Department of Education's Office of Special Education Programs. These projects are designed to deliver a common message about the 1997 landmark amendments to the *Individuals with Disabilities Education Act* (IDEA) to four specific audiences:

   • Policymakers: Policymaker Partnership (PMP)
   • Local Administrators: Local Implementation by Local Administrators (ILIAD)
   • Service Providers: Associations of Service Providers Implementing IDEA Reforms in Education (ASPIRE)
   • Families & Communities: Families & Advocates Partnership for Education (FAPAE).

MOVING FORWARD TO ADVANCE EQUITABLE SPECIAL EDUCATION

Public education is one of the most vital of all governmental services, and it is primarily the responsibility of state and local governments to administer and finance public schools, colleges, and universities. The importance of this responsibility creates controversy on how public education should be implemented and what policy directions state and local governments' should take (Engel, 1999). In the United States, federal education policies focus on equal opportunity and equal access of all students to education. And, educational policies that act to remedy past discrimination or provide additional resources to disadvantaged students are important in bolstering academic achievement for all students. However, educational policies do not always translate into practice, and very often, when changes do occur, they are slow. Furthermore, laws that intend to provide equitable learning experiences for students sometimes not only fail to extend equal opportunities to all students but also mask inequalities.

In education reform, it is necessary to consider whether the resources that schools receive through legislation, from the social capital of the local community to textbooks and to professional development, are sufficient to initiate or sustain change. Educational policies should ideally take these factors into consideration, but the links between the availability of local resources and policies, local needs and policies, and educational research and policies are often not forged (Reimers & McGinn, 1998). Policies targeted toward providing equitable education to all children may fall short because of the inability of stakeholders to carry out the law or because the policies themselves lead to unintended outcomes that act to perpetuate inequality. For instance, it has been nearly 50 years since Brown, but schools are now headed toward resegregation and many schools never truly desegregated in the first place (Orfield & Yun, 1999). Segregation could happen in other, less noticeable ways, such as the overrepresentation of African-American males in segregated special education programs (Artiles & Trent, 1994; Harry, 1994). In order to better serve students with disabilities, government agencies must continue to play a vital role. In fact, there is a pressing need to help educators meet the needs of all children. A useful process for improving public education is by reviewing the various concerns of researchers, scholars, and advocates who are calling for changes in the way educators provide services in both rural and urban schools. The call for a change came in earnest with inclusive advocates such as Will (1986) urging public education and administrators to become more responsible for the education of students who have special needs in schools, including those who are economically disadvantaged. Her views have been supported by many scholars and educators in recent years. At a national level, the National Center on Educational Outcomes (NCEO, 1997) estimated 40−50 percent of all students with disabilities were excluded from National

Assessment of Educational Progress (NAEP; McGrew, Thurlow, & Spiegel, 1993; Vail, 1997). As McGrew et al. (1993) argued, "The treatment of most students with disabilities as outlined in our national data collection programs is a concern from an equity and philosophical perspective" (p. 348). Such exclusion is also seen in state-level assessments where there is a wide variability in the extent of special education students' participation in statewide assessments (Erickson, Thurlow, & Ysseldyke, 1996).

It seems clear that fundamental changes will have to take place in all educational programs to address the needs of all students. Knoll and Obi (1996) suggested that (a) practitioners currently working in schools must be provided with resources, training, and time needed to develop effective cooperative and collaborative working relationships; (b) universities, engaged in preservice teacher education, need to break down the barriers between urban schools and rural schools; (c) the State Departments of Education must have a restructuring task force for every school that provides an opportunity for all stakeholders to buy into the vision and contribute to the local design of reform; (d) the State Departments of Education, regional special education cooperatives, local districts, and universities should collaborate to design regional support teams to assist individual educational programs in working through the process of restructuring; and (e) professional development activities that allow all teachers to examine basic topics in education of all students must be established.

The organizational structures of education programs for students will vary, but the State Departments of Education must strive to introduce policies that help school districts provide services in terms of good principles. State governments must enforce best practices, in all school districts, so that professionals will continue to provide high-quality educational programs for our children in the new millennium. An example is a project for a statewide system change that was implemented in the state of Utah some years ago. This effort has focused on developing coordinated preservice and in-service initiatives in rural areas. It has also been a collaborative effort between the Utah State Office of Education, university program faculty, and rural school district personnel. Teachers and administrators might apply Utah's initiative in developing effective programs for all students. Effective projects must be spearheaded by the State Office of Education for individuals, organizations, and schools that share the vision for school reform. In addition, State Departments of Education must make sure that minimum standard for curriculum, pupil promotion, and graduation, and for specific education programs such as kindergarten, vocational education, and high school. States must have detailed courses of study for specific subjects such as social studies and math and adopt textbooks that are distributed to local schools. They must have detailed regulations regarding the physical features of school buildings and the size of school libraries. They must also define the length of the school day and year, and they must have regulations that are very detailed with respect to requirements for the certification of teachers and financing local schools. In some states, tax limits are set for local districts and requirements are made for certain local budget breakdowns. States must assume greater shares of educational expenses since state courts recognize that existing systems of financial support provide unequal educational opportunities. State Departments of Education's activities must include the actual operation of state schools for students with disabilities and involvement in the operation of vocational programs and teacher preparation colleges. The regulatory activities of State Departments of Education can extend into areas such as curriculum and teaching standards, school construction, school buses, civil defense and fire drills, and other items specified in the state code or constitution.

CONCLUSION

In this chapter, I have presented an overview of government agencies and their roles in enhancing special education. IDEA entitles every student to free and appropriate public education in the least restrictive environment. And, all local school districts must adhere to the standards set by federal and state educational agencies. That is to say, special education programs at the district level are structured upon a cooperative federalism model and therefore governed by both state and federal laws. IDEA is frequently described as a model of cooperative federalism. It leaves to the States the primary responsibility for developing and executing educational programs for students with disabilities, but imposes significant requirements to be followed in the discharge of that responsibility. State policymakers have many tools which influence school practices, but the effects of policies tend to be limited rather than diverse (Stevenson & Schiller, 1999).

IDEA mandates cooperating and reporting between state and federal educational agencies. Participating states must certify to the Secretary of Education that they have policies and procedures that will effectively meet the Act's conditions. State educational agencies, in turn, must ensure that local schools and teachers are meeting the state's educational standards. Local educational agencies (school boards or other administrative bodies) can receive IDEA funds only if they certify to a state educational agency that they are acting in accordance with the state's policies and procedures. Disputes over the application of the law begin at the local school district and travel through an administrative law process that is subject to judicial review. In order to enhance special education for students with disabilities, government agencies must direct their attention to local school districts. Local school districts must make every effort to meet the needs of all students in the most effective ways. Legislators must realize that public education must strive to improve. It is encouraging to see that even before legal mandates were put in place (e.g., IDEA), several states (e.g., Kentucky) took the initiative to create agencies to better serve all students. Finally, all levels of government agencies – federal, state, and local – must share in the responsibility of providing adequate and equitable education for all children. The operation of effective special education requires strong and sustained efforts from all government agencies.

REFERENCES

Artiles, A. J., & Trent, S. C. (1994). Overrepresentation of minority students in special education: A continuing debate. *The Journal of Special Education, 27,* 410–437.

Bennett, K., & LeCompte, M. D. (1995). *The analysis of education* (2nd ed.). White Plains, NY: Longman.

Engel, M. (1999). *State and local government.* New York, NY: Peter Lang.

Erickson, R. N., Thurlow, M. L., & Ysseldyke, J. E. (1996). *Drifting denominators: Issues in determining participation rates for students with disabilities in statewide assessment programs.* Minneapolis, MN: University of Minnesota, National Center on Educational Outcomes.

Harry, B. (1994). *The disproportionate representation of minority students in special education: Theories and recommendations.* Alexandra, VA: National Association of State Directors of Special Education.

Hill, J. L. (1999). *Meeting the needs of students with special physical and health care needs.* Upper Saddle River, NJ: Prentice Hall.

Huefner, D. S. (2006). *Getting comfortable with special education law: A framework for working with children with disabilities* (2nd ed.). Norwood, MA: Christopher Gordon.

Knoll, J., & Obi, S. (1996). *Analysis of inclusive education in Eastern Kentucky* (ERIC Document Reproduction Service No. ED 414 678).

McGrew, K. S., Thurlow, M. L., & Spiegel, A. N. (1993). An investigation of the exclusion of students with disabilities in national data collection programs. *Educational Evaluation and Policy Analysis, 9,* 171–178.

National Center on Educational Outcomes. (1997). *State special education outcomes: A report on state activities during educational reform.* Minneapolis, MN: University of Minnesota.

Orfield, G., & Yun, J. (1999). *Resegregation in American schools.* Cambridge, MA: The Civil Rights Project at Harvard University.

Reimers, F., & McGinn, N. (1998). Informed dialogue: Using research to shape educational policy around the world. *International Review of Education, 44,* 269–270.

Stevenson, D. L., & Schiller, K. S. (1999). State education policies and change of school practices: Evidence from the national longitudinal study of school. *American Journal of Education, 107,* 261–288.

Thomas, M. D., & Bainbridge, W. L. (2000, December). The truth about all children can learn: The bookshelf: Education week on the WEB. Retrieved from http://edweek.org

U.S. Department of Education. (1994). *The Goals 2000: Educate America Act.* Washington, DC: U.S. Government Printing Office.

Vail, K. (1997). Special pioneers. *The American School Board Journal, 184,* 16–21.

Wenkart, R. D. (2003). The No Child Left Behind Act and Congress' power to regular under the spending clause. *Education Law Reporter, 174,* 589–597.

Will, M. C. (1986). Education children with learning problems: A shared responsibility. *Exceptional Children, 53,* 411–415.

Zirkel, P. A. (2004). NCLB: What does it mean for students with disabilities? *Education Law Reporter, 185,* 805–818.

CHAPTER 11

DIFFERENT ROLES AND SIMILAR MISSION IN THE EDUCATION OF STUDENTS WITH SPECIAL NEEDS: THE COMPREHENSIVE SUPPORT MODEL AT WORK

Festus E. Obiakor, Michael O. Afolayan, Pauline Harris-Obiakor and Precious O. Afolayan

ABSTRACT

Individuals with special needs encounter multidimensional experiences in identification, assessment, labeling/categorization, placement, and instruction/intervention. These experiences call for multidimensional strategies that require different educational practitioners and professionals. These individuals must bring with them different ideas on how to remediate problems experienced by children and youth with special needs. Sometimes, in dealing with these issues, we forget that collaboration, consultation, and cooperation (the 3Cs) are keys. To advance these 3Cs, the Comprehensive Support Model (CSM) must be at work. Based on the CSM, students, families, school personnel, communities, and

Interdisciplinary Connections to Special Education: Important Aspects to Consider
Advances in Special Education, Volume 30A, 185–194
ISSN: 0270-4013/doi:10.1108/S0270-40132015000030A009

government agencies must work together to maximize the fullest potential of all students, including those with special needs.

Keywords: Special needs; education; Comprehensive Support Model; collaboration; consultation; cooperation

More than 10 percent of students in the United States have disabling conditions that justify being placed in a special education program. In fact, when gifted students are included in the statistics, the figure increases. Educational opportunities for this category of students are, therefore, not only essential but must be given proper attention, guidance, and provisions. Hayford (2010) raised the critical question of inequity in the distribution of educational opportunities to all students, most especially those that fall in the category of the underrepresented in terms of gender, special needs, and ethnic representation. Obiakor, Eskay, and Afolayan (2012) tackled the same issue in their view of the fate of students with special needs. They argued that the social and cultural attitude as well as a lack of government concern put students with special needs in difficult circumstances. Douglas and Stack (2010) recounted John Dewey's assertion that "the democratic faith in human equality is belief that every human being, independent of the quantity or range of his (her) personal endowment, has the right to equal opportunity with every other person for development of whatever gifts he (she) has" (p. 21). For Dewey, then, equity and social justice without a universal application of, and access to, public education and exposure to economic possibilities is an assemblage of contradictions in terms. They only reflect an underhanded definition of these concepts because "the right to equal opportunity ... for development of whatever gifts" presupposes a comprehensive acceptance of the individual within the socioeconomic endowment of his or her community, regardless of natural or superficial abilities of the individual. In other words, the only credible way to attain true equity is through the provision of education to everyone, including those considered to be individuals with special needs in the society. The constitution of the United States, through the *Americans with Disabilities Act* (ADA) has made provisions for the accommodation and protection of individuals with disabilities. For example, it is explicitly stated on the website of the US Department of Education that:

> The Americans with Disabilities Act (ADA) gives civil rights protections to individuals with disabilities that are like those provided to individuals on the basis of race, sex, national origin, and religion. It guarantees equal opportunity for individuals with

disabilities in employment, public accommodations, transportation, State and local government services, and telecommunications. US Department of Education (1973)

Equal opportunities for students with disabilities is not only an intense moral imperative, it has become a legal mandate, a violation of which carries heavy punitive sanction against institutions and individuals in the United States. Apparently, as mentioned above, the ADA provision and similar laws and reauthorization that follow are anchored on the ethical principle that the way people treat the weakest among them speaks to who they are as a group. It is an understatement to say people are as strong as their weakest links. Therefore, the ethical principle works itself into a legal mandate, which is enforced strictly in all spheres of the American life, and more so in the education of students with special needs.

In providing education to the underrepresented members of the society, whether it is for addressing the educational needs of culturally and linguistically diverse (CLD) children, who are fast becoming a growing critical mass in public schools in America (Ladson-Billings, 1994; Sims, 2008), researching the growing stress of urban education (Gersten, Baker, & Lloyd, 2000; Schaffel, 1996), or in the education and reeducation of indigenous people (Browne, 2014), there is the need for a specialized approach, which has a comprehensive guide to it; this is even more critical when the individual exceptional learner falls within the definition of the CLD population. This comprehensive guide for advocating education for the CLD exceptional learner is the focus of Obiakor's (2008) Comprehensive Support Model (CSM). This model calls for wide-ranging intervention techniques necessary to support CLD exceptional learners. In what follows, then, we essentially explore the CSM and apply its espoused principles as an intervention technique for the provision of functional education to students with exceptional needs.

THE COMPREHENSIVE SUPPORT MODEL

According to the CSM, there is a quintuple (five-way) approach to addressing the issue of exceptional learners. They include the self (that is the learner by him/herself), the family (which includes the nuclear family as well as the extended family), the school (which entails all formal educational institution in which the child acquires knowledge – from womb to tomb), the community (which entails all individuals and institutions in the immediate and remote proximities of the child), and the government (which includes, but not limited to, the local, state, and federal governments).

The Self

The role of self is an age-long criterion in the provision of empowering education for all students. Self is always critical in the pursuit of true education (Hobson, 1996). This is because personality cum character development is salient to the acquisition of knowledge at all levels (Abourjilie, 2006). When these are not taken into consideration in preparing students in school, regardless of the volume of knowledge impacted or quantity of what instruction they are being given, the equation will remain unbalanced. It is tantamount to being overfed but undernourished. Alfred Bandura is a psychologist who has given a lifetime attention to the significance of the self, especially in advocating for and advancing one's cause. Self-advocacy is what Bandura (1983) referred to as self-efficacy. For him, self-efficacy is the notion that there is an innate tendency in an individual that propels the ability to organize and carry out the courses of action considered necessary for achieving a goal and managing a particular given situation. That self-advocacy tendency is what must be encouraged, triggered, and nurtured for students with special needs to attain their utmost potential. This is what will influence future choices they will make, the physical and emotional efforts they will put forth in achieving their goals, and their insistence and persistence in combating obstacles they face in their attempts to achieve like anyone else.

As noted, self-advocacy encourages deliberate efforts and according to Bandura (1983), there are three fundamental efforts that buttress self-efficacy and personal efficacy. First, individuals' efforts at making smaller steps towards the fulfilment of their goals should be noted and encouraged. Second, educators should motivate students to invoke sensational experiences where they are able to observe the achievements of those who are similar to them and who they are able to identify within any sphere of social or emotional experiences of life. The goal is for them to develop the determination that their goals in life are also achievable. Third, there is the need for verbal persuasion from those who play important roles in the life of the individual. This is capable of increasing self-efficacy because it helps to build self-affirmation, confidence, and legitimizes competence. Being acknowledged for what may seem like small efforts encourages the individual to aspire to do more and cultivate the desire to go further. Bandura's (1983) principle of self-efficacy is relevant to the education of students with special needs because the most important factor that could promote these students is for them to believe strongly in self so as to resist the disempowering tendency for dependency. Educators and all service providers for CLD students who are also with special needs must recognize the need to accommodate this group of students without stereotyping them or dismissing them as the "unteachables." These students have personalities which, when nurtured by well-trained educators and professionals, could pilot them into a fulfilling and satisfactory educational experience capable of setting them up for a life of professional and social fulfilments (Donmoyer, 1989). General and special educators, therefore, should endeavor to build self-confidence and self-efficacy in the child. One way of doing so is by involving them in the process of their own schooling. This pedagogy is an extension of the principle of constructivism in which the learner is involved in the process of constructing his or her own learning.

The Family

This is the next appropriate component in the CSM. Studies have shown that the family plays a crucial role on the education of all students (Obiakor, 2008). Aldridge and Goldman (2007) jointly gave a wide array of the mosaic composition of today's American families while reflecting the multicultural configuration of the society. These families include married-couple families, grandparents as parents, gay- and lesbian-headed households, Black families, Asian American families, Latino families, Native American families, and families described by religious affiliations. Taub (2006) provided an important perspective on the growing concern over educators and service providers' understanding of the critical roles of parents in the overall education of their children with special needs.

It is critical that general and special educators understand parental concerns, acknowledge them for their roles, and do what they can within the limits of their professional training to help those parents as well as their children. No doubt, having a deeper understanding of the needs and emotions of parental needs is important to the full implementation of providing workable solutions for students with special needs. Cultural sensitivity is crucial when it comes to understanding parents, their styles, approaches, and values. More often than not, parents discover about their students' disability through the school; therefore, it is so important for the school system to let them have the kind of support they need to cope with their children. They have to understand the intricacies of special needs and the fact that there is a community of support to help them through the process. Finally, families should be helped in understanding the significance of support groups, and how they could partner their children with special needs with other students. The role of the family is essential to the success of students with disabilities.

The School

Between the ages of 7 and 14, it is estimated that a student will spend an average of 6,714 hours in the classroom under the direct instruction of a teacher or other educators (OECD, 2012). Therefore, the school environment is always an integral part of the education of the whole child (Dewey, 1990), and it must be conducive to learning (Conley, 1995). Choreographing the school culture with the life of the child is not only important; it is also a life-saving pedagogy. This is particularly so for the CLD student who also has special needs. Thus, there is the growing need for crafting specialized and proper school-focused pedagogies for accommodating CLD students and giving them the kind of education that would not only ensure their success but also guarantee a perfect adjustment in an environment not particularly designed for them when they live the school.

"*Non scolae sed vitae*" (Not for school, but for life) is an old adage that is relevant to students after they leave school. There is a direct connection between the school environment and the cognition of the CLD student who also has special needs (Sims, 2008). It is important for every education preparation program to require in-service teachers to spend quality time in acquiring knowledge of the impact of the school environment on the CLD student with special needs and how what they are taught in school could help them transition into the world where their education would be translated into empirical or practical applications. Integrating school life into the student's life is more complex than it looks; therefore, an individual educator cannot implement this by himself or herself (Miller, 1990). It is an effort that has to be carried out collaboratively, not only within the school but across the school district, state, nation and even across the globe (Rigden, 2001). Among other pedagogies necessary for implementing relevant pedagogies for students with special needs is inclusion. In corroboration, Burden and Byrd (2003) wrote:

> The Individual with Disabilities Education Act (IDEA) committed the nation to a policy of mainstreaming students who have handicapping [disabling] conditions by placing them in the least restrictive environment in which they can function successfully while having their special needs met ... the regular classroom is the preferred, least restrictive placement. (p. 105)

Teachers and related professionals need to be given specialized preparations and trainings to know how to work with students with special needs. They must know that teaching is not just lecturing; it is everything, including research, social interaction, and all spheres of social life (Duckworth, 1986). When teachers see teaching these students as routine lectures, they are bound to make mistakes, and misunderstand and mis-diagnose them. Misunderstanding personalities of children often lead to those wrong diagnoses, inappropriate placements, and even derogatory labels, and inadequate instructions. Even the brightest of them could easily be mistaken for children with challenging cognitive abilities (Rimm, 1995). Therefore, the burden for providing an appropriate Individualized Educational Plan for a child with special needs is on the school through its multidisciplinary team. It would logically amount to an understatement to state that the role of the school is of utmost importance − it is the only environment where students with special needs could intermingle with other students and gradually develop necessary skills for integrating into the lar-ger society. The best opportunity for becoming a citizen of the society at-large would be lost or acquired in the way the school prepares its students with special needs.

The Community

Dewey (1990) spoke intensely about the role of the community in the over-all provision of the child's education. The mainframe argument of the CSM is that the work of educating students requires a community of sup-porters to actualize success. Vollmer (2010) decried the tendency to think that the school is the primary implementer of a child's education. The CSM is in alignment with the African adage that "*It takes a village to raise a child*," a concept made popular by the book of the former First Lady, Clinton (1996).

The "village" concept alluded to above and in the CSM is a metaphor for a close-knit community around the child. The village becomes the watchdog for the child's welfare just as the physical community within the society provides a part of the safety net for ensuring the child's suc-cess. The CSM posits that for the success of a child, the community in which he/she is growing must be an integral part of his/her education. The first transitional stop for students with special needs is the commu-nity from where they come. Through community involvement, students with special needs will integrate faster into the larger society. Clearly, the community that works together stays together. Recent unrests in US cities and communities (e.g., Baltimore, Cleveland, and Ferguson) have shown that we need to come together to resolve and/or eradicate issues of poverty, unemployment, police brutality, racial distrust, and political extremism. Religious organizations (e.g., churches, mosques, and synagogues) and social organizations (e.g., YMCA, Boy Scouts, and Girl Scouts) can play exemplary roles in building healthy communities.

The Government

Jacoby's (2013) review of Christopher Loss' pivotal book, *Between Citizens and the State: The Politics of American Higher Education in the 20th Century*, pointed to the historical pattern of government involvement in the education of the citizens of the United States, even at the higher education level. The child's education, generally speaking, is always refereed by the government, even in private institutions since the state has the oversight on the establishment of every school within its geographical jurisdiction. The government is involved in the planning and development of curriculum and even in the knowledge the child acquires (Apple, 2000). Therefore, the role of the government cannot be overlooked in the process of providing quality education to students with special needs. As noted earlier, the government has criminalized any form of discrimination against a child with special needs in school, and so including them and providing them with quality education are required.

One critical area in which the government must play a pivotal role in the education of students with special needs is in financing educational possibilities or funding innovative programs. Serving students with special needs requires a substantial amount of innovation, creativity, and money. In these days of economic crisis, it has become a commonplace practice to cut important programs that are supposedly considered as nonessentials in government fiscal plans. States and school districts are known to reduce significant services that students with special needs enjoy. It would be a counterproductive and an antiprogressive venture to carry on such actions because they have negative effects on all students, especially those with special needs. If anything, governments — state or federal — should further reinforce existing laws that support students with special needs. Of late, people and institutions are getting away with violating the civil rights of the disadvantaged, disenfranchised, and disillusioned. It is the government role to make sure that all its citizens are treated equitably and honorably. From our perspective, the federal government should provide avenues for penalizing states that do not have adequate financial support for students with special needs.

CONCLUSION

We have different roles but with the same mission in helping students with special needs to succeed in school and adjust well in life. Across history, there has been some degree of attention to the education of this important segment of our population. One thing that has not been done specifically is providing a model that would align the education of students with proven pedagogical techniques that involve the collaboration, consultation, and cooperation of social institutions. This in essence is what the CSM does! It provides the model for addressing the education of students with special needs through the constructivist strategy of including the student with all pertinent social institutions – the family, the school, the community, and the government. While this model could be applicable to any aspect of educational sector, it is particularly more relevant, useful, and efficacious in its provision of a functional framework for delivering education to students with and without special needs.

REFERENCES

Abourjilie, C. (2006). *Developing character for classroom success: Strategies to increase responsibility, achievement, and motivation in secondary students.* Greensboro, NC: CDI Groups.

Aldridge, J., & Goldman, R. (2007). *Current issues and trends in education* (2nd ed.). Boston, MA: Pearson.

Apple, M. W. (2000). *Official knowledge: Democratic education in a conservative age.* New York, NY: Routledge.

Bandura, A. (1983). Self-efficacy determinants of anticipated fears and calamities. *Journal of Personality and Social Psychology, 45*(2), 464–469.

Browne, D. L. (2014). *Culture: The soul of Africa and the coming gold rush.* North Charleston, NC: CreateSpace Independent Publishing Platform.

Burden, P. R., & Byrd, D. M. (2003). *Methods for effective teaching* (3rd ed.). New York, NY: Allyn and Bacon.

Clinton, H. (1996). *It takes a village to raise a child.* New York, NY: Simon & Schuster.

Conley, T. K. (1995). *Race, ethnicity, and an American campus.* Peoria, IL: Bradley University.

Dewey, J. (1990). *The school and society: The child and the curriculum: An extended edition.* Chicago, IL: The University of Chicago.

Donmoyer, R. (1989). Theory, practice and the double-edged problem of idiosyncrasy. *Journal of Curriculum and Supervision, 4*, 257–270.

Douglas, J. P., & Stack, S. F. (2010). *Teachers, leaders, and schools: Essays by John Dewey.* Carbondale, IL: Southern Illinois University.

Duckworth, E. (1986). Teaching as research. *Harvard Educational Review, 56*, 481–495.

Gersten, R., Baker, S., & Lloyd, J. W. (2000). Designing high-quality research in special education. *The Journal of Special Education, 34*(1), 2−18.

Hayford, B. K. (2010). Improving access and equity in tertiary education in Ghana: The role of private tertiary educational institutions. In M. O. Afolayan (Ed.), *Multiculturalism in the age of the mosaic: Essays in honor of Rudolph G Wilson* (pp. 203−214). New York, NY: Nova Science Publishers.

Hobson, D. (1996). Beginning with the self: Using autobiography and journal writing in teacher research. In G. Bunaford, J. Fischer, & D. Hobson (Eds.), *Teachers doing research: Practical possibilities* (pp. 1−17). Mahwah, NJ: Lawrence Erlbaum Associates.

Jacoby, L. (2013). Between citizens and the state: The politics of American higher education in the 20th century: A Review. *Teacher-Scholar: The Journal of the State Comprehensive University, 5*(1), 61−64.

Ladson-Billings, G. (1994). *The dreamkeepers: Successful teachers of African America children.* San Francisco, CA: Jossey-Bass.

Miller, J. L. (1990). Creating spaces and finding voices: Teacher collaborating for *empowerment.* Albany, NY: State University of New York.

Obiakor, F. E. (2008). *The eight-step approach to multicultural learning and teaching.* Dubuque, IA: Kendall Hunt.

Obiakor, F. E., Eskay, S., & Afolayan, M. O. (2012). Special education in Nigeria: Shifting paradigms. In K. Mutua & C. S. Sunal (Eds.), *Advances in research and praxis in special education in Africa, Caribbean, and the Middle East* (pp. 23−36). Charlotte, NC: Information Age Publishing.

OECD. (2012). How long do students spend in the classroom? In *Education at a Glance 2012: Highlights,* OECD Publishing. Retrieved from http://dx.doi.org/10.1787/eag_highlights-2012-24-en. Accessed on March 17, 2015.

Rigden, D. W. (2001). Quality teachers through regional collaborations. In M. C. Wang & H. J. Walberg (Eds.), *Tomorrow's teachers* (pp. 291−306). Richmond, CA: McCutchan.

Rimm, S. (1995). *Why bright kids get poor grades, and what you can do about it.* New York, NY: Crown.

Schaffel, V. (1996). Shifting gears: An urban teacher rethinks her practice. In G. Burnaford, J. Fischer, & D. Hobson (Eds.), *Teachers doing research: Practical possibilities* (pp. 23−31). Mahwah, NJ: Lawrence Elbaum Associates.

Sims, D. J. (2008). *Hardwired by nature: What we as educators underestimate about our minority students* (Vol. 1). New York, NY: Xlibris Corporation.

Taub, D. J. (2006). Understanding the concerns of parents of students with disabilities: Challenges and roles for school counselors. *Professional School Counseling Journal, 10*(1), 52−57.

US Department of Education. (1973). *Americans with Disability Act (ADA).* Retrieved from http://www2.ed.gov/about/offices/list/ocr/docs/hq9805.html. Accessed on March 17, 2015.

Vollmer, J. (2010). *Schools cannot do it alone.* Fairfield, IA: Enlightenment Press.